REMEMBERED WITH ADVANTAGES

Growing Up Between Two World Wars

Jean Langdale Williams

Published by Prioryswan

Publications 2012

14 Priory Close, Swanland, HU14 3QS

All rights reserved. No part of this publication may be reproduced, stored in a retrieval system, or transmitted, in any form or by any means, without the prior permission in writing of Prioryswan Publications, or as expressly permitted by law, or under terms agreed with the appropriate reprographics rights organisation.

ISBN No. 978-0-9573887-0-3

The author's moral rights have been asserted.

Printed and bound by Central Print Services University of Hull

*"Old men forget: yet all shall be forgot,
But he'll remember with advantages
what feats he did that day."*

Henry V

Shakespeare

Contents

The Two Families 7
Acknowledgements 8
FOREWORD 10
PRELUDE 12
BEGINNINGS 18
MAY TAYLOR AND FRANK LANGDALE 23
RAGLAN STREET 34
GRANTHAM 40
    Family History 53
Facts and Anecdotes 53
MIRRIE TAYLOR AND TOM HOGGARTH 55
ANNIE ELIZABETH LANGDALE 65
AUNTIE ANNIE AND UNCLE WILL WRIGHT 70
GRANDPA AND GRANDMA TAYLOR 81
GRANDMA AND GRANDPA LANGDALE 92
AFTER THE FIRST WORLD WAR 99
    Back in Hull 114
A NEW HOUSE AND SCHOOL 115

ANOTHER HOUSE: ANOTHER SCHOOL	129
A NEW LIFE	136
CORNWALL WITH NORA AND BILL STORM	151
UNWELCOME INTERRUPTIONS	163
SHIRLEY STORM	173
HOLIDAYS	182
WELCOME BREAKS	193
VISITS AND VISITORS	202
PLEASURES	215
PROBLEMS	227
THE SCHOLARSHIP YEAR	240
NEWLAND HIGH SCHOOL	253
Norwich	259
A NEW HOUSE AND A NEW SCHOOL	260
EASTER 1938	276
BLYTH SCHOOL	282
MINOR PROBLEMS	291
WAR BREAKS OUT	302
TETTENHALL	312
OUR NEW HOME	313
WOLVERHAMPTON GIRLS' HIGH SCHOOL	321
NEW FRIENDS	335

VISITORS AND OTHER PROBLEMS... 342

THE SCHOOL CERTIFICATE YEARS 354

OPTING OUT.. 374

THE LAST YEAR AT SCHOOL... 382

WEDNESBURY TECHNICAL COLLEGE.................................... 396

PHOTOGRAPHS

The Taylor Family

MARK AND CATHERINE - my great-grandparents

WILL : their eldest son - my grandfather

FLORENCE : his first wife - my grandmother

MAY : their daughter - my mother

NANCE : his second wife - my grandma

NORA : their daughter - my aunt

SHIRLEY & MICHAEL - my cousins

ANNIE : Will's older sister - my great-aunt

ANN : Annie's daughter - my mother's cousin

MIRRIE : Will's younger sister - my great-aunt

ALBERT : Mirrie's son - my mother's cousin

The Langdale Family

RICHARD AND MARY - my great-grandparents

FRANCIS : their youngest child - my grandfather
SARAH JANE : his wife - my grandmother
FRANK : their son - my father

ANNIE : his sister - my great-aunt

Acknowledgements

I would like to express my gratitude to all those who have helped me with this book:

to Peter Didsbury who, as my tutor during a two-term course at Hull University, encouraged me to believe I could write something others might enjoy reading and, later, gave me invaluable advice and support

to my friend, Mollie Ferns, who cheerfully ploughed through each finished section of typescript, correcting the odd spelling or grammatical error I'd made and pointing out where any clarification was needed

to the friends in Peter's Writing Group who welcomed me so warmly and made me feel my contributions were worthwhile

to Tony Costello, who enhanced, arranged and printed the photographs and their captions with enthusiastic skill.

to Margaret Sugden, who willingly devoted a great deal of time, patience and remarkable expertise to transferring nearly two hundred pages of material from my suddenly defunct word-processor's floppy disc on to a format acceptable to a printer. Without her generous help and advice this book would never have been published.

For the Family – past, present and future.

FOREWORD

Many times over the last thirty years I've thought of questions I wish I'd asked my parents and near relatives about our family history. Some of the facts are now untraceable and it is too late to get more details of the personalities and events which interest me. The realisation of this adds poignantly to the loss I have felt since their deaths. I decided therefore to put together some kind of record of my own early years and to include as much information as possible about recent ancestors, relations and friends who had a significant influence upon my life.

By doing this I hope to give any of our descendants who may eventually be interested, some idea of how those who came before them lived their lives and, maybe, influenced or contributed to later generations. So many of the characters who directly (or indirectly through anecdotes) enriched my childhood died childless, with no one to recall the impact they made upon the people around them or to recognize the ways in which they added to the fabric and variety of local life. I would like their lives to be remembered and celebrated for a little longer.

As their future recorder I happened to be doubly lucky. Firstly, most of my relatives were agreeably garrulous and they relished kindly - rather than malicious - gossip, especially about any items which might amuse or astonish. Secondly, I was the only child in a large, extended family until a cousin was born when I was six. Therefore - however undeservedly – I enjoyed a special place in their affections. I was always pleased to visit friends and relatives with my parents and usually very content to sit quietly with a book while the grown-ups forgot I was there and talked over my head. I understood and absorbed far more of their discussions and chat than they realised, and what I learned then is the basis of much of the material I shall be drawing upon in the following pages. Of course I can't be sure how much was distorted, decorated, enhanced or suppressed by those who talked - or falsified by my faulty interpretation of what I heard - but I shall try to present the facts and impressions as honestly as I can.

Jean Langdale Williams.

The names of some people - though not family members - have been changed.

PRELUDE

Great Aunt Mirrie's kitchen was a rather unexpected mixture - rather like Great Aunt Mirrie herself. She was really far too young to be my great-aunt but she and her kitchen were a familiar part of the fabric of my life until I was eleven years old, and I unthinkingly accepted the oddities of both. My mother and I visited her often and always spent most of our time in the kitchen. Auntie Mirrie was generally busy there: cooking, baking, gossiping, drinking strong tea, or calling instructions through the ever open door to the little skivvy at the sink in the scullery. Her front room - with its plush, three-piece suite, a piano, some highly-polished occasional tables and formal arrangements of expensive ornaments - was for "real" visitors . . . and parties.

The kitchen itself was quite a good size and there was a large sash window in one wall which looked out on to a flagged yard with some dilapidated stables for two horses at the far end. Uncle was a fish merchant, but only in a very small way so, in an attempt to hide the far from attractive signs of his trade, the sash window was screened with thick net curtains in a deep shade of ecru. We therefore couldn't see the rubbish piled near the stables or the rough barrels full of fish and crushed ice waiting to be carted off - unless, of course, we looked very hard. But I never looked very hard. There was always too much going on in the kitchen for me to be concerned with the world outside.

As a young child I was more than content to be perched up on a couple of cushions in the middle of the sofa behind the kitchen table. From there I had a grandstand view of all that was going on and it certainly didn't matter to me that the sofa, crushed against the wall to make room for the surprisingly large, square table, was lumpy and covered in stained cretonne. A big, black range took up most of the wall opposite to where I sat, and the table was usually pushed right up to the sofa so that Auntie could stand on the hearthrug to work. The heat on her back can't have been all that comfortable for her, especially as it was necessary, even in the summer months, to keep the fire well-stoked, but she rarely grumbled. And, of course, I was far enough away from it to enjoy the leaping brilliance of its flames and the way it made the kettle sing, and its lid rattle as it bounced up and down.

Above the range was a broad mantel shelf. It often had the remains of the last year's Christmas decorations pinned round its edge; Auntie Mirrie loved Christmas and was reluctant to take down the last signs of it till well into July . . . or was it just laziness? On the shelf itself was a jumble of bills, postcards and unframed photos carelessly stuffed behind the shiny, black china dogs which were placed one at each end. Uncle Tom had won them for her at Hull Fair years ago and it didn't occur to me then that they made the beautiful carriage clock and the delicately graceful art deco figurine look a little incongruous. I eventually found out that these were wedding presents from members of our family who considered that, even though she had married (as they privately put it) "beneath her", she ought to have one or two things of good quality around her.

The range was flanked by two built-in cupboards stacked with crockery, cooking utensils and a medley of what we then called "dry goods". The deep drawers beneath them held cutlery, linen and the many dozens of things that Auntie Mirrie wanted to keep by her but didn't know where else to put. If Uncle came in shouting for a length of strong string or "that book about hosses' illnesses that came free with the drench I got for Daisy", he knew Auntie'd be able tell him exactly in which part of the four drawers she could find it for him.

All the walls were covered with a thick, beige paper garlanded with bunches of autumn leaves which - if I gazed at them for any length of time through half closed eyes - began to look like the profile of a Red Indian Chief's head, complete with a feathered head-dress. (When I was six years old Red Indians had not yet been reclassified as Native Americans or First Nation people!) This bold leaf-pattern detracted a little from the effect made by the pictures on the walls which were suspended on fine wire from the thin wooden rail fixed twenty inches or so from the ceiling. I never found out who had chosen these pictures. It didn't occur to me to ask, for I was on such familiar terms with them that they seemed to be a natural part of the room. In fact, until I was about four, I think I assumed they'd grown there along with the bunches of leaves. There was a brightly coloured photograph of Princess Elizabeth ("Only four months older than you!" it was frequently pointed out) and her sister Margaret Rose, lovingly draped around their mother. There was an exciting-looking print of a lighthouse flashing its beam across an extremely rough sea towards a ship which was clearly in considerable difficulty, and next to it a vaguely biblical scene of depressed-looking women gleaning in a twilit cornfield. All, except the calendar given away each year with Pears soap, were tastefully framed and - usually - lightly spotted with fly dirt.

The rest of the furniture was made up of a collection of nondescript wooden chairs. Several had gaily coloured cushions on the seats and the rest were piled with old newspapers and back copies of "Titbits" and "Answers". Overall a surprising and, superficially, a rather uninspiring mixture! So what made this kitchen so fascinating? So memorable that I remember it in detail and with great affection after over seventy years? It was, of course, Auntie Mirrie herself.

She radiated warmth. She brought to everything she did a kind of weary energy, a stylishly physical expertise. She suffered from a fairly mild type of diabetes which she maintained she could control by strict dieting rather than with insulin injections, but her preoccupation with providing quantities of good food for everyone who came to the house made dieting difficult. I loved watching her baking, especially bread. She would lift the large brown stein from the side of the hearth, whisk the clean tea-towel from the top, scoop up the risen dough, and slap it on the floured table top with a satisfying plop. The strings of dough left round its sloping yellow sides were then scraped up with a dramatic flourish and the kneading could begin. As she leaned over the table, stretching and pushing the dough into itself and flopping it over into the freshly-sprinkled flour, I could see the top of her full breasts moving and matching the colour and texture of the dough. I was intrigued by the likeness.

Aunt Mirrie always cooked in whatever clothes she wanted to wear later in the day, however unsuitable. Her frocks tended to be draped quite low across her bosom and, for the larger ladies, the fashion (currently revived, but with improved design and techniques) was to pin an oblong of embroidered silk or lace to the shoulder straps of their petticoats with tiny gold safety-pins. This "modesty vest", smoothed down inside the Vee of the dress, was intended to mask any suggestion of cleavage. Just fussy prudery in Auntie Mirrie's opinion. She also objected to covering her good dresses with more than a simple apron tied round the waist. This was useful for wiping her hands on but it did mean that her afternoon dresses often had unidentifiable stains or dusty patches of flour on their bodices or skirts.

Once the kneading was finished she sliced off chunks of dough, shaped them roughly, and dropped them with yet another flourish into the greased tins to rise again. It seemed magic to me how somehow they had always expanded to fit the tins snugly by the time they were ready to go into the hot oven. Oh, that tantalising smell when she later took the first one out! Gasping at the fierce heat, she would slide it out of the tin onto her cloth-draped hand and tap briskly with her knuckles on the bottom to listen for the hoped-for hollow sound. Done! And it was at this point that I became impatient, longing for the left-over dough, patted into flat cakes by my own hot hands and pushed twenty minutes ago into the oven bottom, to be ready too. They would come out with crisp crusts like English muffins and we could hardly wait for them to be cool enough to eat. She would call the little maid in from the scullery and we would all sit round the table to split and eat them greedily, their warmth melting the lavish butter deep into the softness within. Risky, of course, but there was always a tin of baking soda handy, wasn't there? - and warm water in the kettle for any grown-up who felt pangs of indigestion afterwards. A few necessary burps were entirely forgivable.

She rarely made sponge cakes (the oven in the range was perhaps a bit too unpredictable for that) but treacle or jam tarts, pies, pasties and rich fruit loaves were all her specialities. As I got older, though, I began to notice that when fruit loaves were being mixed my mother kept eyeing the loaded spirals of sticky fly-paper, hanging above the table, with nervous attention. The trapped flies buzzed angrily and occasionally one would break free and fall, far too sticky to fly away. Until Uncle Tom decided that buying and selling loose fish in barrels was no longer a paying proposition and started a coal business instead, flies were a constant problem in Auntie Mirrie's house. So we were not sorry to lose them and very glad to exchange the slight but persistent smell of fish for the salty tang of coal.

But such drawbacks did not, in any way, mar my pleasure in being in that kitchen. One of its main attractions for me was Auntie's gossipy chatter and her anecdotes through which I began to learn something of the histories and foibles of members of our extended family, gradually building up my knowledge and understanding of the background into which I'd been born.

BEGINNINGS

I was lucky. My father had reason to be proud of me from the day I was born - well, two reasons to be precise.

'Look!' my father would crow. 'Just look. Aren't they incredible?'

My mother would smile indulgently, philosophically accepting that when visitors came to see the new baby, Frank would rush them to the cot or pram and - without giving anyone time to look at my face - he'd turn down the coverlet and twitch the long skirt of my soft, winceyette gown aside.

'There! What did I tell you? I'll bet those are the longest feet you've ever seen on a young baby - or ever will see.'

He was right, of course, but my mother could never quite work out why he should be so proud of them. I was ten before they began to look in proportion to my height and weight, and - believe me - it took quite a while longer for me to live down friends' and relatives' teasing.

It was July 1926 and May and Frank had married in the previous September. They'd come from very different backgrounds and I've always enjoyed feeling I had roots in both. It's a significant milestone in children's development when they realize that other people existed before they themselves were born, that there was life going on before they appeared on the scene. Until it became fairly commonplace for children to be pages, bridesmaids, or - at least - honoured guests at their own parents' wedding, many people were able to tell amusing stories of their offspring asking, 'Where was I when that photograph of you in that long white dress was taken?' Or 'What was I doing when you were doing that?' - and then failing to understand why they were not there. I think there was very little time for me to experience any such problem. Taking and developing snapshots of interesting family occasions had been one of my father's hobbies since he was eighteen and, perhaps because living in Grantham made my mother somewhat homesick for Hull, we often spent a happy half hour looking through our shoebox of photographs. True, I might be forgiven for wondering why everyone and their surroundings were a pale brownish colour, but I was very used to phrases like 'That's us in Whitby where Daddy and I used to go sometimes with Grandpa and Grandma long before you were born,' or 'That's the house where you were born and that's Mummy standing at the gate just a few days before you arrived'. And once I was back in Hull I was surrounded by reminiscing relatives and a mass of memorabilia.

When two people become a couple their two names are almost immediately combined into a single, portmanteau word. So we get Janet'n'John, William'n'Mary, Darby'n'Joan. When I was about twelve my parents and I had quite a lengthy discussion about who, among a couple's friends and relations, decided which name should come first - and the possible reasons for choosing that particular order.

'It's because it sounds right,' was my contribution. My father looked doubtful.

'Well, just think how clumsy Bob'n'Phyllis sounds compared to Phyllis'n'Bob,' I pointed out. He agreed, but then my mother ran through a few names of couples we'd all known for years, proving that they sounded just as good - or as silly - either way round. There had to be another factor which influenced the choice of lead name.

'Could it be the dominant partner's name that comes first, do you think?' she suggested. We went through the list again. It was unlikely.

'No. It's who you knew first,' said my father firmly. 'Your own relative or friend comes first. You simply add on the new name to theirs. So the family of, say, Peter will call them Peter'n'Joy, and her family will use the word Joy'n'Peter.'

'So what about your two names then? Why are you May'n'Frank to both families and all friends? Would Frank'n'May sound better or worse? Or does it show that Mum is the dominant one? Or what?'

There was no satisfactory answer. In all our minds the two names were permanently united: May'n'Frank it is and always will be. Which is why - when I became curious about what my mother and father had been like as children and how they had lived when they were young - I found it hard to think of their leading separate lives before they came together. But their early years' experiences were so different from each other's (and from mine) that I had no difficulty in accepting that I was not around at the time.

The Early Years

MAY TAYLOR AND FRANK LANGDALE

My mother's childhood had, in most ways, been a happy, loving one and by the time she was twenty she'd become a serene young woman, quietly confident of her own ability to cope cheerfully with whatever life had in store for her. But, as a young baby, her life had not been so easy.

The Taylors were quite a large family, even for Victorian times. Will, May's father, had four brothers and three sisters and they were brought up in comfortable circumstances on the income from the family business: a modestly successful printing works in the centre of Hull. They lived in a large terraced house on what was then the outskirts of the city and, when each son left school, he first had to learn every practical aspect of printing and was then expected to take over some area of the firm's production. The eldest daughter was also employed there, but only in a minor clerical capacity. The other two girls were kept at home to help their mother and the live-in maid to run the house - no easy task as, despite their daily lives being firmly controlled by their strict, Nonconformist father, most of the family continued to live at home until their late twenties.

Will was the eldest son. He was responsible for the running of a large section of the business and, as he was therefore in a reasonably secure financial position, he was able to marry comparatively young. He had fallen in love with a girl from the other side of Hull and they settled comfortably in a small house not far from his old home, and looked forward to starting a family. Sadly, three weeks after the birth of their first child, his wife died of puerperal fever and it was obvious that he couldn't cope with a tiny baby on his own. His wife's mother, for some reason, had little interest in helping with her new granddaughter and made no objection when his own parents suggested that Will and the baby should come home to Elm Terrace to live. His mother, in effect, simply added May to her own family. After all, her youngest son, Alec, was only about nine at the time. Sadly, from then on, May had almost no contact with any of her mother's relations.

May was a pathetic little scrap, difficult to feed of course, pale and sickly, and liable to catch any germ going. Grandmother Taylor had already begun to feel the physical and mental strain of having brought eight children into the world (ten, counting the two who had died) and - though still an impressive-looking figure - she was beginning to feel older than her years. Not surprisingly, she fairly quickly handed over a large part of the responsibility for the tiny baby to Mirrie, her fifteen-year-old daughter who welcomed her, quite literally, with open arms. Inevitably a bond was built up between this young aunt and her tiny, delicate niece that was deep and lasting: almost a mother and child relationship which, over the years, gradually developed into the easy, relaxed affection of close friends. And when Will remarried, Mirrie was immensely relieved that her mother insisted on keeping May "to give Will and Nance time to themselves and get off to a good start", as she put it.

Naturally, May wanted to stay where she was. The Beverley Road house was her home - the only one she knew. Mirrie and Grandmother were there, the school she would soon be going to was nearby, and her two youngest uncles felt like brothers. They teased and petted her and made her feel special. Understandably, Nance had no objections to the arrangement and, though May missed the daily contact with her father very much indeed, she had no wish to live with his new wife - even after her half-sister Nora was born. It was enough to go to stay with them for a few days every six weeks or so, and then come home to familiar surroundings and routines.

But when war broke out in 1914 these routines were changed for ever. The three youngest Taylor men enlisted quite quickly and left for France. Will, though working all hours with his brother Mark to keep the firm going, volunteered to do regular ambulance duty helping to cope with the horribly wounded men who were arriving on stretchers into Hull several nights a week. Food was short and, although none of the civilian Taylors suffered directly from the bombs, the Zeppelin raids on the docks meant that they were often in personal danger. The brothers all survived the horrors of Flanders, but Holborn never lived at home again. He emigrated to Canada in 1919. Bert married Ethel early in the war and in 1920 decided to leave the family firm to work for the Hull Daily Mail. Alec, suffering minor after effects of a German gas attack, came back to live at home - somewhat uncomfortably - for a few months until he too got married.

The changes they all found at Elm Terrace were quite drastic.

A few months before Armistice was signed, May's grandmother had died and Mirrie, at last free to rent a house of her own, set about making a home for her sailor husband and their little son. And May had already gone to live with her father, stepmother and half-sister in Keyingham - a small village twelve miles or so east of Hull. Will had moved his family there towards the end of the war, partly because of the bombing raids but mainly because he'd always wished to live in the country. Nance, too, was happy with the idea. A job had been found for May at the printing works and she thoroughly enjoyed having her father more or less to herself as they travelled to Hull each day by train. She also enjoyed having some money of her own. Though her wages were quite small she welcomed the feeling of independence the money gave her.

She had always been rather small for her age though, as she grew older, she was usually healthy. By the age of sixteen, having avoided the worst of the physical problems of adolescence - spots and lumpy puppy fat - she was still only a little over five feet tall, delicately slender and graceful, and had stopped growing. She had soft dark hair which hung in loose, glossy curls almost to her waist, a thick, creamy skin, and her deep brown eyes were made even more attractive by the natural beige shadow which dusted her eyelids. She generally gave the impression of being calm and gentle, but those who knew her well frequently enjoyed another facet of her personality: her down-to-earth approach to life which was often spiced with unexpected touches of sharp humour. Her arrival at Elm Cottage made quite an impact on the village youngsters, including several men who had been too young to fight in the war. Harry Etherington, Florrie Jackson and her cousin Frank Langdale were particularly impressed - especially Frank Langdale.

*

From the mid-eighteen hundreds onwards the Langdales had been in business as grocers, millers and seed-merchants just outside Hull and, well before that century drew to a close, they were firmly established in Keyingham. Richard Langdale had taken a farm and a thriving windmill there. Two quite sizeable houses went with the farm, there was a small tied cottage opposite, and another was attached to the mill. Frank, his grandson, was born in the Mill House. He went to the village school and spent a good deal of time in and around the farm until he left to go to the Hull Technical School and take up an engineering apprenticeship with Earle's Shipbuilders. Because it was clear that he loved the countryside and, from a very early age, was keen to take part in all the activities on the farm, the family expected that he would follow his father and his uncles into some form of agricultural work and - as all Richard's sons except Frank's father had been set up when they married in places of their own – it was assumed that he would eventually inherit the Home Farm, Mount Airey. To Frank, however, farming was just one of his many interests: lasting, but of little more importance than any other of his hobbies. Engineering, mechanical and electrical, was his passion.

'If cows had engines and horses ran on electricity, we might keep the lad here,' was how his grandfather summed up the situation, 'but, as it is, well . . . ' - and he would click his tongue and shake his head in resigned disappointment. Working with cart horses and pigs, milking and stooking corn sheaves by hand couldn't compare with taking a motor bike apart or learning how complex electrical circuits can be designed.

Naturally, though, Frank was content to stay in the village until he started his apprenticeship. He had, in effect, two homes - Mount Airey and his parents' house - and two mothers. Jinnie was his natural mother but Auntie Annie, his father's only sister, had willingly taken charge of him so frequently since he was three years old that she looked on him as her own son. She lived at home until she married in her late thirties and, as Frank had always spent more than half his time at Mount Airey, she was at least as much involved in his upbringing as Jinnie was.

'It's a wonder that lad isn't ruined by them two women,' Richard Langdale once grumbled to the village schoolmaster. 'Jinnie feels he should always look to her - but doesn't always want the bother of him. So she often tries to "buy" him by giving him whatever she thinks he wants. And our Annie dotes on him - thinks the sun shines out of his backside - so *she* gives him what he wants as well, and never thinks he's a scrap of bother. They're both so determined to mek him theirs that he must feel sometimes like he's being pulled apart!'

Luckily, it seems that Frank really didn't want a great deal and, in any case, he lived so much in his own world that he was hardly ever aware of the struggle going on between the two women. And when May came to live at Elm Cottage he was even more content to stay in the village as long as possible.

Naturally, Frank had hardly noticed her when she'd visited her family as a child, but as soon as this attractive sixteen-year old girl took up permanent residence in Keyingham, he was immediately keen to get to know her. During the past two weeks he'd seen her every day on the train into Hull - she and her father on their way to work and he with his closest friend Harry as they travelled to their different schools. Several times he'd managed to catch her eye and exchange a cautious smile, and he was determined to find a way to speak to her. He wanted to persuade her to join his five or six friends who met up as often as they could to walk, talk, and attend all the local dances and social activities together. They were a pleasantly lively group of youngsters who had all been in the same class in the village school and came from similar backgrounds. He knew Mr and Mrs Taylor slightly of course and, though they'd only lived in the village for two or three years, they were known to be a quietly sociable couple. They enjoyed being members of a rural community and had proved to be very willing to play their part in Chapel duties and in local affairs. He felt there would be no objections from them - it was simply that, where she was concerned, he lacked the confidence to approach her directly. But at least he knew who to call on for help – his cousin, Florrie.

'Go on Flo!' he coaxed. 'See if she'd like to come with us to Kelsey Hill on Sunday.'

Florrie Jackson's mother was Jinnie's sister but, though the two women didn't much care for each other, Frank and Flo (as she was known to her friends) were affectionate playmates and allies throughout their childhood. She, too, had noticed May's arrival with pleasure - a fresh face in a village is almost always welcome, especially if it's an attractive one. So she was only too happy to pass on the invitation . . . and May accepted. It was the beginning of a lifelong friendship.

So began some years of shared activities. As a foursome they enjoyed the occasional weekend and an annual holiday with the Taylor family at their Robin Hood's Bay cottage, and the bonds between them remained rock solid despite the various, inevitable changes in their lives. May continued to work with her father in the firm, so the only change for her was when her family moved from Elm Cottage to East Mount, a double-fronted, detached house next door to the Congregational Chapel. Flo still lived at home but she started work as a pupil teacher in another village some miles away. Harry went off to train as a teacher and Frank completed his apprenticeship, lodging during the week in very basic "digs".

'Do you like pickled beetroot?' his landlady asked him when he first arrived at her house. 'Yes,' he said - and from then on that was what his dinnertime sandwiches contained. But, as lodgings went, it was clean and cheap, and Frank had something worth saving his money for. So he stayed.

May and Frank got engaged on her 21st birthday, and Harry and Florrie followed their example a few months later. Their two-year engagement seemed endless but May and Frank were able to spend a good deal of time together and Frank was always automatically included in all the Taylor outings, parties and holidays. It was on one of these holidays at the Bay cottage that May had an accident which was to have serious, long-term after-effects. She caught her heel in a piece of loose carpet as she came out of the attic bedroom, her feet slid forward, and she fell from top to bottom of the very steep stairs, bumping her back and neck on the edge of every step. She seemed to recover in a fortnight or so but, a few weeks afterwards, she began to put on weight quite rapidly. A direct link was never conclusively established but most of the doctors who subsequently treated her various illnesses believed that she must have damaged something vital (a gland?) when she fell, and that this led to her uncontrollable weight gain. Over the next eighteen months her weight almost doubled and she was never able to shed any of it, though I can vouch for the fact that she had quite a small appetite and that she never ate anything between meals.

In the long term, because her small frame was not designed to support this burden of solid flesh, her health suffered in many ways, but all her life she refused to let her weight be seen as a problem - for herself or for others. Frank seemed simply unaware of any significant change in her appearance. If anything, he loved her more than ever, and her cheerfulness and popularity with old friends and new never waned. As a child and as an adult, if I thought about it at all, I felt that this was how a mother should look, and was proud of her. I'm ashamed to say that it was many years after she died before I really appreciated how difficult it must have been for her to accept and cope with the limitations being so overweight inevitably imposed upon her.

*

One fine Saturday in September, 1925, my mother and father were married in the village church with Nora and Florrie as bridesmaids and Harry as best man. It was a pretty wedding, as the photographs show, and a very happy family occasion. Frank was working at the time as an engineer on the new waterworks being built at Dunswell and, on the morning of his wedding, he had a telegram telling him there was a serious crisis and he must be back at work on Monday. He and May made a quick decision. They set off in their decorated motor bike and sidecar, showered with confetti and the guests' good wishes, but only Jinnie Langdale knew that they were not heading for the Lake District honeymoon they'd planned so carefully. Instead they travelled just a few miles to their future home in Hull, with a box of leftovers from the reception which Jinnie had managed to smuggle out of the

Church Hall and secretly tuck into the space at the back of the sidecar.

'Nobody'll know where you are, so you won't be disturbed,' Jinnie whispered to May just before they left. And it worked out well after all. They had a whole thirty-six hours all to themselves, and the persistent thunderstorms and torrential rain - which they heard later had struck the whole of the north of England an hour after they'd arrived at their cosy little house - had failed to make any impression on them whatsoever.

I joined them ten months later.

RAGLAN STREET

Because I arrived less than a year after they were married, it could be said we were a threesome almost from the very beginning, and it was my good fortune that that is what we remained for the first twenty years or so of my life - a threesome. Because of this close relationship I can't say that I ever consciously missed having brothers or sisters, especially as we were fortunate enough to be part of an interesting, close-knit family and were blessed with a fair number of long-standing friends. As I was the only child in the family for some years I, naturally, enjoyed many privileges but I was always expected to behave sensibly, and it was taken for granted that adults were the really important people at any gathering, not little girls.

Looking back I think that I must have been a very biddable child, certainly not given to tantrums or rebellious behaviour, and I've often wondered if this was because of what Granny Langdale did to me when I was around two months old. True, I have to rely mainly on what my mother told me some years later - and she was hardly unbiased about the event even then - but the facts were never denied by Granny herself. She even boasted about it to me occasionally. It seems that, as a very young baby, I took to crying loudly throughout most afternoons and all of every night. By early morning my inexperienced mother would be worn to frazzled shreds and I would be yelling, rigid and purple-faced, with desperate frustration and temper. When Granny arrived one afternoon she was so worried to see her son and daughter-in-law's obvious distress that, after ten minutes of suffering the violent din, she unceremoniously grabbed me in her arms, mid-scream, and hurried me over to the kitchen sink. She turned the cold tap full on and, fully clothed though I was, thrust my head and shoulders under the gushing water. Apparently I took a startled gasp, looked (according to Granny) completely gobsmacked, and stopped crying immediately. It must have been a fairly shattering experience for all concerned and its effect upon me seems to have been permanent for, from then on, I cried no more than absolutely necessary and I have never lost my temper in my life. In fact I really do not know what it feels like to have a temper to control.

A happy outcome for me, but the incident did little to improve the already slightly cool relationship between the two women involved. This rather edgy atmosphere had probably, originally stemmed from Granny's claim that I'd inherited all my good points from *her* side of the family - she even insisted, to my father's complete mystification, that my back was exactly like her own - but her "water cure" was pushing a young mother's forbearance dangerously near breaking point. Of course I may be mistaken in linking Granny's treatment with my subsequent lack of a temper. It might be genetic. Both my parents had calm, equable dispositions and so were excellent role models, however it seems I could still occasionally become vociferously irritated if things didn't go my way - as my earliest memory proves.

Until I was three we lived in a small rented house in a quiet terrace in Hull. I can vaguely remember playing on the grass in the back garden but there was no garden at the front, just a strip of concrete between the skimpy bay window and the low wall topped with iron railings. If the gate was shut there was no way I could get to the footpath or the street, so it was safe for me to play there if the grass in the back garden was wet. I have a clear recollection of being buttoned up into a thick coat, my hands pushed into clumsy woollen mittens, and my mother lifting me down the front step onto the concrete strip. An old doll's pram was then handed down for me to play with. Even now I can feel the glow of excited pride as I confidently prepared to push it up and down in front of the window, and the sudden rush of baffled disappointment as it careered from side to side, crashing first into the wall beneath the window and then into the wall with the railings.

I can hear myself yelling furiously, 'It won't go where I'm pushing. Silly pram! It won't go right.' I can still feel the tears of frustration running down my cheeks. But there the memory fades and I have no idea when, or even if, I learned to steer the obstinate pram - though I do have a snapshot of me in a summery dress in the back garden, sitting beside it on the little chair which had been made for my mother more than twenty-five years ago. I'm nursing a doll and it rather looks as if I'd accepted defeat and was using the pram as a cot rather than a means of transport. But that is pure speculation and I hope I'm wrong.

Soon after my third birthday my father's work connected with the building of the new pumping station at Dunswell was nearing completion and he applied for a job in Grantham. It was 1930, a time of widespread unemployment, so he had to be prepared to move to wherever he could find work. He was lucky that his boss's strong recommendation led to a successful interview and he was able to start a new job without a worrying period on the dole. Because we had to move more or less immediately it wasn't possible to find a house to rent until we were actually in Grantham, so our furniture had to go into store while we went into lodgings. This could have been very difficult for my mother. She was leaving a supportive family and a number of valued friends and, because time and money were short, she had to rely on my father to find suitable lodgings for us. She had never before lived in a stranger's house, she was separated from her furniture and most of her familiar possessions and - perhaps worst of all - she was going to have to share another woman's kitchen. But it wasn't her way to be easily daunted and she arrived in Grantham determined to enjoy the new experiences and make sure that my father and I enjoyed them too.

I have quite a few happy memories of our months at Auntie Ida's, as I called her. It was not a large house - just three bedrooms - so she and her husband had the back one, their two boys had the smallest, and I slept on a kind of pallet at the foot of my parents' bed in the front room. We were very welcome there as Ida's husband was on short time and they desperately needed the money. So all the adults were prepared to compromise and overcome any problems which might arise from living together in such cramped conditions. Harry and Eric, ten and eight respectively, seemed to enjoy having a little sister, even on a temporary basis, and I loved having big brothers who would listen to my chatter and try to answer my constant questions. I learned quite a lot during our months in their house, including how to beat Eric at nibbling the fancy borders off our suppertime arrowroot biscuits. This was a skill I continued to practise for several years, but I never found anyone else willing to accept my challenge and by the time I had children of my own - who just *might* have been interested - those biscuits had shed their lacy edges and were boringly smooth.

My mother, too, learned some useful information from Auntie Ida - where to buy bargain groceries and cheap vegetables, which shop was best for children's shoes, and what local customs should be followed if she wanted to be accepted by neighbours. Not difficult, but I think the custom which really surprised her, judging from her expression when she later told her friends and relations about it, was the routine Ida always followed if there was a call over the fence from next door.

'I'm going into town. Can I get you owt?'

'Wait a sec, Mrs Digby. I'll just write you a little list,' was the usual response, and in due course Ida would hand over a small piece of paper and a shilling or two.

The first time this happened my mother was intrigued to see Ida, half an hour or so later, set a cup, saucer, sugar basin and a biscuit on the kitchen table, with two pennies arranged neatly beside them.

'What's that for?' she asked.

'It's for Mrs Digby, of course.' Ida sounded surprised to be asked. 'She'll expect a cup from our pot when she gets back.'

'But what's the tuppence for?'

'Oh, well . . .' said Ida, 'that's for going.'

It was quite an education for my mother. She quickly realised that she had a lot to learn if we were to be accepted as fully paid-up members of Grantham society

GRANTHAM

By the time I was four we were able to move from Auntie Ida's to a council house on the outskirts of Grantham. It was a newish, well-designed estate. The houses were semi-detached and most tenants took great pride in keeping their little front garden bright with flowers throughout much of the year. The side plots were generally filled with trim rows of vegetables and there was a patch of grass at the back for children to play on; it also provided space for at least one clothes line. Our long living-room had a window at both ends and so had my parents' bedroom above it. I had the tiny bedroom next door and there was another bedroom opposite mine for any visitors. A small kitchen, bathroom and separate lavatory took up the rest of the ground floor.

We were very fortunate to acquire such a comfortable house so quickly and, looking back, I can only think this was because we were considered well able to afford the rent; the early thirties was a time of growing unemployment and these houses must have been too expensive for many families. At first, though, we didn't feel very lucky or very comfortable.

Ida had found us a woman to scrub out the house for a few shillings and she looked after me while my mother went back to Hull to make arrangements for our furniture to be removed from storage and transported to Grantham. Getting everything sorted and in its place in a home of our own again must have been a pleasure my mother really looked forward to but, a couple of days after we moved in, she noticed that I had a few red spots on my neck and - though I cannot remember much about the events which followed - she told me, years later, of her horror and disgust when she found several insects lurking in my bed. My little bedroom was infested with fleas! They had been hiding in the cracks between the floor-boards and were beginning to spread throughout the house.

The Council's methods for dealing with this situation were complicated and involved sealing off each room in turn and fumigating it for twenty-four hours. So it was over a week before we could begin to live normally, and nearly a month before we got rid of the unpleasant, acrid smell of the cleansing fumes. Sometime later, when she got to know our pleasant next-door neighbour, my mother learned that the previous tenants (apparently evicted by the Council for non-payment of rent) had dealt in old clothes and rags, and kept them in my bedroom. It took her quite a while to rid herself of an unwarranted sense of shame and I've often wondered if this early experience is why, ever since, these pests seem to find me irresistible. If there is a flea anywhere within hopping distance it will come to me for a quick bite and insist on trying to take up permanent residence in my clothing.

It was decided, soon after I was four, that I was more than ready to start school. This may partly have been because my mother was ready for a break. I was once told by my Aunt Nora that, when she asked what it was like having a three-year-old daughter, my mother replied, 'Oh, it's lovely!' and then added wearily, 'Or it would be if only she would stop talking for a bit.'

I understand that, even when I grew older, the situation did not improve much.

The other reason for wanting me to start school early was that I had no-one to play with. On one side of us lived Douglas, a small, delicate boy whose mother seemed to spend most of her days in fine weather dead-heading the hundreds of pansies which covered her front garden borders. When asked if he could come over to play, she nearly always said she had put him to bed with a tummy ache. But he did come over once or twice and was no fun at all. On the other side was sixteen-year-old Leslie who was tall, ungainly and severely mentally retarded. He couldn't speak properly but was very eager to be friendly, and our mothers encouraged me to go to his house occasionally to see his completed jigsaw or the pictures he'd painted in his colouring book. I quite enjoyed this - and listening to endless repeats of his scratchy record of "The Laughing Policeman" - but any real talk was impossible and I learned later that we could never be left alone in case he became so frustrated when I couldn't understand what he was trying to say that he lost his temper. He could be physically violent. So, for me, school was the obvious solution.

My mother found out that many of the children on the estate, instead of going into Grantham to the nearest Council school, took a few minutes' walk to catch a bus to a small village just over a mile away. The little Church School there was reported to be excellent so, one night after tea, my parents took me to the Headmaster's house to see if he could be persuaded to admit me months before my fifth birthday. I remember my excitement at walking from the bus in the twilight and being welcomed into a warm sitting-room. I still have a clear picture of its cheerful red curtains and bright fire. After a few minutes the pleasant man we'd come to see smiled broadly and said I could start next week (the beginning of the Spring Term) and that he would arrange for one of his "big girls" on our estate to call for me and take me to and from the bus for the first few days. I could hardly wait. I saw school as the Promised Land.

On my first day, Big Girl Susan left me holding my dinner-time sandwiches in the Infant playground, waiting to be collected by the teacher and taken into the cloakroom with the two other "new" children. I was then put to sit in a double desk with a kind but bossy little girl who clearly knew all about this place called school and I was given a lump of brownish plasticine to play with. Across the aisle was one of the new boys, in a desk of his own. Throughout the morning huge tears rolled down his cheeks and, until playtime, he sat desperately clutching the apple I'd seen his mother give him before she left. Despite the teacher's efforts to persuade him to go out to play with the rest of us, he persisted in sitting there, sniffing and gulping, and a small damp patch appeared on the front of his trousers. The next time I looked I saw he'd decided to sit on the apple. I found this rather surprising and when, ten minutes or so later, I noticed that he'd decided to eat it I felt disdainfully disgusted. Nothing, though - then or later - could rob me of the pleasure and excitement of being at school - not even the horrible old earth-closets across the yard. I simply learned not to "go" until I got home - a valuable skill which stayed with me for many years to come.

I was extremely lucky of course: it was a very good school. The big room held both the infant and the junior departments and our desks were arranged in five or six vertical lines, with two women teachers in charge. Children progressed from the Infants to Standard I (Juniors) simply by moving across to the next row, and this routine continued up to Standard 4, when children were transferred into the neighbouring room. Here the Head himself taught the elevens to fourteens. I realise now that he was a man ahead of his time, determined to provide an orderly, happy place where children would feel comfortable and secure. At playtime, in the winter, we could have - for a halfpenny - a mug of hot Horlicks (prepared on the coke stove by a carefully supervised senior monitor) and, as most of us couldn't get home for dinner, we could bring sandwiches or a small tin of stew or baked beans (complete in those days with a tiny cube of pork). These were heated up for us in a large vat of water and eaten with a piece or two of bread. Once a fortnight a visiting teacher came to instruct the older girls in cookery and homemaking and a group from the top class was always set the task of preparing a simple hot meal which we could buy for tuppence.

It is possible, of course, that the selling of Horlicks was a commercial venture which made a small profit for the school fund and, obviously, the Horlicks company would gain useful publicity from the fact that the mugs, and the crates which held them, were decorated with the product's name but, surprisingly, I have never heard of any other school which had such a scheme. However, none of the dinner arrangements could have had any financial benefit - and they can't have been easy to organise, given the building's limited, inconvenient resources.

I can recall very little about how and what I learned there over the next eighteen months - just one or two hazy memories of fitting strips of printed sentences into the blank spaces left on cards of nursery rhymes, and doing something with coloured counters which kept slipping into my desk shelf through the hole where the inkwell should have been. I certainly don't remember learning to read - it seemed I'd always known how. But I do remember waiting eagerly on a Saturday morning for "Chicks Own" - my first comic - to come through our letterbox and I know I was able to read the simple storylines under the strongly coloured pictures without any help from anyone. I remember, too, happily wrapping strong-smelling green raffia (why do I remember its taste?) round a hollow circle of stiff cardboard. This was later decorated, with some difficulty, by the addition of a spaced-out wrap of red raffia to form a gaudy little porthole. Several strands of yellow embroidery silk were then attached to hang it up by and I was allowed to take it home so my mother could paste a photo of me on to one side. I gave it to Grandma Taylor as a Christmas present and, until it eventually fell apart, it hung by its yellow loop at the side of her fireplace

Clearest of all, though, is the memory of being taken back to school by my father one dark night and the excitement of seeing its two rooms lit up, with a large Christmas tree in one of them. It had unwrapped presents hanging from its boughs and, at the end of the party tea and games, we were called up in descending order of age to choose one to take home. I realise now that the gifts most suitable for the older children were tied on to the higher branches and the infants' toys were right at the bottom, level with their eyes. For some reason, though, by the time it was my turn to choose, there was still a pretty necklace of blue beads just a little above my head. There was no question, no coaxing me to pick a furry bear or bubble pipe set instead - it was mine! There were tiny, sophisticated black beads between all the square-cut blue ones and when I got the necklace home my mother persuaded me to store it in her leather jewellery box until I was old enough to wear it. But I used to open the box and gloat over the lovely beads about once a week. They were such unexpectedly good quality that I was happy to wear them from being about fourteen until they broke, many years later, as I ran for a train and half the beads rolled down onto the line.

Because the Thirties was a time of serious financial depression, almost everyone had difficulty in making ends meet and we certainly had little to spare for luxuries. Most of our Yorkshire relatives and friends were in a similar situation so few were able to make the hundred miles trip to visit us. Only Uncle Tom had a car and, because the Humber estuary formed an effective barrier between the East Riding and Lincolnshire, there were no direct bus or train routes from Hull to Grantham. My mother must have missed her family and the wide circle of old friends very much. Fortunately she met up with one kindred spirit, Jess, who lived just a few streets away and they frequently entertained one another with cups of tea and chat. Despite the fact that they both moved away from Grantham, they kept in touch for the next fifteen years. Jess had a son only a little older than me and, though he didn't go to my school, Roy and I happily played together whenever we could. Otherwise, as a family, we made our own entertainment in our own home - and books were a vital part of this. No day seemed complete without at least some time spent reading.

My mother had little talent for dressmaking but she was a keen knitter and I never lacked pretty jumpers and cardigans. I *did* have cause to regret her enthusiasm, though, when I was about eight. She knitted me a stylish bathing suit which, to my shame and horror, sagged swiftly down below my knees the first time I wore it in the sea. As a change from the boring drudgery of housework without any of the labour-saving devices which later became commonplace, she also enjoyed embroidering tablecloths, dressing-table mats, and nightdress-cases in pretty coloured silks. This she called "my fancywork" and most days she would spend an hour or so on it, listening to a wireless programme at the same time. It involved very little creativity but she despised the currently popular designs featuring two or three Georgian ladies, standing in a thatched cottage garden of roses and hollyhocks, with their billowing skirts and bonnet ribbons blowing in the breeze. These could be bought already printed on pre-hemmed fabrics, often with the silks included or, at least, their colours dictated. Instead she preferred to choose her own material, and the transfers which she carefully positioned and ironed on. She could then make her own selection of coloured silks to suit the rooms or the person the article was intended for.

My father had many hobbies, some of which interested him all his life and others which preoccupied him for months and were then abandoned for ever. He always had a deep interest in building, making and mending things, and his training as an engineer meant he could invariably reason out the way anything mechanical could or should work. He could mend clocks and watches, repair cars, motor bikes and faulty electrical appliances - and really enjoy doing it - and we could be sure that, if he took something apart, he would put it together again without having any bits left over. My mother could also be sure that whatever he started he would finish. There were no rooms in our house left half-decorated! He liked gardening, coarse fishing, and making things of wood, and he found the challenge of both verbal and practical problems relaxing. I had a polymath for a father - could any child ask for more?

Coming from a farming family, he had grown up surrounded by animals and birds and he had a deep, if unsentimental, affection for them. We nearly always had at least one animal or bird in the shed or the garden recovering from some injury or other, and several remained attached to my father for the rest of their lives. Somehow, though, perhaps because he didn't want to burden my mother with any extra work during my babyhood, he managed to resist acquiring a dog until after I started school. Then he began preparing the ground.

'What's your favourite kind of dog?' he asked casually one day.

'Brown.'

'No, I mean what's your favourite breed?'

'What's breed mean?'

'Well, you remember Auntie Ann's dog; it's a Sealyham. That's its breed. The mountain dog in your storybook with the barrel of brandy round its neck is a St. Bernard - that's its breed. Tip on the farm is a Collie and that white dog with black spots we saw by the canal yesterday is a Dalmation.'

'You told me that was a Dismal Desmond!'

'Yes, but . . .'

But now my mother interrupted. 'Jean - which is your favourite dog?'

'A Sealyham,' I replied promptly.

I liked the sound of the word and I was fond of Auntie Ann; I simply forgot that her dog was always yapping and inclined to snap. There were no more questions.

On my fifth birthday I was told that I must wait for my main present till my father got home. He arrived carrying a sturdy box with large holes in the top. It jerked from side to side when he put it down on the floor and a kind of whining came from it.

'I hope that's not another rabbit with a broken leg,' said my mother, with a rather false note in her voice and a funny look on her face.

But when he unfastened and raised the lid she seemed as surprised as I was. A beautiful (if somewhat bedraggled) black Cocker spaniel puppy was doing his best to clamber out, panting and frantically wagging his little stump of a tail.

'He's yours,' smiled my father. 'We sent to the kennels in Norfolk for a Sealyham, but when I collected him from the station there was this letter to say that the one we were going to have is ill. The woman knew it had to be here for your birthday so she's sent this one instead so that you wouldn't be disappointed, love. We can send him back in a few days if we like and wait for the other one to get better.'

But of course we never did. We never even considered it. And, of course, he wasn't mine - he was ours: a much loved part of the family for the next ten years. I didn't even get to name him.

'We'll call him Paddy,' said my father. 'Is that O.K.?'
I nodded, overcome with sheer happiness. The name sounded just right to me and, until I saw a film of it some years later, I had no idea that - when I was five - there was a very popular play running in London called "Paddy, the Next Best Thing".

*

In 1932, with just a week's notice, my father was made redundant. He joined the hundreds of thousands of unemployed, with little hope of getting another job in the foreseeable future. Within another week we had packed up our furniture and travelled back to Hull, crushed together in the cab of the removal van. We had left Grantham for ever and, apart from Jess and her family, we lost contact with everyone we had known there. But once or twice, in recent years, it has amused me to speculate what might have happened if we had stayed in the town.

Presumably I would still have passed my scholarship to the local High School and, as we are the same age, I would probably have been in the same class as Margaret Roberts. For various reasons I think it's highly unlikely we would have been friends - I suppose it's just possible that I could have beaten the future Mrs Thatcher to the position of Head Girl? - so I have a lingering feeling that there is just a faint chance I might have changed the history of Britain quite significantly, if not the world . . . But we'll never know.

It had been arranged for our furniture to go back into store and we would stay with my mother's Auntie Mirrie until my parents could plan what to do. I remembered Auntie Mirrie well as she and Uncle Tom had driven over twice during our time in Grantham. Each time she'd arrived with presents for all of us, including Paddy, and a large box of over-sweet cream cakes for everyone to share. There was even a new colouring book for Leslie next door, for my mother wrote to Mirrie frequently, telling her details of our daily lives. She had been the first to know when my father lost his job and, typically, had offered immediate practical help. In fact, when we got to their house that first night - after being welcomed with a good hot meal - she passed my father a copy of the Hull Daily Mail with the adverts for every remotely possible job already ringed in red. She knew him well enough to realise he would want to take positive action immediately.

To everyone's surprise and immense relief, within a couple of weeks my father had actually started a job as maintenance engineer at a Hull metal box factory and our furniture had been moved into a rented house just off Beverley Road. I have no recollection of our short stay at Mirrie's. Any pictures of those few days are overlaid with dozens of vivid memories of Auntie herself and of the many happy hours I later spent in her shabby kitchen. Quietly perched on the old sofa behind the big, deal table, I was able to listen to adult conversations, to absorb news and gossip about members of our extended family circle and – occasionally – to persuade Auntie and my mother to tell me something of their past histories. Gradually, without consciously realising it, I was building up some pretty clear pictures of how our two families lived in the early 1900s.

Family History

Facts and Anecdotes

MIRRIE TAYLOR AND TOM HOGGARTH

Of course Auntie Mirrie had been brought up in very different circumstances and must have had to compromise in many ways after her marriage to Tom. Even after her first marriage to Henry Boot, a young officer in the Merchant Navy, Mirrie had stayed on with her parents in their comfortable, middle class home to help run the house and look after her motherless niece, ten-year-old May. This suited her for several reasons. Her husband was away at sea for many months at a time, and living rent-free at Elm Terrace meant she could very easily save a substantial amount towards setting up her own home in due course. And when Mirrie's son, Albert, was born in 1914 it seemed sensible for her to stay at home until the war was over and her husband was out of danger.

The relief all felt when the Armistice was signed was marred by the fact that her mother had died some months before and would not be there to welcome her sons home from France. But Mirrie was in a state of feverish excitement. Her husband had sent a letter to say he would be home in a couple of months and would be able to spend the long leave due to him with her and their little boy. After the death of her Grandma, May had left to join her father and his family, and start working at the printing works. This meant that Mirrie was free to rent a little house so that she, Henry and Albert could be together as a real family. She bought furniture, moved in, and stocked up the pantry as best she could so that she would be able, at last, to welcome him to the comforts of his own home with a lavish spread. All she had to do now was to wait for the telegram telling her the date and time of his arrival. It seemed incredible that he had come through four years of brutal war unscathed – but it was so long since she'd seen him that she trembled with nervous joy.

The telegram came . . . He had been struck down with the terrible Spanish influenza and had died two days ago . . . It was little Albert's wails, as he crouched by his mother's inert body that brought the neighbours into the house. And it was one of them who took a message to the printing works, so that a brother and sister could come over to help her into bed, and comfort the anxious little boy.

*

By the time I was born in 1926, Tom had already married my Auntie Mirrie so, from my point of view, they'd always been a couple: a fixture. It therefore never occurred to me to ask anyone where or how they had met, but it seems to me now that I was aware from a very early age that it was an unlikely match. Tom was several years younger than her and many would have described him as a rough customer because he was tall and solidly built, and his partial deafness meant that he generally spoke very loudly. His mother had died when he was a young boy and his coarse, ill-educated father had taken him out of school at the age of twelve and sent him to work in the stables attached to Hull Fish Dock. It was only by sheer hard work, crafty planning and rigorous saving that he had won himself two valuable assets: a small business as a fish merchant, and a wife of Mirrie's calibre and more genteel background. As a child, instead of being alarmed by his bulk and clumsy, bluff ways, I was quite fond of him -

understandably, perhaps, because he was clearly fond of me. Looking back, I think he probably would have liked to have had a little daughter, preferably dainty and feminine, so different from himself. He and Mirrie had had a baby boy soon after they were married, but he was severely handicapped and died at the age of three. This, too, may have contributed to the rather surly face which he often presented to the world and which others found somewhat off-putting.

But I have many pleasant memories of the times I spent as a child with Uncle Tom. He had an unexpected talent which appealed to me very much - he could play the piano. He loved the popular songs of the day and bought sheet copies of most of them as soon as they appeared in the shops. Whenever I was at their house he would try to finish work early, go and wash and change, then sit at the piano in the front room, as he called it, tempting me to join him by playing his latest purchase as loudly as he could. And I would leave the fascinations of the kitchen, where Auntie was cooking a meal and baking pies, without a backward glance. I would spend the next hour standing by his side - the only way I could comfortably read the words - and joyfully sing the newest songs three or four times through (just the choruses, as we rarely bothered with the less tuneful verses) until I knew them by heart. I would then sort out my favourites from the piles of music kept on the nearby table and pass them over one by one for him to play: romantic songs, comic songs, musical comedy numbers, the lot. Uncle Tom and I didn't care for childish songs. Any such as Shirley Temple's "On the Good Ship Lollipop" held no charm for us. We went for a more sophisticated or humorous selection: "Charmaine", "It

Happened in Monterey", or "Miss Otis Regrets She's Unable to Lunch Today".

It was a family joke that even at the age of two, already able to hold a recognisable tune, I loved to stand in the middle of a room and sing "Always" as a duet with anyone who could provide the bits in between : 'I'll be loving you . . .' followed by the little show-off's contribution . . . 'Arways' . . . 'With a love that's true . . .' 'Arways' . . . and so on for as long as the partnering adult and the audience could stand it. I think Uncle simply took over from there.

What I didn't realize for some years, however, was that Uncle Tom only bought the sheet music for the words and the melody line. He then just vamped the accompanying chords like a run-of-the-mill pub pianist, and I suppose it's quite possible that this was how he'd earned a few shillings in his younger days. He was no great drinker, though, so free pints would hold little attraction. Yet he must have had some lessons in how to read music for, when we were eventually called back into the kitchen to have our tea or supper, we'd steal two or three minutes more so that he could round off the entertainment with a bravura performance of "The Wedding of the Painted Dolls" - not a particularly easy piece, but he played it in full and apparently with all the correct chords. And I could then settle back on the old kitchen sofa and eat my meal in a daze of musical contentment.

Though their characters and personalities differed so obviously, Mirrie and Tom were a firmly bonded couple - a unit. And it was as a unit that they had a number of strong, practical influences upon me. For one thing, although she was by no means the oldest of the eight Taylor children, after her mother died Auntie Mirrie saw herself as the family matriarch, and she felt it was her duty - indeed her pleasure - to make sure that the family members were kept in regular, social contact with each other. This seemed important once several of them no longer worked for the firm, and particularly so after their father had remarried. "Ma", as they called his new wife with little respect and no affection, was a domineering woman who very quickly persuaded him to retire from active involvement in the family firm and to devote his time to entertaining her rather than to keeping close contact with his grown-up sons and daughters. By then, though, all had married and several had children. One son, Holborn, had emigrated to Canada and no one over here had met his wife and daughter. Another had left the firm to work on the Hull Daily Mail. Only three sons and no daughters were now employed at the printing works and when their father died two years later, Ma sold the house, left Hull, and prepared to live for the rest of her life on the proceeds plus a share of the firm's profits.

So, with some unspoken reservations, most of the brothers and sisters, their wives and husbands, reluctantly began to regard Mirrie as their main source of family information and the centre of any social links. Mirrie and Tom were delighted. They were enthusiastic party-givers, picnic planners, and supper providers, and both were prepared to keep the family from drifting too far apart by bullying her relatives into meeting up as frequently as possible. This meant that, whenever my father was working in Hull and we were living locally, I was part of many get-togethers. These were always interesting, often great fun and - for me - often educational. By the early thirties Tom had a decent-sized car and my father had his rebuilt Morgan, so Mirrie would arrange for a little group, including my parents and me, to pack a picnic and drive to spend two or three happy hours at Millington Springs: to take an evening trip to Bridlington: to invite several of us to their house on a Saturday for a hot supper and a game of cards. These suppers were usually either a simple meal of pork sausages, mushy peas and crusty rolls, or beer-battered cod flanked by a generous helping of deep golden chips – again plus the inevitable mushy peas. Even after he'd transferred to the coal business, Tom had kept up his contacts with the Fish Market and he took great pride in being able to buy superb quality fillets and in expertly cooking them for us himself.

But it was the post-Christmas Parties that were the most memorable. The lavish food was planned with detailed care and my mother would go over two or three days beforehand to help Auntie Mirrie with the shopping and complicated cooking preparations. The afternoon before the party Uncle Tom would set his two workmen to sweep and swill out the large, brick archway which was attached to the side of the house and the following morning they would hang tarpaulins at the end which faced the stables. Stout sacking was used to seal off the draughts from the big wooden doors which opened onto the street, more tarpaulins were spread on the concrete floor, and trestle tables set up ready for the borrowed tablecloths and cutlery. By the time the electric light bulbs had been strung across the roof, and a motley collection of benches, stools and chairs had been lined up round the trestles, the place began to look unexpectedly inviting - even cosy. I suppose that, even with a smelly paraffin stove tucked into each corner of the "room", it must still have been pretty cold in there but we were a hardy lot in those days. Everyone knew to dress warmly and, once we'd moved from the house and sat down for the meal, no one seemed to notice the chill. The food and drink, the excitement of lively conversation, the revival of old family jokes and the half-serious bickering rooted in childhood rivalries, all seemed to raise the general temperature and make people forget any physical discomfort.

When the meal was over the trestles were dismantled and pushed out of sight into the stable yard ready for the rest of the evening's festivities. As the only child in the family for many years, I was allowed to stay up after the meal until half past ten but I then had to make my way up to the attic and try to sleep. I was lucky, though. This left plenty of time for me to learn the meaning of real hospitality, and the fun which simple games such as Animal, Vegetable and Mineral, Clumps, and Consequences could be for people of all ages *if* they are prepared to let their hair down. I remember that phrase puzzling me very much when I first heard it. This was the early Thirties and all the women at these parties had bobbed hair, Marcelled waves or semi-Eton crops, and the men were balding or had what was known as a "short back and sides".

The most exciting game for me, though, was Charades. This did not involve individual mimes as it usually does nowadays, but was played according to our traditional rules. Two groups of four or five people were called for - in our family it was the men rather than the women who volunteered to take part more eagerly - and each team retired to a separate room to choose a three or four syllable word and plan the scenes they were going to act. Each scene had to contain one of the syllables, clearly spoken, and the whole word had to be said at least once in the final scene. The audience then had to identify it. Perhaps because, as printers, knowledge of and interest in words were part of the fabric of their daily lives, the choice of a team's word was a serious matter and - even when a very simple one was decided upon as a double bluff - a number of other multisyllable words had to be thought of to trail as red herrings in the final scene.

Once the words and scenes were decided upon, the actors would the ransack Auntie Mirrie's wardrobes, the bedroom where the coats were laid, and any part of the house they thought could provide the necessary costumes. The results were hilarious. Any woman taking part tended to dress conventionally but the men - three normally fairly staid great-uncles of mine, plus my father and Albert - liked to abandon their dark suits and sober shirts and ties. Some would swan into the temporary theatre-in-the-round wearing dresses, hats and heavy make-up, with rayon stockings held up with knotted elastic and their own woollen socks filled with tea towels and thrust into the front of their bodices. Others might choose the blowsy housewife look, rolling up their own shirt sleeves, draping a cross-over pinny around their inadequate skirt arrangements and using a checked duster as a turban to disguise their unsuitable hair style or balding heads. At least one, though, would have to play a male role but generally he'd still manage to make it a comic one. Clothes which were far too big or too small were just right in this case and a wrong-sized cap or hat was a bonus.

Inevitably the audience tended to become so convulsed by the comedy of each scene that they often forgot to listen for the syllable or complete word - but who cared? Of course I loved every minute of it and I still recall the severe attack of hiccups I developed laughing at my grandfather, Will, as he sat with his largest brother perched on his knees and they launched into a take-off of a pathetically unsuccessful ventriloquist act. Occasionally, to my intense joy, I was asked to take a small part in one of the scenes and, once, was given the whole word to say!

My growing interest in acting and obvious willingness to perform songs and monologues for my patient relatives whenever I was asked, were also encouraged by Auntie Mirrie and Uncle Tom's taking me two or three times a year to the theatre : often the Palace or the Tivoli Music Halls. I was sometimes asked to stay with them for a weekend – probably to give my parents a bit of a break (after all they'd only had ten months of married life before I arrived) - and on the Saturday we usually went to a cinema matinee or the first house at a theatre. They particularly enjoyed the comedians' often coarse humour and the conjurers' polished performances, but for me the spectacle of the colourful costumes, the dancing and the music, were all magical. But I also revelled in being able to laugh at most of the jokes along with the audience. None of it seemed garish or crude to me.

Auntie was a firm believer in many forms of fortune telling and would respond to the most unlikely advertisements. I remember her sending off an unwashed shirt collar (with a postal order for the substantial sum of four shillings) in the hope of hearing whether Uncle Tom would soon make their fortune with his coal business. One Saturday, when my mother took me to stay the night with them, I was surprised to see that Auntie Mirrie and a strange, dark-skinned woman were sitting at the kitchen table with a pack of cards spread out in front of them. The woman looked up and stared at us in disconcerting silence as we went upstairs to unpack my little suitcase in the attic bedroom, and she had gone by the time we came down again.

Years later I was told that this woman had said, 'That little girl is destined to go on the stage - but she'll only ever appear for charity.'

This turned out to be true, of course, but Auntie Mirrie chose to ignore the latter part of the prophecy and was happy to see it as her responsibility to start preparing me for my star-spangled future.

ANNIE ELIZABETH LANGDALE

The kitchen at Great Aunt Annie's was quite different from Auntie Mirrie's. It was spacious and usually full of light because its handsome bay window looked out onto the gardens at the side and rear of the house. As a child, even though it was used most mornings as a breakfast room, I didn't think of it as Auntie Annie's kitchen because her maid, Olive, spent more time there than she did and, in any case, in the evening it became Olive's sitting-room for a couple of hours. But I always felt welcome and at home there and whenever the large deal table in the centre of the room was covered with its red chenille cloth I knew there would be no baking or ironing on it for several hours and I could spread my painting things, dolls' furniture, or jigsaw on it without being disturbed.

Nevertheless, I was not entirely comfortable in that kitchen. Except for one old Windsor chair which was used by Olive in the evening and therefore softened slightly by the addition of a rather thin, sad-looking cushion, the seats of the rest were rigidly plump and covered in glossy, black horsehair. As a child I usually wore very short skirts which left my tender thighs bare, and contact with this harsh upholstery made sitting at the breakfast table, or kneeling up on a chair to paint, horribly uncomfortable. Edwardians apparently found its appearance fashionably smart but, apart from the fact that it was almost indestructible, I couldn't see its attraction - and I still can't. Many years later, when I read that nudists - for various reasons - routinely carry a towel around the camp with them to put on chairs before sitting down, I wished I had thought of that when visiting Auntie Annie. As it was I just grizzled and displayed my increasingly angry rash until somebody found me a cushion.

One other thing in the room made me uncomfortable, but in a very different way. On the long wall opposite the bay window, below the line of bells used to summon servants in the previous owners' days, there was a single picture. It was a coloured print in a heavy oak frame and it was quite the largest picture I had ever seen. Even now I cannot imagine why it had been chosen: it was not in any way relevant to kitchen activities or to the lives of anyone we knew, and I found its subject deeply disturbing. It showed a maiden (obviously!) standing forlornly on a rugged mountain top, gazing despairingly heavenwards. She must have been uncomfortable because she was barefoot and very lightly clad, with a mass of dark, wavy hair blowing around her drooping shoulders. Worryingly, her wrists were tied in front of her with a stout rope and, a few yards away, there was an evil-looking man sitting cross-legged on a rock, leering viciously at her. His colourful clothes were vaguely Eastern in design and he was holding a musical instrument which my parents and I were never able to identify. It appeared to be a cross between a hookah and a set of bagpipes but, though there was no indication of why he was playing it, his future intentions were pretty clear, even to me. Luckily, as with all pictures, I eventually ceased to notice it - but I still heartily dislike bagpipes.

Great Aunt Annie was my father's aunt and from the time he

could walk and talk she had struggled with Jinnie, his mother, to become first lady in Frank's affections. Annie had never cared very much for her sister-in-law, and was more or less indifferent to Frankie her own brother, but young Frank was everything she could have wanted in a son if she had been fortunate enough to have one. So it suited her very well that, when Frank's little sister was born with spina bifida, Jinnie was so overwhelmed with the difficulties of nursing her that she was glad to be able to leave the two-year-old boy with her husband's family at nearby Mount Airey Farm for much of the time. This meant Auntie was in charge and she could make Frank feel that this was really his home. So she did.

Annie was the only daughter of Richard, a successful small farmer. After his wife died of what was known in those days as "galloping consumption", leaving three young children and two-week-old Frankie, he was relieved to find a very responsible housekeeper to run his house and look after his family. He could pay for adequate daily help too, so Mrs Boothby (herself recently widowed) quickly realised that acting as a substitute for a farmer's wife - and, perhaps achieving an even closer relationship in time - was a very comfortable position for an honest, capable woman with a twelve-year-old boy of her own to bring up. She stayed there, though marriage was never offered, until she died some thirty-five years later. Annie, therefore, grew up as a favoured daughter who could choose how much or how little she had to be involved with household chores and - perhaps because she realised its practical advantages - she chose to share Mrs Boothby's responsibilities. Consequently, by the time she was eighteen, she had learned to be a highly competent housewife, with all the skills the future wife of a farmer might need.

Unfortunately, no young farmer saw her in this light, and I'm not sure why. She joined in most village activities: she played tennis in the summer, skated on Kelsey Hill ponds in the winter, and by all accounts was involved in many of the Congregational Chapel's social events. Despite being quite small she was strong and energetic, fairly pleasant-looking, and obviously reasonably well-provided for financially. But apparently no one came courting, unless my grandmother's story about her sister-in-law's clandestine meetings with one of the farm labourers could be believed - and Jinnie's stories tended to be enriched for her listeners' enjoyment rather than related to strict truth.

However, this enforced spinsterhood meant that Annie had time on her hands to devote to my father and, as his home-life was somewhat uncomfortable even after his severely disabled sister died before she was a year old, he insisted on spending the bulk of his time at Mount Airey. He was quite fond of his Auntie Annie and tolerant of her somewhat clinging affection. In any case, from the age of five onwards he was always eager to be part of the working life on his grandfather's farm. He even enjoyed helping to pack the eggs, butter, and dressed fowl which, once a fortnight, Annie or Mrs. Boothby would take to Hull market to sell.

The Langdale's farm produce stall was set up in the covered hall there and Annie quite enjoyed sitting behind the carefully set out goods, meeting regular customers and chatting with the farmers' wives at the stalls on either side of hers. It was an outing and a welcome change from farm and village routines but, more importantly, it was a regular source of pin money. Farmers' wives and daughters generally looked after the chickens and the dairy, and traditionally kept the proceeds for themselves. Annie was often teased by her father about the size of her "nest-egg". One day, however, she arrived at her usual stall to find that a Mrs Wright had taken over the one next to hers and, inevitably, they were soon deep in conversation. The Wrights' farm was many miles north east of Keyingham so they hadn't met before, but over the next few months a good deal of family information was exchanged. Mrs Wright must have been impressed by what she saw and heard because, one day, she suggested that Annie should meet her son – ". . . the one who is lame and so can't take on a farm . . .". Annie already knew he was the chief clerk in a Hull solicitor's office, so she felt this might be worth her while.

Within three weeks of their first meeting, according to the story she frequently told me, Auntie Annie was excitedly hurrying over to Prince's Avenue in Hull to tell her favourite cousin, Edie, 'I've met Mr Wright at last and I'm sure he's right both in name and nature.'

And for thirty-five-year-old Annie he certainly was. He proved to have been well worth waiting for.

AUNTIE ANNIE AND UNCLE WILL WRIGHT

They were married in the summer of 1911 and the actual ceremony took place in the Congregational Chapel which was no more than a hundred yards or so from the farm house. It was a fine Saturday afternoon so much of the village turned out to see Annie in her white silk wedding dress walk with her father and cousin Edie down the red carpet spread in the lane in her honour. When she and her new husband walked back to Mount Airey's walled garden for the reception they were followed by a chattering crowd of relatives and friends, eagerly looking forward to the elaborate food which Annie and Mrs Boothby had been preparing over the last few days. It was a courageous beginning to their life together. Will was a tall, fine-looking man but his badly-deformed feet in their expensive hand-made boots were reminiscent of those of Chinese women who'd had theirs bound as small children. The discomfort they'd caused him all his life meant that he could only walk slowly and awkwardly with the help of a stick, so this protracted procession was, in effect, a public announcement of his disability, and this gesture gained him the permanent respect of the whole village. This was important to him because Annie had made it clear she wanted to stay in "her" village rather than move into Hull, and Will was more than willing to travel ten miles daily to his city office. He'd been brought up in the country and still wished he could have inherited and worked his father's farm.

Annie's father, Richard Langdale, had already set up his two older sons with their own farms so – fair minded as always -

he had given his daughter a substantial sum of money towards purchasing a house. This, plus Will's family's similar contribution and the couple's own savings, meant they were able to buy West View several months before the wedding and move into it when they got back from their honeymoon in Scarborough. It was a good-sized house, a few yards down a broad lane which ran at right angles from the main Hull to Withernsea road. The open fields in front of it sloped gently down towards the west so, on a clear day, it was possible - from all the main rooms - to see the glint of the River Humber in the far distance. Sunsets were often a magnificent sight and at night the lights of Hull were strung out like a chain of tiny jewels on the horizon. The vet who had previously owned the house had retired, well-heeled, from his flourishing practice, but it had stood empty for some months and Auntie was faced with the daunting task of cleaning and refurbishing all its slightly run-down rooms before she and Will could start installing any furniture.

Will said she should have someone to help her, now and in the future: the house was too big to run on her own. Annie therefore decided to look for a very young girl whom she could train up from scratch, as it were, to suit her own ways and her own standards. It would be cheaper too, which naturally appealed to Annie's ingrained thriftiness. She knew all the village families well, of course, especially those who attended her own chapel, so the Watsons immediately came to mind. They were an industrious, respectable couple with a family of five children crammed into an inconveniently small cottage and Annie decided that, if their Olive could leave school at Easter, she would be the most suitable girl available.

She was a wiry but strong-looking twelve-year-old, bright but with a pleasant meekness about her which Annie felt should make her easy to train. She was extremely plain - downright ugly some might say - so Annie thought she was unlikely to leave her service to get married. She was also confident that Olive would be in little danger from those who "were only after one thing" as she put it when talking with Mrs Boothby.

I can almost hear her saying smugly, 'I can't see her leaving because someone's got her into trouble, like some we could mention.'

Olive proved to be a cheerful, willing worker who learned the necessary domestic skills quickly, and clearly appreciated the abundant food which Annie provided. Their relationship remained very formal, of course. There was never any suggestion that Olive could be looked on as a friend and she was always kept aware of "her place", but she was rewarded for her hard work by being asked to the wedding, roped in to help with the Reception at the farmhouse, and was given the exciting pleasure of getting her own bedroom ready to move into afterwards. She stayed on as maid until Auntie Annie died at the age of ninety-one.

Despite the restrictions and difficulties following the outbreak of war three years or so after their marriage, Auntie Annie and Uncle Will were able to settle contentedly into a very comfortable middle class life. Over the next few years they spent a fair amount of money improving and furnishing the house quite luxuriously. The vet who had lived at West View before them had needed to travel to outlying farms and villages so he had kept two horses and a gig. There was a coach house set beyond the gravel drive at the side of the house and stabling for the horses at the far end of the garden, so Will bought a pony and trap for Annie and, until a regular bus service ran past the end of their lane, she was able to drive him to the station each day to meet the Hull train. By the time I was a regular visitor White Wings, the romantically named pony, had died and the doorless coach house was used as a store for small mountains of coal and strong-smelling pine logs.

Uncle Will was professionally very successful and his salary reflected the high trust which all the firm's partners placed in him. He was also given much shrewd advice about how and where to invest any spare capital he might have. Most of the house, at least up to the green baize door at the end of the entrance hall, was quite opulently furnished, and their clothes and food were always of the best quality. Soon after the First World War he and Auntie were able to buy a sizeable piece of land a hundred yards or so down the main road and as a hobby, satisfyingly rooted in their farming backgrounds, they kept a flock of free-ranging chickens, and two sows in a purpose-built brick barn. The rest of the land was laid out as an orchard, a vegetable garden and a netted enclosure devoted to growing soft fruit.

Mark Gondell, an elderly man who'd been employed on the Langdale's farm for many years, had always spent two days a week working in the garden at West View. He was responsible for the lawns, the borders, the three little plots of colourful bedding plants surrounded by foot-high box hedges, and the large patches of ground devoted to vegetables and flowers of all kinds which Auntie needed for the house. Uncle liked to do most of the work in the greenhouse himself and he spent many happy hours a week pottering around the waist-high shelves raising seedlings, grapes and exotic pot-plants.

However, once the Paddock, as it came to be known, was bought Mark worked there a couple of hours every day and what had started as a hobby soon began to pay useful dividends - in financial as well as practical terms. Uncle enjoyed feeding the pigs and chickens at weekends and when Olive had any time to spare from the daily housework she could help collect, wash and grade eggs to sell to a visiting market trader, pick fruit for the table and for jam-making, and make herself generally useful in the garden, couldn't she ? It was nearly as good as having a farm!

For the first few years of her marriage Annie was very actively involved in the day-to-day running of the house and in teaching the young housemaid her own domestic skills and methods but, as Olive grew stronger and more experienced, she was expected to take over more and more of the specialised tasks as well as the routine work. Olive learned quickly and despite the very long hours and hard work involved, was always willing to take on extra responsibilities. This gave Auntie a great deal of free time. She still enjoyed doing a little of the cooking and seasonal preserving herself, and would often see to the hens and their eggs, but - except in the harsh weather of winter - she always spent at least an hour every morning doing the flowers: a traditional "lady of the house" occupation. This ceremony involved collecting the filled vases and epergnes from the large dining-room, hall, and smaller drawing-room, and assembling them on the kitchen table so that the water could be renewed and any drooping blooms or sprays could be replaced with fresh ones gathered from the flower garden. The arrangements were always delicately beautiful, especially those in the slender glass cones of the branched epergnes. Whenever we were staying there my mother was expected to sit in the kitchen and chat until the flowers were finished and I could see how hard she had to struggle to hide her impatience and boredom with the fiddly attention Auntie gave to the task. At home she had to make do with one bunch of flowers per week, bought on a Friday from the local greengrocer - as long as they weren't too expensive - and, in any case, desultory chat about the price of pig meal or Mark Gondell's rheumatics was hardly gripping. Far more interesting, if only for their unexpectedness, were Auntie's artistic activities, but she rarely talked about these - she just displayed the amazing results with modest pride.

As soon as Olive could be trusted to be left in charge of the housework and cooking, Auntie had felt free to take up the interests she had apparently longed to pursue since she was a young girl: painting, embroidery and complicated crochet work. Even Uncle Will was surprised at the quantity of finished articles Annie produced to embellish the rooms' walls and high-quality furniture. With the help of expert tutors who ran the classes which she now attended regularly in Hull, she completed four large oil paintings for the dining room (one seascape and three Italian city scenes), several small flower pictures for the main bedrooms, and three quite sophisticated portraits on bevelled glass of romanticised Italian peasants for the drawing room. Uncle had them all framed in heavy, ornately-carved, gilt frames which were the height of fashion in Edwardian times and, hanging from the broad picture rails of these high-ceilinged rooms, they looked impressively professional.

I always felt, though, that the effect of the delicately tinted glass paintings in the drawing room was spoilt by the two vividly-coloured tapestries which also hung there. I was told that these had been made by Auntie's mother and her sister (my great-grandmother and great-great-aunt, now I come to think of it) before they were married, so I can understand why they were proudly displayed, resplendent in yet more flamboyant gilt frames, in a place of such signal honour. But their size and the rather crude colours of the Berlin wool used for the close-packed stitches were somewhat overpowering. Prolonged exposure to bright sunlight, leading to some judicious fading, might have been a good idea. Their subjects, too, were not altogether appropriate for their setting. The one of the Last Supper, with Christ and his disciples in their traditional Da Vinci positions, was fairly acceptable - though Judas's chin should perhaps have been unpicked and re-done - but I never felt that the two-foot square representation of a suffering Christ stumbling under the weight of a massive cross (and being cruelly mocked by five or six onlookers) was a particularly comfortable choice for a drawing room. Still - apart from the slightly dodgy chin - the tapestries were expertly embroidered and must have taken hundreds of hours and immense patience to complete.

Once her pictures were finished, Auntie moved on to perfecting other artistic skills which she must have initially acquired when she was a fairly leisured spinster living with her father at the farm. She continued to go to classes and, though nothing she produced was original or more than basically creative (it was essentially painting-by-numbers) she was clearly very skilled indeed and all her work was a joy to look at. She crocheted and tatted yards of silky white thread into deep trimmings and inserts for tablecloths and bed linen. She made tapestry tops for footstools and embroidered beautiful panels for a two-sided screen - three depicting deep-coloured flowers in gorgeous silks and three Jacobean designs in fine wool. One had only to look around the house and garden to know that there was no shortage of money or comfort at West View.

So it seemed incredible that, until I was about twelve, there was regular traffic between the back door and the far end of the coach house - and not just to fill the coal scuttles and log baskets. There was a dark, open corridor down the far side there and, at the end of it was a privy with a mahogany seat - a two-holer. The fitments included a bucket of ashes complete with handy trowel and, inevitably, squares of paper on a loop of string hanging from a nearby hook. It was the only lavatory at West View and we hated it. Even on a bright spring day I dreaded going there. It was dank and smelly and a refuge for spiders, and I was always disappointed to find that the paper squares were ripped from "Farmers' Weekly". They made very boring reading – though, now I come to think about it, any more interesting material would have been equally frustrating. The torn segments would very rarely have contained even one complete sentence. My father swore it was fifty yards from kitchen door to the wooden throne (and "swore" is an apt word in this context) and on bitter cold, winter nights the unavoidable visits to its horrors required thick coats and scarves, a flashlight and gritted teeth - quite difficult when once they started chattering. We tried to synchronize our trips whenever possible and would take it in turns to stand at the entrance, stamping our feet and slapping our crossed arms around our shoulders. I remember my mother saying she wasn't surprised that there was always a box of Bile Beans, a popular 1930s remedy for constipation, on Auntie's night table.

Over the years my father had been able to introduce several new ideas and beneficial changes into some areas of their lives. After all he had lived at West View - loved by them both and regarded, more or less, as their son - from 1915 till he'd begun his apprenticeship. His father was in the Yeomanry and was called-up soon after war began to serve as the Regimental rough-rider, buying and breaking-in horses in Ireland, and Jinnie had joined him as soon as it became possible, relishing the social "perks" stemming from her position as a Sergeant Major's wife. She had needed little urging to leave young Frank in the care of Annie and Will for the duration.

With his encouragement and advice Annie and Will had bought their first wireless set, and a Hoover for Olive to use. They tried and enjoyed a luxury coach tour of Scotland, and even a cruise of the Norwegian fjords. In 1938 my father's persistent nagging finally persuaded Uncle Will that Auntie's health might suffer if she had to continue the disagreeable, routine trips to the coach house annexe. For some years they had both maintained that there was really no need to spend money unnecessarily on a water closet. They pointed out they'd been used to privies all their lives and that, in any case, it was healthier to keep "all that" well away from the house. Reminders that they weren't getting any younger and that my mother's family, who lived only five minutes' walk away, had had a water closet for many years, carried little weight.

'Even when I was in bed with the 'flu,' protested Annie, 'Olive managed.'

'Well, she shouldn't have to!' was my father's reply. 'And what if she'd caught the 'flu at the same time?'

That question hit hard - and the battle was won. *We* were delighted, of course, and I rather think Olive must have been too, but it would never have occurred to her to presume to say so.

As we were living in Norwich at that time it was several months before we visited West View again and we were somewhat surprised to be taken, as soon as we arrived, to see the new lavatory. We were even more surprised when we saw it. A section of a sturdy old building which was used to store bins of grain and poultry food had been neatly sliced off. It was very professionally done and the toilet (now so called) which had been installed there was a great improvement on the wretched privy over at the coach house. My mother, I know, was bitterly disappointed that a trot from the back door across a flagged yard would still be necessary, and I was sorry to see that the only light in the place came through the gaps at the top and bottom of the door, but I realised that - apart from the effect upon the temperature in the bleakly whitewashed cubicle – this economy hardly mattered; the deeply uninteresting "Farmers' Weekly" was still in use. Overall, though, it was progress and we praised it as enthusiastically as we could manage.

My father, however, could say what he liked without offence.

'Couldn't the architect find room to put it in the house then? I'd have thought the bathroom was plenty big enough to . . .'

'Oh no!' Uncle was obviously surprised by Frank's lack of sensitivity. 'We didn't feel it would be hygienic to have it in the house.'

My father accepted the fait accompli philosophically. He begged the old privy's mahogany lid from them and, the next Christmas, gave them a beautiful, highly-polished side-table to keep their new wireless on. I don't know if they ever realised what he'd made it from but I was delighted, eventually, to inherit it - and it's just the right size for the Word Processor I'm typing this on.

GRANDPA AND GRANDMA TAYLOR

Once back in Hull we enjoyed living near Keyingham and being able to visit the Taylor grandparents with so little effort. My mother was especially glad that, when her father asked if he could come and eat with us on Wednesday lunchtimes, she was able to make him something he was particularly fond of, and have some time with him on her own. She wasn't in any way jealous of her half sister, Nora – indeed they were quite close – but it can't have been all that easy, once she had married and moved away, to know that his daily life and almost all his attention were centred round her step-mother and Nora. And he was not only very special to her, he was a very special man.

I realise now that he was a mass of contradictions. Superficially he seemed a very reserved, rather taciturn man; indeed he often appeared to be quite shy, even self-conscious, but he won Debating Society prizes for public speaking (I still have several beautifully bound volumes of Dickens from the set he won in 1903) and, until his active allegiance to the Non-conformist movement faded, he was in great demand in surrounding villages as a lay preacher. Despite his generally giving the impression of being very serious-minded and somewhat aloof, he had a wicked sense of humour. He would often dissolve into helpless laughter at others' jokes, and his own, unexpectedly witty comments enlivened many family discussions. It was typical of him that, when young Frank Langdale and his close friend Harry Etherington – acknowledged experts in identifying small animals from their footprints and other, less savoury, leavings – joined the Taylor rambling parties around Robin Hood's Bay, Grandpa said he appreciated being able to call on the services of two resident turdologists! For many years he was a very active member of the Keyingham drama group and in the charades at Auntie Mirrie's parties he could act the fool with hilarious subtlety.

My mother was immensely proud of him: of his standing in the village where, as chairman of the Parish Council, his help and advice were constantly sought by worried people about all kinds of problems: of the three act play he wrote for the village Dramatic Society, and the two or three humorous articles he had published in "Titbits": of his knowledge of antiques and the fairly valuable pieces of china and other items he managed to buy at various auction sales. Some of these interests and achievements I knew about at the time, but I only learned of other facets of his life many years later. I don't remember seeing his "Titbits" articles but I clearly recall being taken to see his play, "The Mounteagle Letter", which was based on local involvement in the Gunpowder Plot. I was most impressed by the costumes and by references to the church tower at Welwick - only a few miles away – where conspirators went to watch anxiously for Guy Fawkes' ship to come sailing up the Humber.

Grandma Taylor also had some slightly unexpected facets to her character. Her real name was Sarah Ann Charlotte but she was known to all relatives and friends as Nance. I have no idea why, and it never occurred to me to ask because – at least by the time I knew her – she was quite a formidable lady, and hardly one who might be expected to be given a pet name or to encourage the use of a nickname. She came from a comfortably-off family in Birmingham and at sixteen she had been apprenticed to a fashionable tailoring and dressmaking firm in the city. Grandma had worked hard to become successful in all areas of her training but she specialised in highly-skilled cutting and was soon, therefore, very much in demand.

However unlikely it may sound, a well-known Court Dressmaker – Madame Clapham, would you believe? – was based in Hull in the 1900s and, when Nance was still quite a young woman, she was bribed with a substantial salary rise to leave her well-paid post in Birmingham and become Head Cutter at Madame's prestigious establishment. Nance was tall and carried herself with a faintly regal air, and it was noticed that she bore a slight resemblance to Princess Mary, who was soon to become Queen. So, just occasionally, she was expected to leave whatever she was working upon and model some of Madame's newest dresses for any distinguished customers who were finding it difficult to choose which gowns to order for the Season - an Edwardian mannequin in fact.

The Taylors were staunch Baptists and so was Nance, and she arrived in Hull in 1905 with letters of introduction to the Chapel which my relatives attended. She was made very welcome, of course, by all the families of the congregation, but the Taylors were particularly impressed with her and entertained her so frequently that she quickly felt at home in Elm Terrace and joined in most of their social activities. By now Grandpa had been a widower for over three years and, since his wife died, had lived back at home with his baby daughter, my mother. So, inevitably, he found himself spending a good deal of time in Nance's company. She and Will were married within a year of her arrival in Hull and Madame Clapham lost her Head Cutter.

Nora, their daughter, was born two years later and soon after the War began they decided to move out of Hull to the safety of a sizeable cottage in Keyingham. There was no deliberate attempt to remove themselves from the rest of the family but, from then on, Nance saw them rarely and this tended to limit Will's contact with his brothers and sisters to the workplace. Only May, after she came to live with them in Elm Cottage in 1918, kept in close touch with her Hull relatives, both through her daily work and as a visitor to their homes. In any case, Nance had plenty to occupy her in Keyingham. She was an excellent housewife and mother and a very good cook and, as the invaluable Mrs Rogers came in every day to do the rough work and the laundry, Grandma was able to take part in almost all the village's social activities and "good works". Before long she was made President of the local Women's Institute and wasn't allowed to give up this responsibility for nearly twenty-five years – and then only on condition that she took over the more onerous job of Secretary.

Anyone seeing Grandpa as he travelled to work, sober suited, on the Hull train might have been surprised that he chose to live in a small village, but he really felt at home in the country. After all, as a boy, he had been used to spending most summers in the small village of North Newbald where his father had always rented a cottage so that his family could to stay there for at least two months in order to build up their strength to face the rigours of winter. So in the 1920s, long before it became a fashionable thing to do, he had the idea of buying a fisherman's cottage in the centre of Robin Hood's Bay and using it for weekends and holidays for any family or friends who shared his interest in the rock pools and sands of the beach, and in exploring the surrounding area's many beauty spots. In the late spring and early autumn he and Nance would travel up by train from Hull on a Friday afternoon and prepare to welcome a party of five or six people the next morning to the cramped, three-storey cottage. Grandma and one female volunteer generally spent the weekend catering for the guests' hearty appetites but everyone else - stoutly booted, with sticks in hand and rucksacks loaded with picnic food – would ramble across the moors, clamber up and down the steep paths around Goathland and Little Beck, or take the local bus to Whitby to explore its historic attractions. At the beginning of July, Nance and young Nora would go up to Bay to stay for most of the summer, becoming – to some extent – part of the village community, and entertaining any family and friends who wished to spend their holidays there. Grandpa would join them on a Friday evening and leave on the earliest train on the Monday morning to look after himself in the Keyingham house, travelling to work through the rest of the week as usual. When we'd originally lived in Hull, and just once when we lived in Grantham, we'd been able to spend time there too and it remained my favourite place for many years, with an aura of magic all its own.

For many years Nance cheerfully took on the main responsibilities and most of the housework involved in running Maynor (the cottage had been named after the two daughters) before it dawned on her in 1931 that it had become a burden rather than a pleasure. Though Nance needed no support and was more than capable of dealing confidently with any possible arguments from her husband, she chose to make her unexpected protest at a time when both my mother and Nora were present. She spoke with more than her usual firmness.

'Will! Do you realise that our holiday cottage is a holiday for everyone but me? I spend most of my summers keeping house, changing beds, shopping and preparing meals for other people – and all in fairly cramped rooms and a pathetically primitive kitchen, none of which can be compared with the comforts and conveniences of our own home. I've had enough!'

Will, whatever his and Nora's private regrets, put the house on the market the next day.

Despite being very hospitable, and always making us feel really welcome whenever we stayed with them at Keyingham, Grandma seldom visited to our home. But when we lived in Hull, and Grandpa came to us for lunch every Wednesday, I always hurried home from school so that I could spend a little time with him. One week, when he arrived for his favourite meal – corned beef hash which, for some reason, was never on Grandma's menu – he held up an odd-shaped parcel, awkwardly wrapped in tatty brown paper.

'I went to a sale on Saturday at that house in Ottringham where they're selling up because the family are emigrating to New Zealand,' he told us solemnly. 'One of the lots was a strange assortment of odds and ends in a cardboard box, and I noticed there was a little enamel snuff box down at the bottom. So I bid for it and got the whole box for next to nothing. Your Grandma wasn't too pleased when I got home with it and she said the sooner I got rid of all the rubbish, the better she'd be pleased.' He turned towards me. 'So I thought you might like to help me, Jean, by getting rid of these.'

It was a pair of lady's high-heeled court shoes, the smallest I'd ever seen and – for once – I was happy with the size of my feet. The shoes were a perfect fit.

'Come Cinderella!' he said, taking my hand with a flourish. 'You *shall* l go to the ball!'

'I see someone's been hard at work with the Cherry Blossom shoe polish,' said my mother. Their soft leather gleamed like the glossy skin of a newly-fallen chestnut and she eyed them a little enviously as she added 'Even the heels shine!'

Grandpa looked a bit sheepish. 'Well,' he muttered, 'I didn't want her dressing-up box to get dirty.'

I had a sudden picture of this formally-dressed business man vigorously polishing these wonderful, stylish little shoes just for me – and I loved him even more. Not many men of his generation would have guessed how much such a gift would mean to a little nine-year-old like me.

Grandpa never seemed hurried or harried as he moved from place to place, going from one task to the next with leisurely efficiency, but in fact he worked extremely hard and accomplished a great deal. As young married men – in addition to their daily, very practical involvement at the printing works – he and his brother, Mark, each supplemented their incomes by taking on the business responsibilities and financial accounts of a local Friendly Society : the Forresters and the Druids respectively as far as I can remember. Before the National Insurance Act came into force in 1948, the Friendly Societies' main purpose was to provide cash Sickness and Death benefits for their nine million subscribing members, but they offered other types of insurances, too. Clearly this entailed a fair amount of clerical work for the two brothers and took up several evenings per week.

The original intention was that it would only be necessary for a few years but, when it came to light in the early 1930s that Mark had got his accounts into a serious muddle, Will was determined that all the resultant deficits must be made up as soon as possible and he committed himself to working for some years ahead to help solve the problem. I was too young to understand the background to the affair (though I did catch an occasional remark or two about Mark's wife's absurd extravagances – her insistence, for example, on furnishing their house with antiques, and always using only the most delicate china, the finest lace tablecloths and expensive bed linen) but it soon became obvious that the subject was too embarrassing for me to pursue. Looking back, I realise that I was only ever taken to their house once and that the only times I saw Mark were on my rare visits to the printing works.

I know he was a couple of years younger than Grandpa but he looked much older and, to a little girl, somewhat grey and forbidding. I didn't know him well enough to call him Uncle and, in any case, had no need to address him or hold a conversation. He and his small family didn't come to Auntie Mirrie's family parties and weren't on our Christmas list either!

But, whatever the pretensions of Mark's wife may have been, she was outclassed by Grandma in at least one respect. Nance was a woman of the world: a lady. She had a thorough grasp of all aspects of etiquette, she could deal with people from all walks of life with competent dignity, and woe betide anyone who tried in her presence to step beyond the bounds of good taste. I still remember, when I was fifteen, volunteering to collect money for the Red Cross from some impressively grand houses in Tettenhall, just outside Wolverhampton. We'd moved there in the winter of 1939 and I longed to do something for the war effort. Grandma was paying us one of her rare visits at the time and when I got home I launched into a detailed (and, I thought, humorous) account of my traipsing up a long, tree-lined drive and arriving, somewhat overawed, at the imposing front door of what appeared to be a mini-castle.

'I didn't have the nerve to tug at the huge brass bell-pull,' I confessed, 'so I went round to the kitchen door and spoke to the maid there. She fetched the butler. I've never seen one before - I didn't know there were any still left in wartime – and he told me to go back to the front door. He would see me there. So I did – and when he opened it he said that, if I would step into the hall, he would speak to the mistress.'

I was so wrapped up in telling my story that I didn't notice the increasing horror on Grandma's face, and ploughed gaily on.

'When he came back he slipped some money into my collecting tin, and I saw how much it was. You'll *never* believe it. It was about six pennyworth of coppers – that's all. For the Red Cross! Then he ushered me out and I trudged back down their blasted drive!'

I waited expectantly for my audience's appreciative reaction. It was just the kind of tale my mother would enjoy hearing. But not Grandma. Definitely, it seemed, not Grandma.

'Jean,' she said with solemn emphasis. "Don't ever let me hear again of your going to someone's back door! You are not a tradesman. You are not a gipsy selling clothes-pegs. You go as a visitor, even if you are uninvited. And should you catch a glimpse of someone's contribution to charity, be it large or small, and however good the cause, you will never comment upon it . . . to anyone.' She paused to draw breath and straightened her back still further.

'And please remember, "blasted" is not a word I would expect to hear from a young girl's lips, particularly when used to describe someone's drive. As far as I'm concerned, that word should only be applied to a heath . . . and then only in Shakespeare!'

I was completely deflated, and I didn't feel really comfortable again until I'd told my parents the whole story (in more or less the same words) after Grandma had retired for the night. They certainly seemed to enjoy it and that made me feel a little better but, unless there's a *very* good reason, I've never turned up at anyone's back door again. And the word "blasted" has long gone out of fashion anyway; strong language has definitely got considerably stronger since 1942, even for young girls.

I did learn one more thing that day, though – and it was quite consoling. My father – normally a securely confident man, at ease with everyone – confessed that he still found Nance intimidating sometimes, and that he still often felt he had reverted to a shy eighteen-year-old, hoping to marry May and be adopted into the Taylor family.

GRANDMA AND GRANDPA LANGDALE

Sarah Jane, always known as Jinnie to her relatives and friends, was the Granny whose cold water treatment shocked me into silence when I was a tiny, yelling baby. Throughout her life she was definitely a force to be reckoned with - a loose cannon, a pinch of spice in the family fruit loaf - but she was also a charmer and could operate (and I use the word deliberately) at many different levels. Even those closest to her, however much aware of the pitfalls of accepting her veracity and her motives too trustingly, nearly always found themselves falling, time and again, under her spell. Though she could not, in any way, be considered beautiful she was, nevertheless, quite striking-looking - "a fine figure of a woman" she would be termed in Edwardian days. She always dressed to impress, and invariably wore, dangling, slightly flamboyant earrings. She was quite tall, and her graceful carriage and naturally curly hair all added to her attractiveness, but it was probably her bustling energy and lively sense of fun which drew so many people to her side, and blinded them to her one or two less admirable traits. Or, maybe, they simply felt that her faults were of little importance compared with the pleasure they gained from her entertaining company.

She was one of four daughters born to John and Mary Towse, who had met while working as groom and lady's maid to a wealthy county family living in Yorkshire. The Georgian manor-house where they were employed was set in a small park a few miles from the East Riding coast, and the inland village of Keyingham was just about the same distance further west. Their employers did very little entertaining and consequently few domestic staff were needed, so John – in addition to acting as a part-time butler - was eventually given some additional responsibility for overseeing the gardens and the small farm attached to the estate, and Mary took on some of the tasks of a parlourmaid as well as caring for her mistress. When they married, the family were so reluctant to lose them that they were given the tenancy of a comfortable tied-cottage, and their duties were adjusted to suit their living there rather than in the main house. But after a few years, with four healthy, growing girls and two lively sons, John and Mary realized that the cottage was no longer large enough. They had to make a move.

My great-grandparents had always been reasonably well-paid for their work and had been able to live quite cheaply because most of their food - their greatest expense - came from the farm and their own large garden. They had managed to save a tidy sum of money so could look around and consider many options before deciding where to go for the kind of job they felt able to do best. By the time Jinnie was fourteen they'd decided to move to Keyingham and John had taken over the pub in the centre of the village: the Blue Bell. He was a popular landlord and Great-grandmother Mary found she, too, quite enjoyed the work involved in being a successful publican's wife. The whole family liked being part of a larger village community and appreciated the pub's roomy living quarters. Best of all, though, was the fact that the village was large enough (and sufficiently close to Hull) to offer the children a choice of career - and to increase the girls' matrimonial chances.

Within a few weeks of moving, it was arranged that Jinnie should go to a reputable dressmaker in the village to learn the basic skills of her trade and, as she soon showed real aptitude for the work, her father paid for her to have special tailoring classes in Hull. So, apart from being well-prepared to earn her living, she was able to help her sisters make their own clothes and make sure that she herself was always stylishly dressed at very little cost. When she was seventeen, much to the family's surprise, she even made herself a riding habit. She couldn't ride, but there was an underlying reason for this extravagance - Francis Langdale could . . . and frequently did.

Francis (whom everyone always called Frankie) was several years older than Jinnie and he was a fairly frequent customer at the Blue Bell. He was the youngest son of a local farmer and, though he generally had nothing much to say for himself and was quite shy with most people, there were three reasons why Jinny found him highly attractive. Firstly, once his working day was over, he was always impressively well-dressed ("dapper" was the word, she felt). Secondly he was a successful farmer's son - which meant he had a certain social standing in the village, and would eventually have his own farm. Lastly, she felt he could easily be persuaded or coerced into believing that she was the girl he should marry.

It was quite a bonus that, despite his slight build and mild, unassuming manner, he had a real talent for buying young, completely untrained horses and ponies, and selling them later for a profit. This enterprise involved "breaking them in" - as it was then known - so that they became docile enough to accept a bridle and bit, and could be used to pull carts and gigs, or saddled and ridden for pleasure. At that time it was quite a violent procedure and Frankie could quite often be seen battling with a fiercely bucking horse in one of Langdale's fields, or - occasionally - racing madly down Main Street on a pony dangerously determined to shed its desperately clinging rider. This gave Frankie a slightly dashing reputation, but little actual cash. The capital used was his father's, and Richard - in common with most yeomen farmers in those days - had never paid his three sons a wage, but doled out whatever money they required at the time it was needed. Farmers' sons generally accepted this convention because it was assumed that they would either inherit the home farm or (as long as times were good) be set up in one of their own in due course.

Jinnie must have felt she was on to a good thing. An elegant riding habit would be a wise investment - and in some ways she was right! They were married, in somewhat of a rush, when she was just eighteen and his father, Richard, was more or less forced to let them have the house attached to his flour mill at the far end of Church Lane. Jinnie proved to be a good cook and a thrifty housewife, so - despite the lowness of the wages Richard now had to pay Frankie - my father was born into comfortable domestic circumstances. But, by marrying and having a baby so early in her life, Jinny had missed out on some of the pleasures of youth and she was only too pleased that Frankie's older sister, Annie Langdale, was always eager to look after little Frank whenever the young couple - mainly

Jinnie, of course - wanted to go to village dances and socials or to visit Hull Market. In any case, Annie privately considered Jinnie too immature and flighty to be a suitable mother for this beautiful boy. A spinster, such as herself, with time on her hands and a wealth of experience of life could do a much better job! Over the coming fourteen years or so she gradually took on more and more responsibility for Frank's upbringing and, though a variety of circumstances made it inevitable that Jinnie frequently took advantage of this help, Annie got little thanks from her sister-in-law. There was always a strong undercurrent of jealousy between the two women.

nderstandably, Jinnie found the complexities and stress of caring for her new baby girl, born with spina bifida when Frank was less than two years old, so difficult that she was forced to hand him over to Annie for much of the time. Yet she didn't particularly relish the fact that - from then on - he usually seemed to prefer spending his days on his grandfather's farm, eating (and often sleeping) at Mount Airey much of the time. In any case - by all accounts - even when his little sister died a few months later, the atmosphere at his own home was often uncomfortably strained. Jinnie was a forceful young woman, used to fighting at least two of her sisters to get her own way, and - though Frankie seemed to accept, without protest, the role of henpecked husband very soon after their marriage - he found her many domineering tirades very wearing and responded to them with periods of uncooperative silence. Generally Frankie appeared to let her have her own way, but he quickly found ways of quietly circumventing her rules and regulations, instructions and wishes. Most evenings he managed to sink a few pints by sliding out "to see a man about a pony" (or a bull or a sow) and heading for the Ship Inn or the Blue Bell. Later, of course, the evenings he spent training with the local Yeomanry provided rather more genuine excuses for leaving his wife to her own devices.

Jinnie found lots to occupy her time. She continued to make clothes for relatives, went to most village social events, entertained friends, and used her growing nursing skills to help out anyone around who became ill. She loved to gossip and give people her commonsense advice - albeit sometimes too forcefully - but, although she enjoyed men's company and their admiration, she had no interest in them as individuals. She was obviously proud of her power over Frankie, for she often told people the story of their young son's first encounter with a tandem bicycle; she even told it to me several times during my childhood. Apparently Frank had been fascinated by the sight of this peculiar contraption when a man and woman rode one down Main Street in the direction of Withernsea.

'How d'you think your Mam and Dad would like one of those?' old Bert, the cowman, shouted to the boy as he passed by.

'I think they'd like it fine,' Frank called back, 'but Mam'd only want one if she could always have the front seat *and* choose where they were going.'

When Frank was thirteen he was quite happy to go to live in comfort with his Auntie Annie and Uncle Will at West View.

The First World War had started and his father had been sent to Ireland with his Yeomanry unit to buy and train horses and mules for the British Expeditionary Force in France. He was given the rank of Sergeant Major, put in charge of the operation, and he stayed there until 1918. Jinnie sailed for Ireland as soon as she could, determined to share the experience and to enjoy it to the full.

AFTER THE FIRST WORLD WAR

When the war ended Frankie returned to working on the farm with deep reluctance. He was so tired after his years of responsibility as the regimental rough rider that he vowed never to get on a horse again, and he never did. A few pints at the Ship or the Blue Bell were his main comfort and form of relaxation. For Jinnie, though, it was quite a wrench to come back to the restrictions and routines of life in the Mill House in Keyingham, but she soon became a regular attender at all the village socials, Whist Drives, and dances. She generally made quite an impression at the dances because she usually made herself a fairly spectacular new dress for each occasion. However, because she was frequently persuaded to make one for several other women, her own was often not started until the last possible hour – and it even, at times, ended up mainly held together with safety-pins. No one would have guessed, but she made no secret of it. She almost invariably entertained everyone around her by telling how she'd come to be so short of time that she'd been driven to raid the pin box. She might even regale them with details of the unfortunate places the pins were encroaching upon.

Not surprisingly, she soon found herself enjoying a certain popularity with Frank's young friends. Her house was always open to them when bad weather meant they couldn't meet and walk outdoors, and she was happy to provide hot drinks and home-baked pastries whenever they gathered there. They often confided in her and discussed their difficulties, valuing her shrewd, down-to-earth advice as much as they enjoyed the warm welcome and cheerful laughter they always found in her company. They weren't the only ones to call on her sympathetic support when they needed it, either, and a story she once told me was an intriguing example of someone turning to her in time of serious trouble, confident she would be the best one to help.

By then, however, I'd learned that it was wise to remember that Granny was a really talented raconteur. When I was very little she used to tell me stories about a pet which had died before I was born. He was a very large, black tomcat called Tarzan who'd had some amazing adventures, and whenever Granny visited us I was treated to a new episode. I specially enjoyed hearing the one about how he saved Granny's life when she was suddenly taken ill and there was no one else in the house to help. She'd told Tarzan she needed a doctor, and he'd jumped onto Grandpa's bike, cycled two miles, and fetched one. It was all described so vividly, with such a wealth of convincing detail, that I unquestioningly accepted every word, and it must have become firmly lodged in my mind as the literal truth. When we moved to Grantham she was only able to visit once and so there were no more stories. In fact I almost forgot them, but when - soon after I started school - my teacher read us "The Tale of Tom Kitten", they flashed back into my mind and I proudly told the class about Tarzan and the bicycle trip. Only then, as I stood in front of twenty children excitedly repeating Granny's words, the impossible absurdity of the story began to dawn on me and I felt ashamed at my babyish stupidity. I recall blundering back to my seat, hot with embarrassment. I told my parents about it that night and they managed to lessen my discomfort by coining a new family saying. From then on, whenever someone seemed to be telling a suspiciously tall story, instead of saying the traditional 'Tell that to the Marines', one of us would mutter quietly 'So Tarzan jumped on the bike and set off . . .'

Understandably, therefore, when - with all her usual dramatic flair - she told me an exciting story about helping her brother Jack, I mentally reached for the salt cellar. She related how, very late one evening, Jack turned up at the Mill House, desperate for her help. He'd waited till everyone had left and Grandpa had gone up to bed, then he'd crept in through the back door. He was white-faced, shaking violently, and had blood oozing from the side of his mouth.

'You've got to help me, Jinnie! I don't know what to do,' he whispered hoarsely. 'I think I've killed someone.' And he broke down into panicky tears.
It took a while before she could make any sense of what he was telling her, but eventually she managed to piece together a coherent outline of what had happened. Apparently he'd been with a married woman in the next village and her husband had come home unexpectedly. There had been a furious row which led to the two men punching each other quite violently. As Jack told it, he had somehow landed such a powerful blow that the husband fell backwards to the floor, hitting his head on the sharp edge of the hearthstone.

'He didn't move, Jinnie! He didn't move! I lifted his head and there was a horrible, bloody mess at the back. His eyes were half open . . . but I . . . I think he was dead. He wasn't breathing . . . and he didn't move. I've got to get away. I could hang for this! You've got to help me . . . you've got to. You're the only one I could turn to . . .'

Jinnie tried to persuade him to stay, at least until she could find out whether the man had really died, but Jack was so terrified of the possible consequences that he was adamant: he must get up to Liverpool docks, secretly and as quickly as possible, and try to sail to Canada or America as a stowaway. He was her favourite brother. She *had* to agree. She gave him what little money she could rake up, packed a pile of sandwiches into a small flour sack, and promised to tell no one that he'd been to see her. She'd have to pretend, when the news broke, to be as surprised as everyone else and - until then - hide her distress and anxiety about Jack behind a facade of normality. This story seemed so much like the plot of a third-rate novelette that I was inclined to take it as yet another of Granny's entertaining attempts to gain attention, but she did seem genuinely upset as she neared the end of the story. So I had to ask how things had turned out. Had the man died?

'No. . . and it was all hushed up . . . probably to protect the woman. I daren't inquire much round in her village, so I just don't know. But I don't know what happened to Jack either. I'd no means of letting him know it was safe to come back. I don't know where he went - or even if he reached Liverpool. We never heard from him again and nobody could understand why he'd suddenly disappeared. It wasn't like him! My mother and father were that upset . . . they didn't know what to do, or where to start finding anything out,' her voice thickened with emotion, 'and *I* couldn't tell them. It was a real tragedy for all the family, but everybody expected him to turn up again before long. He just never did . . . But I often think of him even now and hope he's doing all right.'

It all sounded so unlikely that I dismissed the story from my mind almost as soon as she'd finished telling it but, strangely for her, she never retold or referred to it again. I simply filed it away and more or less forgot it. But in 2010 Juliet came up to Yorkshire from Winchester and we had lunch together. Juliet is the daughter of Florrie, my father's cousin, and Juliet's grandmother was one of Granny's sisters. Juliet and I meet very rarely but, while we were swapping memories of our own parents' years of friendship, I suddenly thought to ask Juliet if *she* knew anything about our Great Uncle Jack. She thought for a couple of minutes and then told me that *her* grandmother had once said she'd had another brother, but he'd disappeared when he was in his early twenties and nobody knew why, or where he'd gone. So I was probably wrong to have doubted what Granny had told me - at least one basic fact was true. Juliet and I have decided to hope Jack made a great success of his life, became a millionaire, and that we'll one day learn we have been traced as the only heirs to his vast fortune.

In 1919, after a few disagreements and necessary adjustments Jinnie and Frankie managed to settle back fairly contentedly into the humdrum routines of civilian life in Keyingham, and to rub along together without too many problems. But Jinnie always envied her sister-in-law Annie's more luxurious lifestyle, and undoubtedly hankered after the status and comfort of being a farmer's wife - something she'd certainly expected to enjoy when she married into the Langdale family. To her disappointment, Frankie was still little more than a farm labourer.

Two years after the war ended Richard Langdale died. He'd been a good employer, well-liked in the village, and young Frank felt his loss keenly. Jinnie was also affected by the news, but only because it meant that Frankie would now - surely? - inherit the farm. His elder brother John had been set up in his own farm many years ago and had died quite young, leaving it to his widow. Jim, his other brother, had twice failed to make good on the farms he'd been given and had therefore returned, just before the war, to work at Mount Airey. And Annie had had substantial help with buying West View when she and Will had married in 1911. It *must* be Frankie's turn now and this was what Jinnie had been waiting for.

Within two or three hours of Richard's dying, Annie told Frankie that she knew he had been left the farm, as expected. She said that, because the will had been prepared by her husband's firm of solicitors - and Richard had asked Will to be his executor - she had arranged that a family meeting would be held at her house on the morning after the funeral so that the will's terms could be discussed. Jinnie could hardly wait but, when that morning came, she was so tired after all the work she had put into helping with preparations for the funeral tea - spring cleaning the farmhouse (a great opportunity to make a swift assessment of its contents) and the huge baking for the lavish meal provided for the many guests - that she woke with a crippling headache and couldn't face dragging her exhausted body from her bed. She knew the contents of the will, anyway, so they could manage without her for once.

The West View dining-room was a suitably dignified place for that morning's occasion and Will read the document through at a measured pace and in a clear voice, but Frankie found the terms of the will difficult to follow and, even after they had been carefully explained, he still failed to grasp their full implications. The farm *was* his . . . but, in addition to small bequests to several of his long-service employees, Richard had left Jim and Annie a thousand pounds each - a seriously substantial sum in those days. And this money had to be paid out of the estate.

Will explained that there was only sufficient working capital in Richard's bank account to keep the farm ticking over, so Jim and Annie's money had to be found in some other way - and it had to come out of the estate somehow. They had a right to it, and it must be paid in the very near future. Frankie was bewildered and, when he tried to explain it to Jinnie when he got home, she scarcely had the patience to listen, but launched almost immediately into a stream of invective against all the Langdales - and Annie in particular.

'I never did trust that lot,' she told me - several times! - years later. 'They'd had their share. I'd like to know what pressure she put on your great-grandfather Richard while we were away and he was making that stupid will.' She paused for breath, her face scarlet with hot anger and her earrings jangling in supportive protest. 'I told your Grandpa he could just get right back and tell Will Wright to get it sorted – NOW!'

Perhaps, though, she should have insisted on going back with him.

He returned an hour later to say that his sister and brother had agreed to waive part of their claim on the estate and, in exchange, he had accepted the offer of a lump sum and signed away the farm to them. My father, who was seventeen at the time and without any ambition to become a farmer himself, never knew whether this was a fair bargain or not. No valuation of the estate was ever made and the amount of Frankie's lump sum was never disclosed, but the way in which that day's decisions were forced through, without any consultation with Jinnie, rankled all her life. She bitterly resented the fact that Richard had (as she saw it) let himself be manoeuvred into agreeing to the impossible terms his will imposed, and she felt that the Langdale family had, with Will's help, cheated Frankie by playing on his weaknesses. Any respect Frankie had gained in her eyes through his war service now disappeared without trace.

Frankie, though, was secretly delighted. He felt that the lump sum freed him from the responsibility and drudgery of running a farm and would make it possible for him to realise a long-held dream - to own a pub! And one fact made things even simpler: he was married to a publican's daughter with some experience of the trade. So Jinnie had to accept his decision and concentrate on making sure he bought the best they could find.

They made an excellent choice. The Coach and Horses was a sizeable, well-built pub at Dunswell, a village on the main road half-way between Hull and Beverley. Its mock-Tudor facade was attractive, and there was ample room at the side and round the back for a fair number of customers' vehicles; even charabancs could be accommodated at a pinch. The windows of the two main bars looked out onto the road and there was a pleasant little dining-room behind. Jinnie could even plan that, in years to come, a couple of rooms upstairs could be let out on a bed and breakfast basis.

At first, under their care, the Coach and Horses was a real success. Frankie worked hard to learn the skills necessary to become a good landlord and Jinnie's buoyant energy and extrovert personality made her an ideal landlady. In addition to a good number of regular customers, there was a useful amount of passing trade and Jinnie's freshly-made meat pies and sandwiches were especially popular with visitors on their way to and from Beverley's fairly frequent race meetings. My father, throughout the time he was working on the installation of a new pumping station only a mile or so away, found the pub a very handy place to stay during the week, but he fled back to Auntie Annie and West View with great relief every Friday night. He disliked the noisy, bantering atmosphere of the Coach and Horses' larger bar and found the Snug's quiet, parochial chat tedious. And he so loathed the smell of stale beer and tobacco smoke, which inevitably lingered after the pub had closed at night, that he was virtually a teetotaller all his adult life.

Unfortunately Frankie was not. Within two or three years of their moving to the pub his previous recreational drinking had grown alarmingly. As George Bernard Shaw might have phrased it, the maximum temptation to sample his cellar's contents, linked with the maximum opportunity to enjoy it in unchecked privacy, had led to financial disaster. Because, physically, he showed no obvious sign of the effects of his enthusiastic indulgence - other than a gradual increase in his euphoric, come-day-go-day attitude to work and the world around him - Jinnie had continued to devote all her energies and attention to enjoying her success as a pub landlady and was, surprisingly, unaware of what was happening. They tended, in any case, to live parallel rather than interwoven lives so, by the time she realised the seriousness and extent of the problem, he had managed to drink a large slice of the profits, and the debts to suppliers were beginning to mount. There was only one sensible solution: to sell up, bank the remnants of their capital, and move on.

Presumably this capital stayed in Frankie's name, and I suppose he promised to reform, but - whatever the reasoning behind the decision - their next step was unwise to the point of stupidity. They moved back into Hull and bought a small shop which sold beer, wine and spirits: an Off-licence with living quarters attached.

It was around this time that Jinnie began to show signs of becoming noticeably deaf. This was worrying, as one of her younger sisters had - for some unknown reason - become profoundly deaf when she was a very young girl, but Jinnie refused to acknowledge that there was any need for concern, and simply told people to speak up more. It can't have been easy for either of them to face the adjustments their circumstances now forced upon them and, inevitably, the temptation of the readily available stock was again too much for Frankie. The profits dwindled and, after a couple of years or so, he and Jinnie had to move into a shabby terrace-house and he was forced to look for a job: any sort of job. Mount Airey had been sold on so there was no point in their trying to move back to Keyingham, even if he had wanted to return to farm work, and he could offer few skills and little useful experience in other areas of employment. Like so many men at this time, he had to join the ranks of those on the Dole. The result was that, soon after my father and mother were married, Jinnie and Frankie were having such a desperate struggle to make ends meet that, for many months, my mother used to order and pay for two sets of groceries - one to be delivered to her in-laws' house.

Eventually, however, Jinnie managed to get a job as cook-housekeeper in the Nurses' Home in the grounds of an isolation hospital near Goole - and their luck changed. The Home had originally been a large, Victorian house set in several acres of beautiful gardens, and they were given a comfortable sitting-room and a spacious bedroom with their own bathroom attached. Jinnie had a staff of three or four women to help her prepare the meals and do the housework for the nurses (who lived there more or less permanently) and for the Matron, who had her own little suite of rooms there too. Jinnie was an excellent cook, well-able to manage her staff with energetic efficiency and, because she always liked to march to the beat of her own drum, she was in her element.

Frankie must have felt guilty about his past failures and he must have realised that it was now up to him to help her continue to make a success of this new life. It seems he also realised that he needed to cut down his drinking drastically. He accepted Jinnie's domination without protest and, for the rest of his life, he contented himself with jogging along quietly in her shadow. He became a pleasant nonentity – 'Always happy to take a back seat!' as he once said to my father.

Within a very short time of their moving to the hospital, the ambulance driver retired and the job was offered to Frankie. There was actually very little driving to do, so he was expected to help the gardener for the rest of the time, and he became genuinely interested in the work. It was no surprise, therefore, that he was asked to take over the gardens when, in due course, that man also retired and - with the help of a strong and willing "lad" - he threw himself enthusiastically into improving the lawns and flower beds, and developing the size and productivity of the vegetable plots. Gradually he became even more expert and, after a while, he was often able to supply cut flowers for the wards and the Nurses' Home, and fresh fruit and vegetables for the kitchens. I remember very clearly the pride with which he showed us the large asparagus bed he had developed and the prize certificates he'd won for his marrows, roses and chrysanthemums at local shows.

He and Jinnie seemed settled for life. Her deafness worsened, but very slowly, and her extrovert personality seemed to ensure it had little effect upon her enjoyment of their social life in the nearby village, or upon her ability to keep her staff working cheerfully. We didn't see them very often, even when we lived in Hull - their work responsibilities meant they had little free time - but they came to us for their annual holidays and for a very occasional weekend. While I was a small child we were not allowed to visit them (it was, after all, an isolation hospital) but, after I'd been in the Hull hospital with scarlet fever myself, the matron was able to give us permission to visit once or twice a year and I actually stayed there one summer for nearly a week, on my own.

Perhaps because we saw them far less often than some of our other close relatives, Jinnie always came with a carrier bag of gifts for us - including at least two for me. After all she was my Granny and I was her only grandchild. At first, naturally, I looked forward to seeing what she'd brought me, and my mother did her best to keep me from thinking more about the presents than about seeing Granny and Grandpa themselves, but as I grew older I sometimes had an odd feeling that they were really brought to buy my attention and affection. I don't really know why I should feel this - but I hope I was wrong. She could, in any case, hold people's attention effortlessly by sheer force of personality and - though it was always wise to treat most of her stories with a certain amount of caution - she was skilled in decorating her lively accounts of incidents with entertaining, semi-believable details and explanations. It's doubtful, though, whether this talent led to her being rewarded with the deep affection she strove for. A very forceful personality has its drawbacks; most people tend to be wary of succumbing too enthusiastically to its attractions and I was no exception.

During the financially difficult Thirties, when she and Grandpa had to give up the Dunswell pub and, later, the off-licence shop, my parents were sympathetically sad to see that most of the more valuable pieces of furniture had disappeared. This happened over a period of time but if, later, she mentioned - say - the old grandfather clock they'd had from the Keyingham farmhouse, Granny would murmur quietly, '. . . but, of course, that was on the rully that went astray when we moved house.' Similarly, when it became obvious that she no longer wore any bits of good jewellery, she would sometimes refer casually to ' . . . the things that went when we had that burglary.' May and Frank were too tactful to point out how odd it was that they'd not, at the time, been told about either a disappearing vehicle or a burglary, but when we were alone together at home - if one of us mislaid some important possession - we couldn't resist saying, 'Do you think it might be on that rully that went astray?'

Happily, there were other much more amusing examples of Granny's inventiveness to treasure, and some of her anecdotes *were* true, willingly corroborated by Grandpa. One that he always revelled in was her account of how, a few weeks after they were married, a visiting salesman came to the Mill while she was there alone and suggested that they should meet in the barn the next night at nine for what he called " a bit of how's yer father ".

'Yer old man'll be going out for a pint, as usual, so we can have a bit of fun, can't we?' He leered at her, trying to pinch her bottom. 'A slice off a cut loaf'll never be missed.'

Granny was outraged but, before she could make any reply, a horse and cart were heard pulling into the yard and he made off hurriedly, saying he would see her tomorrow at nine. Naturally she told Frankie about it as soon as he got home and, pleased he was so indignant, she persuaded him to get two friends to join them in a plot to teach the man a lesson he would never forget. When the hopeful Casanova arrived in the barn the next evening, Grandpa was waiting for him in the dark, wearing some of Granny's clothes and a good sprinkling of lavender water.

'I'm over here,' he whispered seductively, and let the man fumble around him, breathing heavily.

Just as the questing seducer began to realise that things were not quite what he'd expected, Grandpa smacked him in the face, shouting, 'Cut loaf! Cut loaf! I'll give you cut loaf!'

And then all hell was let loose in the barn. Granny and the two friends had been hidden behind sacks of grain and they jumped out, banging pans and tin plates together and yelling a ripe selection of insults as they chased the man down the lane to the main road. He was never seen in the village again.

Back in Hull

A NEW HOUSE AND SCHOOL

I didn't like our new house much. After the Grantham one it seemed old, dark and cramped, and there was a gasometer looming over the houses at the far end of the street. There was no bathroom. Instead a white, enamelled bath was awkwardly fitted into the kitchen, with a wooden lid on top which could be used as a kind of sideboard or work-surface. The tiny living-room had a black-leaded grate, flanked on one side by a small oven and by a water-reservoir-cum-hob on the other, and its one window looked out onto a walled back yard, a coal house, and a lavatory. The front room, painstakingly distempered a gloomy grey and stippled with little maroon spots, was best ignored - especially as the landlord asked that we 'take *particular* care of these particular walls'. In fact his tone was quite threatening when he explained that it was a new technique 'what took days to do.'

My father watched the disagreeable man ride away on his ramshackle bike, then closed the front door with slightly unnecessary force.

'I'm *particularly* interested in why anyone should choose to spend hours on this *particular* way of desecrating four perfectly innocuous walls,' he called to my mother, who was examining the tapless bath in the kitchen with some foreboding.

'And I'm *particularly* anxious that it shouldn't become fashionable and widespread, aren't you?'

'Can't say I'm *particular* one way or the other,' was her sharp reply. 'Just shut the door on it and forget it. And please get in here and start working out how we are going to manage to have hot baths.'

We did manage, of course, and overcame all the other minor problems, but it was hard work at times for the adults, I think. And though she never mentioned it, I think the fact that this depressing house was only two minutes' walk from Elm Terrace - where she'd lived for fifteen happy years in comparative luxury - made the next few months especially difficult for my mother. True, no Taylors lived there now, but inevitably, as May passed Elm Terrace on her way to and from the local shops, she must have been reminded of so many memories, and been saddened by the changes. Oddly enough, she never pointed the house out to me even though she sometimes told me stories about her childhood there, and it was some years after she died that I realised that I knew the house she had been telling me about.

My immediate concern, though, was that I would be starting a new school. It was only four streets away but there was a choice of two routes to get there. The shorter one included a ten-minute walk by the side of the main Beverley Road and the other involved zigzagging among several side streets lined with rows of identical-looking, terraced houses - a little confusing for a six-year-old. In those days parents rarely took their children to school: it wasn't really necessary. We'd have thought it implied that we were still babies, and would probably have been unmercifully teased about it by our classmates.

As it turned out, initially I had no chance to choose my route - at least not for the first two or three days. Our next-door neighbour had a daughter my age – "Our Letty" - and apparently she was quite willing to take me with her. Because of a spell of very wet and windy weather, we didn't meet until my first morning. A loud knock on the party wall between our two staircases signalled that it was time to go and I was gently pushed out of the front door just when Our Letty was standing on her front step, being handed half an orange.

'I'll have the rest when I come 'ome tonight, Mum,' Letty commanded.

Her mother nodded meekly. Letty and I turned to face each other over the iron railings and, in the minute's silence which followed, a mutual indifference - bordering on faint dislike - was born. I feared that here was another bossy little madam. I'd already met one or two of these at my other school and had just begun to recognise that I, too, showed slight signs of the same tendency - which meant that I wouldn't take too kindly to being told what to do by someone of my own age. And to make matters worse, Letty looked distinctly odd.

It was a cold, damp morning, so her lumpy tweed coat was augmented with a broad, hairy scarf which was draped round her neck, crossed over her chest, and fastened at one side with a large nappy pin. Without exchanging a word we set off. As she stumped along in her wellington boots the yellow pompom on the top of her knitted beret bounced up and down in harmony with the purple tassels of the scarf, and I could see that her chapped, red cheeks were in danger of further irritation from the juice which was inevitably being smeared over them. Woolly gloves made her dealings with the orange quite difficult and led to a fair amount of spitting to get rid of the pips and strands of worsted. It was such a complicated procedure that she had to concentrate all her attention upon it and was unable to say a word to me for most of the way. I was quite relieved when she finally managed to turn the peel inside out and gnaw the pulp down to its white pith, but I was disgusted to see her throw the remains into the gutter. I now realise that my reactions were rooted in prissy snobbishness but I was far too young then to understand these feelings or recognise the dangers of my attitude. I was only acutely aware of the embarrassment of being seen with her and - even worse - of being introduced into the new school by her. And the memory of that morning is still uncomfortably vivid.

We hung our coats on top of other coats in a narrow corridor smelling of wet wool and something unpleasantly unidentifiable, and Letty took me into a large, rectangular schoolroom which had several blackboards fitted flush to the walls of one side. Two rows of connected desk-tops - complete with empty holes for ink pots - ran parallel to these boards, with long benches behind them for children to sit on. This was the "Babies' Class". A plump young teacher, wearing a flowered cotton smock, took my hand and Letty, silently relinquishing all responsibility, trotted off to sit on the back row. The teacher led me to the end of one of the benches and told me to sit down there and listen quietly, then she went and stood in front of the rank of blackboards and began to aim with a white cardboard pointer at the sentences chalked along them. The pointer's red tip bounced jauntily on each word in turn as she chanted these sentences and some of the twenty or so children, struggling to remember them, accompanied her by jerking out an odd word here and there. The rest just sat apathetically gazing at the pointer's progress. The teacher might have been speaking in Chinese for all they knew.

As far as I can remember, each sentence began with a coloured-in letter of the alphabet and was part of a vaguely religious poem - this was, after all, a Church School. I know we started that day with a Biblical quotation: "C . . . Cast your bread upon the waters etc." (memorable all these years later because, inevitably, it made me think of going to a Park to feed some ducks) and it eventually stopped at " L . . . is for Love we must feel for each other. M . . . is, of course, for our dearest Mother . . . " I gathered over the next few days that this was a routine morning exercise, but I've never been sure whether it was intended to help with reading, the learning of the alphabet, or the inculcation of desirable Christian maxims.

For the first time that I could remember, I was bored. Even the novelty - for me - of using a slate, with a bit of damp rag passed round every so often to rub out our chalk marks (not for us the screeching horror of a slate pencil!) had lost its charm by the end of the second day. By the third day I had shed Letty, both as an escort and as a companion, and was determinedly fending for myself.

Oddly enough, I don't recall encountering Letty again until, a fortnight or so after I'd joined the school, I was sent one playtime by the smock-clad teacher to go to the girls' lavatory to help Letty find her spectacles. I hadn't even noticed that she wore glasses but I obediently went to see what I could do, only to find - surrounded by a sympathetic crowd of older girls - a distraught Letty with tears streaming down her face and dripping messily from her chin.

'They've gone down the pan. They've gone down the pan,' she sobbed at me. "You've got to get 'um out.'

I don't know how they came to be down there or what I was expected to do about it, but one of the big girls bravely fished around, brought them out, and ran shuddering to rinse them under the tap. Just then the end-of-playtime bell went and everyone disappeared, leaving me to mop up Letty's face, help her dry the glasses on her skirt, and persuade her to go back to the classroomn. I don't think we ever spoke again; there never seemed to be any need.

Before we broke up for the Christmas holidays a week or two later, it was announced there would be a Christmas Party for the whole school. On the last day of term we would go home at two o'clock and come back to school at three, bringing a tin mug. My boredom completely disappeared and I set off from home excitedly clutching my enamel mug (with a small label tied to it and strict instructions from mother to be sure to bring the right one back) and dreaming of huge Christmas trees hung with presents. Sadly, I need not have bothered: it was nothing like any of my dreams.

We were marched through into the next classroom, slotted uncomfortably into one line of desks similar to our own, and told to wait quietly with our mugs until the resident class was brought in and crushed into the remaining desks. We then sang "Away in a Manger" and passed our mugs forward to be half filled with sweetened, greyish milk. Everyone was then given a fish paste sandwich and a limp ginger biscuit. When these were finished we sang "While shepherds watched" then filed back into our own room to be given an orange and collect a pink paper calendar. This was a free gift advertising Gibbs Dentifrice and bearing the outline of a Christmas tree which we had painstakingly crayoned in that morning as a present for our mothers. Hardly up to anybody's expectations. But let's face it, times were hard and money was very short indeed - and, so it would seem, was a bit of imaginative adult planning. However, unlike many of the children in the school, I had a lovely family Christmas to look forward to.

I was too young to remember where we had celebrated the festive season when we originally lived in Hull, but it seems that a tradition had been discussed and firmly established just a few weeks after May and Frank were married. They were to return to Keyingham and spend Christmas Eve and Christmas Day with her father, Nance and Nora. On Boxing Day they could then walk over to Frank's Auntie Annie's for lunch and tea, and the following day they could visit their local friends or simply relax with May's family. The next year it would be Auntie Annie's turn to entertain them first and all the other arrangements would be reversed. Both "sides" agreed that this was fair, but I don't think my parents had any real say in the matter and if they hankered after a different kind of family Christmas they kept it to themselves.

When we were in Grantham it was understood that it was too far and too expensive to travel to the East Riding just for three days - four at the most - but now we lived in Hull the tradition was unquestioningly reinstated. It was Auntie Annie's turn, and to Auntie Annie's we went. I have no idea how all my Christmas presents were transported there but I have a very clear memory of arriving at West View and being taken immediately into the dining-room by a fussily welcoming Auntie. And there it was! A beautiful tree set up in the corner by one of the frosted lancet windows which were let into either side of the fireplace. Magic! The leaping flames from the fireplace made the coloured glass baubles, hanging from its branches on loops of black cotton, glow and sparkle, but we had to wait until Uncle Will got home before we could see their true brilliance and the little candles - rather precariously stuck into metal, clip-on holders - were lit for a few minutes with Auntie's long taper. Those fragile baubles were passed on to me some thirty years later and I still have many of them. I hang them, with a certain amount of trepidation, on our tree every Christmas but I risk it because of the happy memories they hold. Visiting Auntie Annie and Uncle Will was now part of the pattern of my life, and West View became as familiar and homely to me as Auntie Mirrie's house.

*

There must have been an administrative error when I was first registered at the school for I should never have been put in the Babies' Class. So, immediately after Christmas, I was sent to work with the six year-olds next door. I recall almost nothing of my time in that class because, within a very few weeks, I was transferred to Standard I and into the care of Miss Davis. She was an excellent teacher - lively and enthusiastic, yet patient with any pupils who moved at a slower pace than the rest: another one ahead of her time! We worked in variable groups, according to our abilities in the basic subjects. This was fairly rare in that time of large classes - most teachers "taught to the middle". I liked the quiet atmosphere in her room and the satisfying work she planned for us but, most of all, I loved reading really interesting stories with the top group - no more of the dull, repetitive sentences of the earlier Primers and no more being held back by the hesitant stumblings of those children still struggling to decode simple words. Miss Davis also had a fund of anecdotes about her family and her own childhood which she used to illustrate the principles and attitudes she was trying to foster in us: kindness, courage, and consideration for others.

One day she told us how she had been bullied by three older girls. For some unexplained reason they started shouting names after her in the street and threatened her with stones. One day she got a note from them to say they would be waiting for her after school and, as she wrote on the blackboard for us, ". . . your really forrit this time." She was very frightened and hid in the cloakroom for a long time after four o'clock. She could hear them calling to each other in the playground and bouncing a ball fiercely against the cloakroom wall, and she suddenly realised that - by now - all the teachers had left and she was unprotected. After a while she decided that the only thing to do was to face them. She took a deep breath and walked out with her head held high, pretending she was not afraid - and they fell back and let her pass. They never bothered her again.

I have no means of knowing whether this story was true or not, but I'm sure I wasn't the only one in the class who was determined that, from now on, I too would always be brave in the face of danger and pretend I wasn't frightened. I think Miss Davis would have been distressed if she had known the painful consequences of my following her example (in rather different circumstances) two or three years later.

I made two friends in this class: Millie and Astrid. Millie lived quite near our house and sometimes, if it was cold or wet on a Saturday, we would play at "dressing up" at her house or mine. We both had a collection of clothes we'd been given, but hers were by far the most gorgeous. Her mother, it seems, used to go to smart dinners and dances (Millie's father was the manager of a local furniture shop) and she had saved a number of dresses, shawls and fancy handbags for Millie to play with. I must confess that these clothes may, in fact, have been the main attraction for me: there was little real warmth between us, but Millie and I strutted about, posturing and imagining we were princesses or fine ladies quite amicably together, and we never quarrelled over whose turn it was to have first choice from the old trunk or, if we were at my house, the stout cardboard box.

But Astrid was different. She fascinated me. Even her name seemed exotic. Her father was Norwegian - a merchant seaman - but she hardly ever mentioned him and, as I never saw him, I sometimes wondered if he really existed. She said she had older brothers too, but I never saw them either. She lived in a largish, old house a few streets away from me, on the other side of our school. It had very little furniture and no carpets on the ground floor; I didn't get an opportunity to see the bedrooms but I noticed the stairs were just bare, unpainted wood. I only went there once or twice as I found her mother slightly alarming; she was tall and ungainly, and spoke sternly with a strong, gutteral accent.

Astrid, on the other hand, was small, slender and seemed to dance as she walked. She had a very white skin and sleek black hair cut into a neat bob with a straight fringe. She talked at speed and was very definite about everything, and could always back up her opinions with stories or examples drawn from her own experience.

'My auntie gave me some bath salts when I went to tea on Sunday,' I might say.

'You shouldn't put anything in your bath except water.'

'Why not?'

'My Auntie Freya put salts in her bath one night and it made her bottom sore.'

'She should have put cream on her bottom, then.'

'You shouldn't put cream on your bottom.'

'Why not?'

'I put cream on my bottom once and it went orange.'

'It couldn't have!"

'Well, it did. So I think your mother ought to use those bath salts to wash the pots with.'

'Why?'

'Because it makes them smell nice. The lady next door to us always does that and hers smell lovely.'

And so on. I was enchanted.

One afternoon I went to her house to play for a little while after school and she came back with me part of the way home - to "set" me, as we called it then. It was dusk and the shops along the main street were already lit up to catch the evening trade. As we passed the greengrocers, with some of its fruit and vegetables temptingly piled on racks set out on the pavement, I saw Astrid pick up two or three plums. She did this with such casual ease that I thought I must have imagined it, but about twenty yards further on she handed me one and began to eat one herself. I held it as if it were a live coal and - though I couldn't understand why - I began to shake quite violently.

'Aren't you going to eat yours? They're good.'

I shook my head. 'I'll eat it at home,' I mumbled.

'O.K.! . . . I think I'll go back now. I might just get another one to take home for Mam.'

I ran all the way home, not daring to look over my shoulder, and when I slammed the hall door behind me and rushed, panting, into the kitchen my mother looked up in alarm.

'What's wrong? Has someone frightened you?'

She put her arm round me and hugged me comfortingly to her side. That opened the floodgates and I cried as I told her what had happened. Though I didn't know why I was so upset, once I had seen the shocked and worried expression on her face I knew I was right to be so. She took the plum out of my hand and flung it to the back of the fire, then sat down and turned me round so that we faced each other at eye level.

'Jean,' she said in a slow, frighteningly serious voice, 'That was a terrible thing to do. Are you sure you didn't take it? Are you sure that you didn't ask her to take one for you?'

I just shook my head, but she read the signal correctly and looked relieved. She didn't moralise, or speak of the sin of robbing someone of what was rightfully theirs, or even point out that a shopkeeper's stock was his livelihood. Instead, she leapt straight into descriptions of how people were punished for stealing things: policemen coming round, court trials, prison, and the horrors of the cat-o'-nine-tails! I'm not sure how a child psychologist would react to this approach but it was completely effective. Unlike many youngsters I was, apart from one stupid activity on a building site – of which more later - never tempted to take as much as a leaf from someone's hedge, and the desirable items on Woolworth's open counters were in no danger from me. The ethical issues connected with stealing were, of course, dealt with later.

As might be expected, after that I always felt uncomfortable with Astrid and even, in my own mind, began to question the truth of some of her stories, but there was very little time for me to become less gullible. We were about to move once again.

ANOTHER HOUSE: ANOTHER SCHOOL

None of us had any regrets when we left the gloomy house off Beverley Road. Even Paddy must have been glad when he was no longer confined to trotting round a walled backyard. Our new house was in fact exactly that: new. It was part of a small estate being built on the very edge of west Hull, and Number 36 was at the far end of a terrace of four houses with nothing in between us and the village of Cottingham except a mile or so of fields. We got the chance to live in such a pleasant area through my mother's cousin Mark. His pleasant but somewhat frumpy wife, Amy, had a very glamorous eighteen-year-old sister who had recently married a fairly wealthy man. He had bought her a block of four of these planned new houses as a wedding present and she was to use the rents as her personal allowance. Very soon after we'd moved to Hull and my father had started his new job, the Taylor family realised that we needed a better place to live - and as soon as possible. Enquiries were made, strings were pulled, and within a month we were promised one of the first "wedding present" houses to be completed. We moved in a year later, the very week we were told that the paint was dry.

It was like moving into the country. The front garden was the usual size for a small suburban house but there was a long back garden stretching down to a concrete ten-foot, and there was nothing beyond that but open fields and a scattering of trees. Gradually, of course, other houses were built at the side and in front of us and two more streets were added, but the fields at the back remained as they were until long after we'd left. Overall, if anything, Number 36 was smaller than the house we'd just left but it was so light and airy that it felt much larger, and - to our joy - it had pale, distempered walls and a proper bathroom. We felt at home immediately.

The next four years were happy ones for all of us. We were within comfortable travelling distance of our family and friends, my father had a secure and interesting job, the house was easy for my mother to run, and there was a selection of useful shops only five minutes walk away. Buses ran into the centre of town every twenty minutes from a stop just in front of those shops, and Hull had a very reliable transport system (including trams and trains) from there to the city's other suburbs and surrounding villages. We could visit and be visited with very little effort now, so my Grandpa Taylor was able to come to lunch every Wednesday. We made frequent trips to Auntie Mirrie's and out to the two families living in the "home" village, Keyingham. Never a week went by but some relatives or friends dropped in - no invitation necessary - to spend the evening with us. In those days many people kept open house just as we did, and genuinely welcomed unexpected company. Because such visits were always made after everyone had had their evening meal, cups of tea and a few fancy biscuits, or some homemade scones, were all that need be offered and, if amusing chat palled, an informal musical evening might develop, or a game of cards might be suggested.

My new school had only recently been built and it too was fresh and modern with lots of windows, and most classrooms had a central door leading out onto the long patio which edged a large playing field. It was well over half a mile's walk away and all the pupils had to go home for dinner, but I didn't mind that. There was plenty to see and enjoy as I dawdled, tramped or hurried along the wide roads lined with pleasant houses and gardens. But my first two weeks at the school were a little confusing because, as before, I was put into an infant class - this time the top one. I can only think I must have been small for my age, or maybe it was my mid-July birthday which threw the Head? However, within two days, as soon as it was noticed I could successfully complete five reading/writing cards within a few minutes, the mistake was put right. I was taken by the headmistress herself across to the other side of the H-shaped building and installed in Standard I, and I stayed there until the summer holidays began just a few days later. The next term I moved up with the rest of the class to Standard II and only then did I have a chance to start making new friends.

Fortunately, though, during the summer holidays, I had met Gillian (whose name, surprisingly, was pronounced with a hard "G" as in Gilbert) and we became friends immediately. She was a few months older than me and so would be in the class above me but - having moved to Number 32 only a fortnight before we arrived - she was as pleased as I was to find someone so near who had similar interests. There were no other young girls in our road, then or even after more new houses were built, so we became inseparable. Our parents had nothing in common (hers were at least twenty years older than mine and she had a twenty-five-year-old half-sister sharing her bedroom) but I think they must all have been pleased that we had found someone suitable to spend much of our leisure time with. And, of course, we had a companion for our daily journeys to and from school.

My new class teacher, Miss Wilkins, had us under strict control from the very first day - a vitally necessary move as there were fifty of us to cope with. She had mousy, tightly-permed hair and her fawn-coloured face was generally set in rather sour lines, which tended to make her look much older than she was. But in fact, by the end of our year in her care, most of us liked her and, I think, unconsciously realised that she worked us hard for our own good. We sat all day in double desks in long columns facing the blackboard, and our seating position was dictated by the results of the last end-of-term exams, with the child who was top of the class sitting in the extreme left-hand corner at the back of the room, and the one who had the lowest marks sat in the front seat on the extreme right of the teacher. At this school this practice was adopted in every Junior classroom and the desks themselves were regularly opened for "tidiness inspection". At the end of every term we had to bring a bit of furniture polish and two cloths and rub their lids until they shone!

Our daily timetable, which was strictly adhered to, was divided into periods of named subjects, and every period was packed with activity - not always particularly enjoyable. Miss Wilkins herself worked throughout the day with tireless energy and she drove us on relentlessly to learn, by rote, tables, spellings, short poems, basic maths processes, and simple rules of grammar. We were also taught meaningless - to us - geographical facts about Hull's imports and exports, a few historical dates, joined-up handwriting, and polite behaviour. The good thing was there was never time to be bored in her class (indeed there was hardly time to draw breath) but the bad thing was that, for some, it must all have been a bit of a jumble.

However, she could be rather frightening at times. One of her favourite exercises was to have us all standing behind our chairs, a few minutes before playtime, while she rapidly fired a maths question at each of us in random turn, and we couldn't leave unless we got the answer or the table correct. I did realise eventually that she tailored her questions to each child's possible capability, and I'm pretty sure (for I met her years later in rather different circumstances) that her occasional irritability and frequent use of snapped-out orders were a deliberate ploy. We did no art or craft at that stage, but full use was made of the parquet-floored assembly hall, and of the small apparatus kept in the curtained recess leading from it. In particularly good weather we were taken out into the playground or field for "drill", as it was called, and in the winter Miss Wilkins even taught us a few simple country dances when drill in the hall became monotonous.

As soon as the Register had been taken on a Friday afternoon, a boy and a girl were chosen to put a special book on every desk and we were each given a clean sheet of lined paper. The books were in pristine condition and their stiff, buttercup-yellow covers were decorated with an attractive black tree pattern. The glossy pages inside were a pleasure to see, with clear diagrams and several photographs per chapter. We were given no opportunity to read the books but they seemed to be about plants, insects and small animals. This was our Nature

Study period, though we didn't realise it at the time. Miss Wilkins would write the number of a page on the blackboard, retreat to her own high desk, and we were then expected to sit in absolute silence and make a careful copy of that page in our very best writing. It was always the beginning of a chapter, the text was never read out or explained, and - although our papers were collected up before playtime - they were never commented upon, marked or even returned to us. I remember being slightly mystified by all this, but it was a pleasant enough Friday afternoon occupation. It created a peaceful atmosphere and there was no pressure - we could work at our own pace at a not too demanding task - but I did sometimes wonder if any of the others knew what pistil, spawn or hibernation meant. I always intended to ask, when the silence rule was relaxed later, but I forgot because Miss Wilkins suddenly became alive again and rushed us through an oral spelling test before reading us a short story: our treat to round off the week.

It was some years before I understood that Class Registers were regarded by the Local Education Authorities - and therefore, of necessity, by headteachers - as sacrosanct records of attendance, and at the end of every week teachers were required to enter accurate totals of each child's presence or absence (mornings and afternoons separately) and calculate the percentages for every child, then for the whole class. At the end of the month the overall totals etc. had to be worked out and entered again, and the whole operation was repeated with end of term totals and percentages. They not only had to balance but, for some reason which I never discovered, they had to be on the headteacher's desk by playtime. To add to the teachers' difficulties there were unbreakable rules about using red pens for attendance slash marks and black ink for any absence circles. There was also a complicated set of symbols, one of which had to be fitted inside the circles to show the reasons for absence - and some (such as a stay in hospital) then had to be counted as attendances! With around fifty children in every class the teachers' Friday afternoons must have been a small, recurring nightmare.

Presumably all this palaver dated from the time when school staffs were paid according to the number of pupils attending, so mistakes were verging on the illegal and could not be tolerated. For some unfathomable, bureaucratic reason the rules and requirements were not simplified until the 1960s and, in some areas, well beyond that. And to many teachers' continuing distress even small mistakes corrected with Tippex or delicate scrapings with a razor blade were not just frowned upon but resulted in a summons to the Head's office or sharp, humiliating reprimands at Staff Meetings.

So Miss Wilkins' need for undisturbed peace on Friday afternoons is understandable and I hope her Registers were the things of beauty those in power demanded - but I still wish her efforts could have been followed by a little discussion about pistils and hibernation. I was never very enthusiastic about Friday spelling tests.

A NEW LIFE

My father had settled into his new job very quickly. His employers at the Sheet Metal Company were Jewish: Harry Parry, his sister Lola, and her Russian husband, who was always called Mr Joss. The brother and sister were, apparently, equal partners (Harry was in charge of the manufacturing and sales side of the business and Lola looked after the wages office, personnel and accounts) but Mr Joss, who was very wealthy, also had some kind of financial interest in the firm though he took no active part in its running. They all lived together in a luxurious house in Pearson Park, with two maids and a "daily" to relieve them of the burdens of housekeeping, and a chauffeur to drive any of their three cars as needed. My father came to have a great regard for Harry and, in time, a strong bond of affection grew up between them, but the other two were such eccentric characters that he found them more a source of gentle amusement than deep respect.

The first morning he reported for work he was shown to his little office-cum-workshop and immediately set about tidying up the mess his predecessor had left and arranging his own tools, etc. He heard someone come and stand at the door but was too busy lifting some boxes to a high shelf to turn immediately.

'What a nice-looking man.' That must be Lola, he thought.

'Such goot white overalls. So clean.' Mr Joss's thick accent was, in those remarks, hardly noticeable, but it was clear that their comments were not addressed to him, only to each other. Lola bustled away, but Mr Joss lingered. After a couple of minutes' awkward silence he came over to the wooden bench and leaned across it towards my father.

'Have you godd a liddle file in your so tidy tool-box?' he whispered confidentially, and held up his index fingers about three inches apart.

'Of course.'

'Would you be goot to lend it to me . . . for one minute only, pliss?'

My father smiled and handed him the smallest file he could find. Mr Joss took it, removed the top set of false teeth from his mouth, then turned politely away and applied the file vigorously. He slotted the plate back into place and ran an exploratory tongue around his mouth with loud sucking noises, nodding his satisfaction as he handed the file back.

'It's goot.' he said, and left.

It was one of my father's favourite stories - but for close friends' entertainment only, of course.

It soon became obvious that my father could not only be relied upon to keep all the firm's machinery and vehicles running efficiently and carry out any necessary repairs without undue expense, but that he was always willing to help with any other problem - large or small - the three might have. They took full advantage of this.

If, for example, one of the regular lorry drivers was ill and no one could be found at short notice to take a promised load over to, say, Liverpool my father would say, 'Leave it to me. We can't let them down, can we? It would be bad for trade, wouldn't it?' and rush home to grab a packet of sandwiches before setting off to drive through the night.

He would work all through a weekend rather than see a production line stand idle, with men laid off till Wednesday, even though experience soon taught him that the promised overtime pay did not always materialise - and then never in full. After a few months it was decided that the firm would pay to have a telephone installed in our house: a very good idea - at least for them. It meant that he could now be summoned at any time of the day or night and, though he never grumbled (in fact, I think he relished the variety of the work he took on) my mother began quite quickly to dread the sound of that phone's bell. It always meant we were losing him for the next few hours.

Within a year they had become so attached to Mr Frank, as they all called him, that he was frequently asked to help in various areas of their private lives too. For some reason, they began to prefer his driving to that of their perfectly capable chauffeur. Harry or Mr Joss would make some excuse or other to justify taking my father from his regular work so that he could drive them to wherever their business appointments might be - Nottingham, York, even London. And, with him, they would always sit in the front passenger seat so that they could talk. Needless to say, he relished the opportunity to drive the Rolls or the Humber but his own work still had to be fitted in - usually by working extra hours over the next day or two.

His trips with Lola were very different. She would arrive in his workshop without warning, probably wearing a richly-coloured silk dress with one of her fur coats slung around her shoulders, and looking like a voluptuous opera singer about to embark upon her favourite aria.

'Come along Mr Frank,' she would say, ignoring the fact that he might be up to his elbows in an engine's entrails. 'Get the Rolls out. We are going shopping.'

There was no way he could refuse. And she almost always insisted, too, that he didn't wait to remove his overalls - just wash his hands. Once or twice he found she was wearing a pair of Harry's large, woolly socks over her silk stockings, their tops cascading awkwardly down her ankles and over the tops of her shoes. When he tactfully pointed this out, all she would say was, 'Well, my feet are cold.' And that was that; he would drive wherever she directed him with no further argument. Her favourite destination on these occasions was Whitefriargate, a narrow street of shops which snaked through the centre of Hull's Old Town, and which was generally crowded with a mass of pedestrians.

'Stop!' she would call at the first shop she fancied and, embarrassingly, he would have to park there until she came out laden with parcels to be stowed in the boot. But she wouldn't get back in the car at that point. Instead she would totter, Harry's socks no doubt making her high-heeled shoes extremely uncomfortable, to the next shop which attracted her, calling and beckoning my father to follow her with the Rolls. The spectacle must have been quite hilarious, especially as she always finished up - exclaiming its name with anticipatory pleasure - at Woolworths. I wish I'd been lucky enough to see it.

My mother, I know, felt he was being shamelessly exploited but, surprisingly, she didn't grumble when he turned up one day in the Rolls to deliver a large cage containing a ragged-looking bird hunched on a wooden perch. It was Harry's beautiful African grey parrot which my father had often told us about: a great talker and a real character.

'When Harry came down into the conservatory this morning,' he said, 'he found Poll had been attacked - we think by a rat. There were feathers all over the place and some blood, which certainly didn't come from her because it was smeared on the floor a long way from the cage. Harry said she was clinging desperately to the top of her cage and shaking violently. She must have been terrified and I think she's broken a wing. Harry thought she ought to be put down but I said he should let me have her. We'd look after her and I think I can get her right again.'

Poll lived in our kitchen for the next twelve months and we all learned to love her. Her wing healed, her feathers regrew to their former grey and scarlet glory, and she gradually got over her shock and started to talk again. There were only three additions to her repertoire when she lived with us: the sound of our telephone ringing, the ice-cream man's bell, and my mother's voice calling Paddy in from the garden. They were all so convincing that they became irritating and it must have seriously bewildered our poor dog that, when he bounded eagerly in through the back door – expecting food or a walk – half the time he was totally ignored.

Poll would, however, rattle the bars of her cage insistently when my mother was dishing up dinner. She wanted a share of it - and, of course, generally got it. I loved to see her standing on one leg, holding a teaspoonful of rice pudding in the other claw, and pecking delicately at it - grain by grain - looking for all the world like an over-refined lady of quality. If it had been possible, I'm sure she would have had a little extra claw cocked daintily in the air. Her brilliant, boot-button eyes, in their distinctive chalk-white circles, would glint sideways at me as if to be sure that I was appreciating her gentility.

Only my father, though, risked taking her out of the cage, and never while I was in the room. I believe she always behaved like a lady and would perch on his shoulder to nibble at his ear but her beak was cruelly strong and could have inflicted some real damage on my tender flesh - you only had to watch her get the kernel out of a nut to know that. We all felt bereft when, about a year after my father brought her to us, Harry suddenly remembered to ask how she was and, when he was told she was now recovered, said it was time she returned home. It was unexpectedly hurtful, but that was that.

Eventually, though, my ever-patient mother did begin to complain a little about the calls the Parrys made upon her husband outside normal working hours, and she was worried by their increasing dependence upon him. Lola and Mr Joss - and, to a lesser extent, Harry - observed the rules of their Orthodox religion very strictly. Their Sabbath began at sundown on Friday and until the following day's sunset they were forbidden to do any work whatsoever. If their maids were not able to be with them for any part of that twenty-four hours, they would leave them ready-prepared meals which could be eaten cold. Sometimes, though, the arrangements would go awry and our weekend plans would be completely upset by a panicky telephone call for my father to bike down to Pearson Park to light their drawing-room fire or set the complicated burglar-alarm system, rescue the cat from up the apple tree or mend a fuse. When he got there, there would always be other "little" tasks which provided them with an excuse to keep him talking for an hour or two - and, as he would say, how could he put in a claim for overtime for that?

One request, though, was welcomed by my mother. As soon as they knew the plans for the King's Silver Jubilee, the Parry trio booked seats - at great expense - in one of the official grandstands which were to be set up along their Majesties' route from the Palace to Westminster Abbey. They booked rooms for two nights at one of London's best hotels and all three bought new clothes in readiness for the great day. One of the maids told my father that Lola's silver fox furs had had to be specially made to match her silver grey and crimson outfit. It was considered unwise to leave their Pearson Park house empty while they were all in London (they were taking the chauffeur and one maid with them). Hull was going to celebrate with a huge fireworks display in the evening and Mr Joss felt there might be drunken rioting which could lead to some damaging of property. So, rather than ask the remaining maid to stay there alone, Mr Frank was asked if he and his family would be good enough to stay at the house, too, that evening - at least until the most vulnerable time was over.

We therefore spent some hours there and were able to sit out on the front balcony and watch the fireworks show in considerable comfort. I must admit we also made a surreptitious tour of the house so that my mother and I could at last have some idea of its glories, but I was so overwhelmed by the sight of the mirror-lined bathroom with its Hollywood-type sunken bath and gold taps that I have no recollections of any other rooms. I do remember very clearly, though, that - apart from a cup of tea and a biscuit or two - no food was offered, so as soon as we got home my mother had to set about making us baked beans on toast and hot cocoa.

'What did the Queen look like?' was my father's first question to Lola when she got back home.

He told us that Lola drew herself up proudly and looked at him in surprised scorn.

'I don't know. I didn't look. I was there to see my King.'

As far as I can remember my mother and I enjoyed just one further treat from the Parrys. Several years before the Coronation they had bought a very expensive car which they hardly ever used. I think it was a Bentley and it had been made for the Prince of Wales but, apparently, when it was delivered to him, he took an immediate dislike to it and it was put up for sale. It was midnight blue, had all kinds of luxurious fitments, and was upholstered in heavy, white brocade which my father said reminded him of Cicely Courtneidge's Double Damask Dinner Napkins - the subject of a very funny sketch frequently broadcast on the wireless at the time. I've wondered since whether Harry or Lola had, at some point, suddenly been made aware that my mother was getting impatient with their demands upon my father. Perhaps - when she answered the phone - her reaction, for once, was rather less than friendly. Whatever the reason, though, it pleased us very much when they suggested my father might like to take us out one Saturday in the Bentley. We drove out in style for a picnic on the moors, but somehow it wasn't any fun. It was too grand. In fact my mother said it felt as if she was being driven in a hearse, and I was so worried that I might stain the white brocade that I forgot all about my plans to pretend I was a princess on my way to visit the Queen, waving to the cheering crowds of admiring peasants. We were quite happy that it was never offered again. We wouldn't have gone, anyway.

*

There wasn't much money to spare in our house but, compared with many people in the thirties, we were very comfortable and I look back upon the five or so years we spent in Linkfield Road, on the outskirts of Hull, with great pleasure. I remember how I used to come home from school looking forward to telling my mother all the interesting things that had happened that day and how she always listened willingly to every last detail. I now wonder how genuine her interest really was - she didn't actually comment very much and I was so full of myself that I probably wouldn't have been aware if her eyes had begun to glaze over with boredom - but the close attention she appeared to give to my stories and enthusiasms meant a great deal to me: then and now. I expect, nowadays, it would be thought of as our "quality time". She was fun to talk with, though, once I had got the day's "news" out of my system, and it was always interesting - even educational - to listen to her conversations with other people. Her comments on events and others' behaviour were shrewd and often witty, and I was fascinated by her anecdotes about our family's past.

Somehow - I'm not sure when or from whom - she'd acquired a store of words, phrases, sayings and superstitions, which spiced up her everyday language.

'I don't know why,' she would exclaim occasionally when my father arrived home, 'but I've been flying round today like a paper kite.'

My father would look across at me, his eyebrows raised.

'I really don't think so, May,' he would say, with a sly grin, and she would look ruefully down at her all too bulky figure and chuckle.

'Well, I've been in quite a kerfuffle anyway, and it felt as if I was being blown from pillar to post.' We would nod sympathetically in unison.

I did find some of her sayings extremely irritating, though.

She knew it and would use them deliberately as a tease. 'What's for dinner, Mummy?' I might ask, then feel cheated when she replied with the old, 'Wimwams for weasels to wind up the sun' or 'A quick jump at the pantry door and a bite off the sneck.'

And I was always infuriated by the much more obscure reply she would give if I asked about something I'd just missed during an adults' conversation. 'He's gone round the corner with a wheelbarrow,' she'd say briskly, 'and he isn't coming back.'

I knew she didn't really believe in the superstitions she quoted or the actions they imposed, but I enjoyed all the little rituals like tossing spilt salt over my left shoulder, or going out in the dark to look at a new moon and turn my money over, and - in any case - it was sensible to be on the safe side, wasn't it? When I was old enough to stay up late enough, I found it exciting when my father went out into the cold night at five to twelve on New Year's Eve, carrying a lump of coal, some bread and some silver coins, so that he could knock on the door a few minutes later and be welcomed in as the dark-haired first-footer. Like Tevye in "Fiddler on the Roof", tradition meant a lot to us, but only as a source of pleasure; it was not a central issue in our lives.

My mother's daily round was, I suppose, pretty routine. She very efficiently cleaned the house and polished the furniture, cooked our meals, baked cakes and pies, and did most of her shopping without going beyond the garden gate. This was because the large grocery shops in the city were, at that time, so desperate for the housewives' custom that they would send a salesman round to any respectable household that requested it, to take down their orders personally; and their van could be relied upon to deliver the goods the very next day. I was always fascinated by the way the man who came to us would – without a printed list to help - rapidly reel off dozens of items to remind my mother of things she might have forgotten. It was almost as good as seeing a Memory Man perform on the music hall stage, for he never included any item she'd already ordered. This service suited her very well as, being so overweight, she couldn't walk around town for very long and found carrying heavy bags for any length of time made her worryingly breathless.

There were also several vans which visited our road regularly: a butcher's, a fishmonger's, a baker's, and a soft drinks lorry. And, of course, there was a twice daily milk delivery – a godsend in the days when ordinary households didn't have a fridge - and a fortnightly visit from the coalman. There was a library van too. This came once a week and, for a very small charge, my mother was able to choose some light reading from the surprisingly large stock of books the man had packed into the back of the shabby vehicle. It was hard to see how anyone could make a living this way (though, with the aid of a Tilley lamp, he did manage to work through until late evening) but she welcomed that van, whatever time it arrived. It effortlessly supplemented the more serious selection available in the Public Library which was a tuppeny bus ride away. Convenient, too, were the various men with handcarts who used the ten-foot at the back of the houses to ply their trade: a knife-grinder came occasionally and so did a rag-and-bone man who would offer children a balloon or a pathetic little gold fish in a jar in exchange for a bundle of rags, a few jam pots, or a bit of scrap metal. Each had his own way of announcing his presence but my favourite was definitely the old man pushing a cart loaded with bedding plants. His chant had a real melody and rhythm to it.

'Any asters . . . any stocks . . . any blue lobelias . . . any plants,' he would sing, dropping his voice half an octave on the last word. Its tune would echo in my head for hours afterwards.

My mother washed and ironed most of our clothes but the bed and table linen, heavy garments, and my father's overalls were sent to the laundry. This was her one extravagance and I now realize that she funded it (and any other little luxuries we enjoyed) by careful management of the family budget and by spending very little on herself. My father handed over his wages into her care every Friday and was entirely content to keep just a few shillings for immediate expenses and leave the spending of the rest of it to her. They both smoked but neither of them drank - except a great number of cups of tea - and it was a rare treat for us to go to the pictures or to eat in a cafe. There was often, therefore, just a little money over which could be put aside for the proverbial rainy day.

Soon after our first Christmas back in Hull, my father decided we needed our own transport as soon as it could be managed, though he was quite content, on a daily basis, to cycle to work like many hundreds of others over the blessedly flat streets of Hull. The old motorbike and sidecar, though useful to some extent when we lived in Grantham, was no longer much use now that I couldn't be packed in with my mother, and it really wasn't possible for either of us to ride pillion. In any case, we had Paddy to consider too, and the bike was definitely on its last legs - or wheels, to be more precise. It sold fairly quickly and most of my mother's little savings fund was removed from the rainy day section and earmarked for the time when a very cheap car could be found which my father could dismantle, refurbish and rebuild.

By the next summer we were the proud, if somewhat bemused, owners of an odd-looking Morgan - though its original manufacturers might have had difficulty in recognizing it as such. It had, of course, only three wheels: two at the front and one at the back, and the body work looked rather as if it were coated in thick plaster. It was painted a dark, matt brown and, although it had a shabby hood, it was not easy to manoeuvre it into position and didn't really offer much protection against the weather anyway. So we tended to treat it as an open sports car and dressed accordingly. Still, we weren't car snobs: we just rejoiced that the bench seat in the front held two adults (with a spaniel sitting comfortably upright between them) and that I was safe and snug with any bits of luggage in the little "dicky seat" in the back. All my father cared about was that it would go and was reliable. All my mother cared about was that Frank had some sort of a car at last and that it made it easier for us to visit people or take short trips to pretty places. As for me, I was just glad that I could travel with the wind blowing in my face - not because I was addicted to fresh air, but because I knew I wouldn't feel car-sick. I had suffered this sickness in every closed car I'd ever travelled in and, though I was never actually sick, even the smell of leather (and that was what cars in those days were usually upholstered with) could make me feel desperately queasy. Now we could pop over to Keyingham, to East Mount or West View whenever we wanted. We could join Auntie Mirrie and Uncle Tom for a Sunday outing to the coast or visit friends and relatives for an hour or two in the evening - if, of course, my father wasn't working or attending to some of the Parrys' personal needs. The little Morgan very soon proved to be worth all my father's efforts for, two months after he had finished working on it, it took us all down to Cornwall.

Apart from visiting the Robin Hood's Bay cottage, we had never - as a family - had a real holiday and my parents had even been robbed of their Lake District honeymoon. So an unexpected invitation to stay for a week with Nora and Bill in Cornwall seemed as wonderful as winning the football pools. The Parrys' reactions to my father's request were predictable.

'Mr Frank, you can't possibly leave us like this. What if something goes wrong? We won't be able to get hold of you! And if we could, you'd be too far away to come at once.' That was Lola.

Mr Joss: 'But I might want to go to London. This is not goot, not goot at all.'

But Harry just said, 'Go. You deserve it. But mind you come back safe. We need you.'

CORNWALL WITH NORA AND BILL STORM

Nora Taylor was ten when my mother left Elm Terrace in Hull and went to live in Elm Cottage with her father and stepmother in to Keyingham. Until then Nora must have felt like an only child. May's fairly frequent visits simply added a little variety to the even tenor of the little girl's life, so she probably didn't even think of her as her "big sister". Will and Nance were not particularly indulgent parents (by all accounts little Nora was pretty strong-willed and definitely liked her own way, so she needed the firm handling that her mother was well-equipped to provide) but she must have been unconsciously aware that she was central to their lives in a way that May was not. Nevertheless, it seems that despite the six years' difference in their ages, the two girls were quite fond of each other and my mother would occasionally tell me stories about Nora when she was a toddler or a very young child.

One of my favourites was about her "good night" routine. Apparently Grandma used to make all her own curtains, bedspreads and cushion covers on her treadle machine and tended to work enthusiastically at renewing them quite frequently. There was no electricity in Keyingham when they first went to live there, so Elm Cottage was lit by oil lamps. The Taylors were lucky – from the ceilings of their main downstairs rooms they had some rather impressive lamps suspended on chains which could be pulled up or down to allow them to be cleaned, filled and lit easily. Nora insisted that the moving chains made a "miggle" noise, and it was certainly loud enough to be heard clearly in all the bedrooms.

Every night, when she was put to bed and her mother had lit the night-light on the chest of drawers, there was no chance that Nora would settle down unless a certain obsessive ritual had been completed, in full, with the child's voice rising nervously as it became more and more dictatorial.

'Leave the window shut.'

'I have.'

'Don't shut the door prop'ly!'

'I won't.'

'Leave it open a bit.'

'I will.'

'Are you going down now?'

'I am.'

'W – e – ll . . .' A deep breath would be taken in, then there'd be a sudden rush of words.

'Don't treadle! Don't miggle! And don't let the cat come up!'

When she was old enough to travel in daily, Nora attended a girls' school in Hull where she received a sound education, but when she left it was never suggested that she should have any kind of further training or take a job of any sort. She was expected (and was very content) to stay at home, perhaps helping a little around the house and – with a good friend, Mollie, who spent her time similarly engaged – being generally useful in village affairs. Keyingham had by then a number of families whose head was in business in Hull and who had moved into the village when the regular train service made commuting easy. So Nora and Mollie were able to enjoy the company of several others who shared their interests. They played tennis, went for long walks, visited friends or people who were housebound, and helped organise picnics, tennis teas, and musical evenings. There were dances, parties and charity whist drives in the winter, so there was little chance of their being bored. Nevertheless, it must have been a fairly welcome change for Nora when it was time to open up the Robin Hood's Bay cottage again, even though her friend could rarely leave her widower father to join them there.

Over the years, of course, the family got to know quite a few people in Bay (as it was usually called) and in the village of Thorpe close by. Even my mother, who was at the cottage far less than Nora, had become very friendly with Lilian, a young woman about her own age and they met as often as they could. Lilian's father kept the grocery and general stores in Thorpe and she was part of an interesting network of family and friends who made the Taylors very welcome.

And that is how Nora came to meet Lilian's younger brother, Bill.

From being a small boy, Bill's older brother wanted to join his father behind the counter of his flourishing grocery shop in Thorpe, and Bill's younger brother had no strong inclination towards any particular trade - he just wanted a quiet life. Bill, on the other hand, had one overriding ambition - to become a sailor in the Merchant Navy. He was thirteen when he first followed the time-honoured path beloved of adventure story writers: he ran away to sea. Naturally his father tracked him down and hauled him back, but eventually he had to admit defeat when Bill made another, slightly more successful attempt a couple of years later. So Bill was allowed to start his chosen career through the proper channels and very soon showed real aptitude for the job and a willingness to study hard for a succession of well-deserved promotions.

It was his older brother who first became interested in Nora and she, of course, was quite happy to have someone very presentable to take her to one or two of Bay's social occasions but, when Bill came home for a few weeks' locally-based training, she lost all interest in Andrew, and Bill became the centre of her world. He was irresistibly charming - not only to her but to three-year-old me. He was my second favourite man for the rest of his life, almost overtaking my father in the popularity race. It's difficult to describe him without using so many enthusiastic adjectives that he sounds like the hero in a woman's magazine and becomes unbelievable. He was tall, broad and good-looking, full of fun and kindly warmth, and his pleasantly low voice was made even more attractive by his North Riding accent with its occasional Geordie grace-notes. Everyone in our family took to him without reservation.

I was about four when he and Nora married. It was a simple wedding because, having passed the necessary exams very successfully and climbed the promotion ladder rapidly, he had been able to join a reputable shipping line as First Mate on a sizeable freighter. These ships generally picked up cargoes in Britain, and from ports in Holland, Denmark or Scandinavia, before crossing to Canada and America, where they sometimes took freight on through the Panama Canal to Chile. This meant, of course, that he would be away for many months at a time and could never predict how long each voyage would last. Soon after they became engaged Bill was told his next trip might well last for over a year. So, with only a few days' notice, he got a Special Licence, Nora got a coat with a fashionable fur collar and a stylish hat, and they were married in a Hull Register Office. The honeymoon was brief, of course, but at least they were married and, when his ship docked in Cardiff - happily only a few months later - Nora was able to join him there for a week. She continued to live with her parents at East Mount, though. There was little point at that time in trying to set up a home of their own. This was the thirties, money was short, there was a trade recession, and - if they were to have any time together - she had to be ready to take a train, at a moment's notice, to journey to wherever his ship docked.

The Recession, of course, soon became a very serious Depression and there was little or no demand for our cargo ships to cross the Atlantic - or any other ocean, come to that. Many were therefore "mothballed", the somewhat inappropriate term used at the time, which meant they were sent down to the River Fal and laid up in rows to await the possibility of a global financial recovery. 'Or to rust away!' many people, particularly unemployed sailors, were saying bitterly.

A seaman was left aboard each ship to act as caretaker, and Bill was fortunate to be given this job on his own ship - presumably because the firm wanted to retain him for when the situation improved and she would sail again. Nora joined him there and they were able to spend many months together, leading a normal married life - except that there were all the added pleasures of living on board a fascinating ship, on one of England's most beautiful rivers, surrounded by gorgeous scenery. It also meant that they were able to ask us to enjoy it with them for a little while and our Cornish holiday was one of pure pleasure.

The journey down in the Morgan was an adventure in itself, at least for my father and me, but I expect my mother had a few qualms. The old car was untried over such a great distance and, as there was so little money to spare, the possibility of our being stranded because of a mechanical breakdown or the unforeseen need to replace a tyre or some vital component of the engine, must secretly have worried her very much. But my father's confidence in his own work on the car was amply justified and we had no problems going there or coming back. The weather was dry and I slept part of the time, leaning sideways against a small cushion in the triangular space in the back. It was too far to travel all the way in one day, so my father found a farmhouse near Tewkesbury which offered bed and breakfast quite cheaply. The farmer's wife had no objection to our sharing a family room, and we were so comfortable that we stayed there on the way back too.

We were dazzled by the beauty of the thickly wooded banks of the River Fal when we arrived at King Harry Ferry, though I've no doubt that my parents were distressed by the sight - and the depressing implications - of so many fine ships lying silently idle, but I was too young to be anything other than happily excited by it all. The ships were anchored in rows across the river, parallel to the banks, as if ready to head for Falmouth at a moment's notice, but they looked permanently static rather than prepared to cast off. Bill's ship was berthed at the far side of the front row and there were four others between it and the Ferry, so I don't know how contact was made to tell Bill that we had arrived, but within five minutes of our parking the car we saw him rowing a small dinghy round the ship's bows towards the landing-stage where we were waiting. The dinghy was sparkling white - we learned later from Nora that Bill had repainted it only a few days before - and I was delighted to see that the name on the bows and on the seat rail in the stern was JEAN.

'Oh, Uncle Bill! Isn't it wonderful that your boat has the same name as me?'

Of course, he'd done it as a special surprise for me - typical of his thoughtfulness - but he let me think it was just a happy coincidence, or sheer magic. I can only regret that, because I was a bit scared of the new experience of getting into a rocking boat, the snap he took of me sitting alone in the stern shows I am nervously cowering there rather than smiling my thanks. Some years later, when I read "Swallows and

Amazons", I wished I'd made more of the opportunities that dinghy offered.

Bill rowed us round to the far side of the ship, and there was a rope ladder hanging from the deck down almost to the water! My mother was horrified.

 'BILL! You can't mean I have to climb up THAT?' Bill nodded sympathetically.

 'I'm terribly sorry, May, but that's the only way you can get on board. You'll manage it if you take it slowly and don't look down. You'll be fine,' he said soothingly.

'NO! I can't. I WON'T!' The dinghy rocked dangerously as she became increasingly agitated. 'And what about Jean?' I now began to feel a bubble of panic rising in my throat too.

'She'll be O.K. I'll give her a piggyback up,' he said, looking directly at me and winking jauntily. 'Sorry, but I really can't manage to take you up the same way.'

But then it must have become obvious to him that May was on the verge of becoming seriously distressed, for with a mischievous grin he said, 'Tell you what, I'll see what I can find on the side of the Ocean Maid!' and he rowed us round the row of ships' bows to the one nearest to the Ferry.

There, of course, was a solid-looking set of wooden steps sloping gently down the hull from the ship's deck to meet the water, and Bill slid our boat alongside and tied it up securely. My father clambered out onto the small platform at the steps' base, then helped us out too. My mother waited there until I was halfway up the steps and gripping their handrail safely, then she bent and removed one of her leather shoes. Slowly and very deliberately she leaned down and filled it with water from the river, and with ceremonious dignity poured it on Bill's head just as he looked up to hand a suitcase up to my father.

'Nice to be in Cornwall, Bill,' she said, 'and just in time for your christening, too.' And she sped up the steps as fast as she could manage. I could hear her laughing as we crossed all the other ships' decks and negotiated the gangplanks which linked them with each other. I could also hear someone clapping his hands. It was Bill giving her a round of applause. I expect it made having to put her foot back into a wet shoe entirely worthwhile.

We had a wonderful holiday, full of sunshine and laughter. I had a lovely little cabin of my own, complete with a porthole and a real bunk, of course, and we took our meals in the officers' saloon. I could play on the main deck and in one of the lifeboats, while the adults lazed around, chatting, reading, listening to Uncle Bill's yarns about the sea, the sailors he'd met, and the ports he'd visited, playing deck quoits, or arguing with joking fierceness over one of the board games from the ship's store. They seemed quite old people to me, I suppose, but I now realize that they were young and really enjoying being together in such a beautiful place in such marvellously fine weather. Every morning I went with Uncle Bill as he rowed across to the Ferry to fetch fresh milk. Sometimes we would leave my father fishing from the ship's stern and my mother enjoying the novelty of preparing a meal in the galley, and I would go with Auntie Nora and Uncle Bill to shop for groceries in the village. I'd sit, still a little nervously, in the stern of the boat, and give myself a stiff neck because I couldn't resist turning my head, however awkwardly, to gloat over the sight of the name in bold, black letters behind me. Twice Bill rowed us all to a deserted little beach on the shore of the river so that we could bathe, build a driftwood fire and picnic. The sunsets were spectacular.

We were still in fairly high spirits as we drove home at the end of the week, occasionally singing one or other of the songs Uncle Bill had introduced us to, but I remember my mother suggesting to my father that it might be best if he just stuck to the first two verses of "Barnacle Bill the Sailor" - for Jean's sake. And I never did get to hear the rest.

*

Although our Cornish trip had been wonderful it was good to be home again and back at school. Having come second in the final term's tests, I left Miss Wilkins' class with few regrets and joined Miss Murray's, hoping for a calmer twelve months ahead. This teacher was a little younger than Miss Wilkins and definitely plumper. She was what my mother would call "quite bonny", by which - coming from the north of England - she meant agreeably pretty. As we girls had already enjoyed regular sewing lessons with her while Miss Wilkins took the boys for drawing with pencils and rulers, we thought we knew her quiet, pleasant approach to classroom routines and to teaching. And we were right - except where her passionate enthusiasm for music was concerned. There, we soon found, she was a tyrant . . . a whirlwind . . . a dictator.

She conscientiously taught us all the appropriate subjects according to the correct timetable, and I'm sure we learned a great deal during our year in her class, but her real interest was in teaching us to sing from the tonic sol-fa and by sight-reading from conventional music notation. For nine-year-olds this was quite an uphill task and involved intensive practising for about fifteen minutes every day, as well as one of the half hours per week allocated to "Singing" on the timetable. Whenever there was an opportunity or a few minutes to spare, she would roll down the canvas chart which was kept permanently attached to the top of the blackboard, seize the white cardboard pointer with its scarlet tip, and grab a tuning-fork from the pen-tray on her desk. That was our signal to be absolutely quiet and listen for the clear note which sounded after she'd tapped one of its prongs on the side table and held the stem at right angles to the board. We were then expected to follow the pointer's movement up and down the tonic sol-fa list and sing, accurately and sweetly, the syllables which represented notes of a musical scale. Somehow she made it fun and, by Christmas, we were ready to transfer our skill to singing from music written on a five line staff, giving each note its correct number of beats.

There were just over fifty children in the class and I can't help wondering now how many of them were desperately bored or confused by all this, but lots of us - including me - were not and, for us, it had two good outcomes. For the rest of our lives we could read at least a single line melody at the correct tempo and (if we could sing in tune and were willing to give up some of our playtimes to practise) we got to go, in our Standard 4 year, to the children's Music Festival at the City Hall. This was competitive and involved each group sight-reading unfamiliar tunes, as well as singing folk songs in chorus. It was a memorable experience which most of us, I think, wouldn't have wanted to miss. As a class, though, we enjoyed even more the weekly session in the school hall when we practised the hymns for assembly and had a "real good go" at singing songs like "The British Grenadiers" and "Dashing Away with a Smoothing Iron" with Miss Murray accompanying us on the piano. I still have the little blue book of the folk song words we were encouraged to buy for sixpence; I just wish I had some opportunities to use it now.

But, however good the school, in the thirties few young children achieved perfect attendance records, and – through illness - there were some very unwelcome interruptions to both my home and my school life.

UNWELCOME INTERRUPTIONS

I've always been pleased that my birthday is in July. It's a very satisfactory distance from Christmas and the summer weather can be a very pleasant time for outdoor celebrations. From the age of seven until after I was eleven, I was allowed to invite six or seven classmates to a modest party in our garden, and my mother would make fancy sandwiches, and individual trifles based mainly on jelly, topped with custard, and sprinkled with coloured hundreds and thousands. There would be home-baked butterfly buns, their "wings" carefully angled into sweet butter-cream, and an iced birthday cake with a Madeira-type sponge inside (most of us didn't really like rich fruit cake) complete with the correct number of candles. She always hoped that the day would be warm and sunny so that the tables could be set up on the concrete at the back of the house, and we could play on the lawn afterwards.

Unfortunately this was possible only once. Those who say that 1930s summers were always fine and hot, or who maintain that their pre-war childhood holidays were always blessed with continuous brilliant sunshine are wrong. My mid-July birthday was often disappointingly wet and chilly, with a gusty wind. This meant, of course, that instead of taking turns on my swing, skipping with our clothes-line, or enjoying ball games such as Egg-if-you-Move, we had to play Pass the Parcel, pencil and paper games, or Toilet. The name of this latter game often raised a snigger or two. It involves spinning a trencher or platter, and the person whose name is called out then has to leap to grab it before it falls flat - or pay a forfeit. As a child I could see no connection with a lavatory but I now have a theory that it is really a corruption of the words "Twirl it".

My mother, of course, was always prepared for bad weather, but it can't have been easy to feed us all in our small kitchen so that the living-room was free to play in immediately after tea. I looked forward to these parties for weeks, constantly changing my mind about who to invite, and talking over what sweets and little trifles my mother should buy from Woolworths to give as prizes. But I only enjoyed three of these birthdays. The other two were miserable failures.

I came home from school on my eighth birthday feeling, as my mother put it, "wrong side out". This was unusual for me. So was my reluctance to wash and put on my party dress and, when the guests began to arrive, I really wasn't interested - not even in the little parcels they shyly handed over as a kind of entrance fee. I was too concerned with fighting down the nausea I had felt when I looked at the tea table loaded with food. My mother didn't really have time to notice that anything was wrong with me. She was too busy, at first, pouring and giving out glasses of lemonade, and then having to try to get a message to the mother of one of the little girls who was crying and saying she felt sick! But, once Dorothy had been collected and taken home, she could begin to pay some attention to the group of excitedly chattering guests - and she caught sight of my miserable face which was changing from crimson to a greenish-white and back again with worrying rapidity.

I don't remember much of the next half hour. It's just a muddle of being rushed to the bathroom (thankfully in time), having my forehead felt repeatedly, and being examined for spots. I do remember, however, the bliss of lying between cool sheets and thinking, muzzily, 'It's my birthday, so they won't give me Fenning's Fever Cure, will they? Or Compo?'

These, with Friar's Balsam, were my mother's favourite stand-bys and I never quite worked out which was intended as a cure for what. I'm not sure that she did either. I do know, though, that I dreaded the Fever Cure and I've recently heard that, unlikely as it sounds, it contained nitric acid! True or not, it certainly turned my mouth and throat inside out for three full minutes and left a curiously acid after-taste for five minutes more. I don't think I ever saw my parents dose themselves with it, or with Compo - a cloudy, deep red liquid which I had to drink immediately after very hot water had been added. It was unpleasantly aromatic so I was always glad if she reached for the Friar's Balsam bottle instead. Two drops of that on a lump of sugar were, in comparison, quite palatable. I understand that, as a toddler I was once or twice given Californian Syrup of Figs, a popular remedy in the thirties and forties for constipation and general unwellness. But there was no danger of that being used after my father had tried it himself. The story told to me by my mother was that he came down to breakfast after an extremely disturbed night and hurled the bottle into the dustbin.

'Don't let even a smell of that stuff come near this house again. If that poor little lass suffered a quarter of the stomach pains I've had . . . It just doesn't bear thinking about . . . I've a good mind to sue them. . .' And, uncharacteristically, he glared at her as if she had invented the mixture herself.

My current problem, though, turned out to be measles and most of the party developed it too within the next few days. I was really quite ill, but the thing I remember most about it was the misery of lying day after day in a darkened bedroom, forbidden to read. Nowadays a child in a similar situation would at least be given a radio to lessen the boredom but our one wireless was large and immovably sited downstairs so I somehow had to survive without my daily "fix" of print. And when I recovered, the weeks of deprivation meant that my appetite for books was greater than ever. I read every spare minute of the day. I took a book to the lavatory and I would even prop a book up on my bed so that I could read as I got dressed in a morning and undressed at night. Eventually my easy-going father - himself an enthusiastic reader - took exception to my always dashing from a meal table the moment I finished eating, to retrieve my current book and lose myself in its charms.

'You read too much,' he complained. 'We hardly see you and you've almost stopped talking to us. You'll damage your eyes if you're not careful, you know.'

I was taken aback. It was so unlike him to reproach me for anything, and it seemed unreasonable to me that he should think anyone could read too much. I felt very resentful; he was being unfair. But his next remark was so unexpected that my defiantly defensive reply faded into silence.

'I think you're reading to escape,' he muttered.

This was quite a difficult concept for an eight-year-old to grasp but I somehow sensed there was a core of truth in what he was saying, and I sidled quietly out of the room and into the garden to think it over. Though, to a large extent, I now think he was right, it seems likely that my being an only child (often left - albeit happily - to my own devices) had something to do with it too. My immediate reaction though, as I swung backwards and forwards on the garden swing that day, was to stifle any stirrings of guilt and decide to linger at the table a bit longer from now on, to spend a little more time playing with other children on the ten-foot strip of concrete behind our houses, and to take a torch up to bed with me so that I could read under the bedclothes after my light was put off. In the long term, though, I did read slightly less but my father's remark returned to haunt me from time to time - and, occasionally, it still does.

My ninth birthday didn't even have a chance to get started. I was obviously ill by the time I got home from school and had to be put to bed straight away. The doctor arrived before lunch the next day and an ambulance arrived soon afterwards to take me to the Sutton Isolation Hospital for the next ten weeks. In those days scarlet fever was a very serious illness indeed, so could not be coped with at home and - in order to prevent any danger of spreading the disease - hospital rules were draconian. Patients were not allowed any visitors whatsoever and any books or toys sent in to the children had to be left to stay in the ward permanently or be burned. We couldn't send letters out and the only news parents could get of their child's condition was by ringing the ward sister (not a very welcome procedure - I gather she was always busy and often couldn't come to the phone) or by checking the local newspaper which listed each patient by a given number, never by name. Both these sources gave only meagre information in guarded conventional terms such as "very poorly" or "quite comfortable", so relatives and friends had to be satisfied with that. I later learned that my mother rang every day but I had to be content with an occasional brief message from her - passed on if the sister remembered!

Apparently no one else from my school caught the disease, but I think there may well have been a minor epidemic at the time. I can think of no other reason why I was put into a women's ward and had no contact with other youngsters throughout my stay. So, once again, I was the only child around. This, of course, was not much of a problem for me (though I have since been told that in later years parents were allowed to stand outside the children's wards for a short time some evenings to mouth messages, smile, and wave at their offspring) but it was some days before a sympathetic young nurse thought to fetch me some comics, a book or two, and a doll. My only entertainment, therefore, was listening to adult conversation and watching the nurses at work. We were none of us allowed out of bed - not even to go to the bathroom - and this made things very awkward at times. However, I learned a lot - more, perhaps, than a nine year old should.

Home seemed far away and my only link with it was the postcard which arrived most days from one or other of my parents. I found it very hard to understand why they didn't send me some things to do or play with, but of course they had no way of knowing I needed anything and I had no way of letting them know. So I just put up with it, read the ward's tattered copies of "People's Friend" and bits of the local newspaper, and tucked the celluloid baby doll into the bed beside me. This was quite the wrong thing to do. When I woke the next morning the doll's head had come off and a nurse had to spend some time manoeuvring the hook which hung from the base of its neck, so that it became reattached to the elastic which ran from leg to leg inside the hard, pink body. This was as irritatingly complicated to do as it is to describe, but I was very hurt and resentful when she scornfully remarked to the whole ward that she wouldn't have guessed I would be so destructive with other people's possessions. I had to burrow under the blanket and keep my eyes tight shut after she said loudly, 'I thought she was better brought up, didn't you?'

The only other time I was close to tears was when the Ward Sister came in unexpectedly and told me to sit up as straight as I could and look out of the window opposite. I couldn't believe what I saw. There, looking rather embarrassed and waving at me through the glass, was Grandpa Langdale. I can't pretend that he was one of my favourite relatives. He was pleasant enough, but always so overshadowed by his extrovert wife that one tended not to notice him much. But on that day he was pure gold to me. We couldn't hear what one another was saying but we nodded and waved and grinned at each other for several minutes. I wasn't forgotten! Later I learned that he and Granny had come to Hull for a few days and, without telling anyone where he was going, he'd marched up to the hospital and demanded to see the Matron. She was not available, but he did manage to contact Sister Connolly. He told her he was the head gardener at a similar isolation hospital near Goole and that he sometimes drove their ambulance to collect patients. She could ring and check if she liked. This, he maintained, meant that he was immune to the infection and he could therefore be allowed to see his granddaughter. The Sister couldn't flout *all* the rules but he was at least allowed a window visit – and some months later she became the Matron of the Goole hospital. Grandpa never spoke much of their earlier encounter, but the family believed that Sister had known the post was coming up and had used the opportunity to get as many details about the place as she could.

After he left I was told that Grandpa had left me a present: a fresh grapefruit, of all things. It was a lovely gesture, bless him, but the fruit was too sour for a little girl to enjoy – however weary she was of the hospital diet. And this *was* unbelievably dreary. Presumably it was the considered advisable to give the patients only simple, really bland food and presumably, too, the caterers were on a very tight budget. Their solution was to devise a set menu and stick to it – every single day. We always had porridge (stingily sweetened) for breakfast, and steamed fish with mashed potato for lunch, followed by rice pudding. For tea we had thick bread and butter with red or yellow jelly, and at seven o'clock there was left-over rice pudding reheated to an unappetising stodge. We could have as much as we liked of these dishes. The trouble was we didn't like any of them much, even when washed down with mugs of sweet tea or watery milk. This diet's predominately carbohydrate content, and the lack of fruit and vegetables had another unfortunate outcome - not, perhaps, the best choice of word on this context. Every Saturday night we all had to force down a cup of revolting liquorice powder, mixed with water, whether we needed it or not.

I was kept in hospital longer than most patients because of a kidney infection but after nine weeks I was served very small quantities of minced beef - absolute bliss - instead of fish, and a day or two later a nurse was told to start rubbing my legs and feet to remove all traces of the disease's aftermath: dry skin. I was cured.

My clothes were sent for and I was taken into an unfamiliar bathroom, gently scrubbed down with Lifebouy soap, told to dress quickly, and driven home in the front seat of an ambulance. As I walked up the path to our front door my painfully thin legs seemed oddly shaky and I couldn't understand why my mother's face was so red and her eyes so moist, or why Auntie Mirrie was close behind her in the hall.

'Nice to have you back,' said my mother as she gave me a quick hug and kissed me.

'You need a bit of feeding up,' said Auntie Mirrie. 'Would you like me to take you to Brid for a few days?'

But all I wanted was home. The sun was shining and my father would be back from work soon. There was a wonderful smell of corned beef hash, there were books to read, and

Paddy was jumping up, trying to lick my face. I was surrounded by love again. What more could I want?

SHIRLEY STORM

Fortunately not all my childhood illnesses were linked to my birthdays. One featured, more or less, as an unwelcome Easter present.

I have only two first cousins: Shirley, who was born six years after me, and her brother Michael, who arrived two years later. From being just a few months old, it was obvious that Shirley had a will of her own and a positively alarming fund of physical energy. She walked early, lunging enthusiastically around the house and garden, and cheerfully ignoring the inevitable bumps and bruises she sustained as she crashed clumsily into furniture and flowerpots. Indeed, it was some years before her spatial awareness improved sufficiently to allow her relations and friends to stop putting their bric-a-brac on to high ledges and shutting away fragile items of furniture whenever she was expected to visit.

She talked at a very early age, too. She had an oddly harsh voice for a toddler and invariably spoke loudly at an astonishing speed. Unfortunately the language she spoke was not recognisably English but her statements, requests and commands were delivered with such complete aplomb and expressive hand gestures that we always felt it was our fault if we hadn't understood what she'd said. Grandpa Taylor claimed he was convinced that she was half French or even Spanish. He claimed that this must be due to the fact that her father was an officer in the Merchant Navy and, therefore, widely travelled. Gradually, though, it was realised that, for some reason, she had evolved her own vocabulary and she stuck to it obstinately until she was almost four. It was quite easy for us to remember that "timonnie" was tomorrow, and "morny" and "ackernoo" meant morning and afternoon, even when they were embedded in swiftly gabbled sentences, but "floddies" and "feng" were a little more difficult. Her mother, Nora, had to wait until the day Shirley pointed imperiously at a vase of sweet peas on a high shelf and impatiently demanded to be lifted up to "feng the floddies", before she realised that "feng" meant smell.

The greatest puzzle, though, was a phrase which she used emphatically at least two or three times a day, and always with bitter looks at whoever was refusing to let her do something she was determined to do. It was several years before we were able to decode what she'd been saying.

'No, Shirley. NO.' Nora might say.

'Cassigaydus! Cassigaydus!' Shirley would yell, and one got the impression that - if she had been a stereotypical Victorian heroine - she would have stamped her foot and flashed her eyes dramatically.

Our grandfather suggested that the word was a primordial curse which she was able to use either as a swear word or as a threat of evil to come, while my father decided it made a good nickname for her and frequently teased her with it. But it was quite a relief when we eventually discovered that she was in fact simply protesting - with more energy than accuracy - that, whatever activity she was being forbidden, the little girl down the road was allowed to do it. In other words, "Cathy Gray does!"

Understandably, we all loved her. She was a bright child, bounding to meet life with a cheery confidence, always ready to pick herself up undaunted whenever she collided painfully with unnoticed obstacles. But her mother, coping alone most of the time because her husband was away at sea, certainly found her - as she wearily put it – "a bit of a handful", especially after Michael was born.

'If only she'd settle down in one place for a few minutes,' Nora would wail to my mother. 'I have to watch her all the time or I don't know *what* she'll be doing. And it's bound to be something she shouldn't be doing - or something positively dangerous.'

So, two or three times a year, until Shirley started school, she would come to stay with us for a few days to give her mother a rest (and baby Michael a bit of peace), or I would be invited to stay with them in the hope that I could entertain the little girl for at least part of each day. My mother's calm firmness seemed to be just what Shirley needed and, though my father only saw her for an hour or so in the evening his patient, humorous ways of dealing with her wriggling energy and occasional tantrums were very effective. I quite enjoyed our days together - most of the time anyway. I was the big sister, the role model, the one who chose and directed the games we played: the Boss. Generally, she was surprisingly biddable, and happy to be involved in any project I might decide upon.

She had a beautiful set of cream wickerwork furniture which her father had brought her from Madeira: a child-sized table and two arm chairs. I liked them so much that I almost always managed to bring them into our games.

'I'll tell you what,' I might say. 'Let's pretend we're going out for cocktails on our way to the pictures and this is our table in the cafe. You choose what you're going to wear, and I'll find that hat with the veil, and I'll wear the red shawl, and we'll go by bus to get there, and then we'll meet some people on the way . . .' and so on. Primitive attempts at Dramatic Improvisation, if you like, but great fun.

It was irrelevant that, at four and living in a village, she had probably never been in a cafe and that neither of us had a clear idea what a cocktail was. Nobody we knew had ever tasted one but I had a vivid imagination and she was very willing to develop one. In retrospect, though, I often wonder why she didn't soon come to dislike me intensely, or at least resent me, for I was not only the domineering organizer of our play but I was also frequently held up by Nora as a shining model of perfect behaviour.

'Jean would never do that!' and 'Why can't you sit quietly? eat with your mouth closed? put your toys away? say please? like Jean does.' These were the kind of sentences hurled at Shirley whether I was there or not, and whether they were true or not. And Nora continued these strategies for the next ten years. It can only have been Shirley's sunny and forgiving nature which prevented her from hating the very sound of my name.

One Easter Shirley came to stay with us for a few days while Nora had a much needed break. The four-year old proved to be even more obstreperous than usual and at the end of the third day my father came home to find my mother uncharacteristically flustered and snappy. He took Shirley onto his knee and firmly held her captive.

'Come on, Cassigaydus! Let's see if you can stay still and quiet for three minutes. If you can, I'll tell you what happened today to Mr P.'s parrot.'

But for once even this didn't work and, as she struggled to free herself, he became aware of the surprising heat of her little body. She had chickenpox.

I was thrilled. I immediately started begging to be her nurse and couldn't believe my luck when I was told I could start by putting her to bed. As I bustled off importantly to find the apron I'd once been given but never worn, I saw my mother apparently twirling an imaginary flag to my father, and he was grinning back with one thumb stuck jauntily in the air.

My mother and father decided to move into the back bedroom so that Shirley and I could have the front bedroom as our hospital. It was the largest in the house, with a comfortable double bed and a decent-sized window which caught the morning sun. I loved the dressing table with its embroidered mats, the glass ring-tree, and the ebony-backed brush, mirror and comb set. I looked forward eagerly to spending time sitting at the little stool in front of it, angling the triple mirrors so that I could see the back of my head or produce countless images of myself receding into the distance.

'She might as well sleep with the little lass,' I heard my father say. 'She's going to get it anyway, isn't she? And Shirley won't feel lonely if she wakens in the night.'

This made me feel even more important. I didn't particularly want to catch chicken-pox and perhaps have to miss the first week or two of term, but the thought of being a nurse was quite exciting and I imagined I would enjoy the experience, later on, of being the pampered patient myself.

The next few days passed pleasantly enough. Shirley had such a mild form of the disease that, apart from being considerably less energetic (and therefore generally more amenable and easier to entertain) she had few of the expected symptoms. Even her spots were easily soothed with calamine lotion. I soon tired of carrying little meal trays and jugs of lemon barley water up and down stairs but, once most of my books and toys had been transferred to the bedroom, I revelled in being given the impression that I was the Nurse in Charge. Chickenpox seemed something to be desired rather than dreaded . . . But I was wrong: completely wrong.

By the time Shirley was considered no longer infectious and well enough to spend time downstairs, I had begun to feel wretched. Suddenly I couldn't wait to have the bed and the room to myself and to lay my aching head on a soft pillow. That afternoon Shirley's things were moved into my little bedroom and I wasn't even aware that, the next day, my father tucked her into our little car and took her home. I was too hot and uncomfortable to care about anything but my own miseries and the frightening fact that, as I lay miserably on my side and looked at the edge of the open door, it seemed that a large black hand kept appearing with its fingers outspread. By next day I was more or less covered in itching spots and, twenty four hours later, they had spread inside my nose, mouth, and even more uncomfortable places. Old Mrs Slide from next door, asked in to see if she could help my mother find something to ease the intense irritation, declared dolefully that I must have "caught a double dose" - my own and Shirley's! I don't really think there is such a thing but it made me feel quite special, and for a while this helped me put up with most of the symptoms fairly stoically. However, after the first few days, the main problem was that - because nothing relieved the itching for more than an hour or so - I had to be dabbed with a prescribed lotion very frequently and I, quite literally, couldn't sleep for the next three days and nights. My parents must have been exhausted.

My mother coped with cheerful patience during the day and early evening, but then my father insisted on taking over. Although he had to leave for work every morning at half past seven, he normally never went to bed before midnight - he maintained that sleeping was a waste of good "living time". It seemed natural, therefore - while I was so ill - that as soon as he'd had his evening meal and skimmed the morning paper, he would sit by my bed in an easy chair hauled up from the living room, with a lotion bottle and cotton wool at the ready, and a small pile of books within easy reach. He seemed happy enough to talk for a bit, read his own choice of novel a while, apply the lotion as needed, then read to me whenever I asked him to. He stayed with me throughout these three grim nights, occasionally dozing, but immediately wakeful if I started squirming in acute discomfort. By the time morning came after the first night, we had finished all my favourites from Grimms' Fairy Tales and so, when he came up the next night, I asked for Hans Anderson.

'Not a chance,' he said, with a surprisingly wicked grin. 'I've brought up a book of Greek myths and legends. I'm going to bore you to sleep tonight.' And he started to read the unexciting prose in a deliberately matter-of-fact monotone.

But the chickenpox won. We ploughed conscientiously through to the end of that drab red book and daylight had come. But sleep still eluded me. My father, however, refused to be beaten. As it was now Saturday and he finished work at twelve, he was able to sleep in a bed for a few hours after dinner and take up the night shift with renewed energy. Before I could ask again for Hans Anderson he produced another red volume from the same set, this time concerned with Roman myths and legends, and - unexpectedly - I found myself mildly interested. Whenever we stopped for the necessary lotion-dabbing he would suggest I tried to have a little nap but, after a few minutes, I would become so restless that he would pick up the book again and we would be back with the gods and their encounters with mere mortals.

I can't pretend that these three nights' memorable discomfort led to a deep and lasting interest in either Greek or Roman legends but the already close relationship with my father was enriched by our shared experiences, and I have always treasured the memory of his loving care. And, though at the time, the stories seemed to have made little impression, I was often astonished in later years to find I knew so much about the characters and events they contained. Without any conscious effort on my part, whenever the gods, heroes and legendary mortals were mentioned in books or conversation, details of their history would immediately rise to the surface of my mind.

So I recognise now that I gained a good deal from having chickenpox: an ability to exist happily on five or six hours' sleep a night (which lasted till my late seventies), and a superficial knowledge of ancient history which has enabled me to read "I, Claudius" and several of Mary Renault's books with informed pleasure. Indeed, until a few years ago - when age began to affect quite noticeably the swift and easy recall of names, dates and specific facts - I think I might have qualified as a Master Mind contestant. But only, of course, in two chosen subjects.

HOLIDAYS

Holidays cost money - and we didn't have much to spare in the thirties. In fact, over the next five years - apart from our expedition to the River Fal - we only managed to afford two trips away. The first one was to Easington, a tiny seaside village only a few miles east of Hull, and the second to the coastal resort of Bridlington, which was twenty miles or so further north. Of course, in the summer, we sometimes went out for the day to picnic in some pretty country place or somewhere on a beach but, if we went in Uncle Tom's car, this was a mixed pleasure for me. I always felt carsick in any closed car, the unsettling motion exaggerated by the unpredictable rise and fall of its soft leather seats. The fact that I wasn't actually sick didn't make the journey much more bearable for me, though it probably made a considerable difference to the other passengers' comfort. I survived by repeatedly reminding myself that all symptoms would disappear three minutes after the car stopped and I could get out into the fresh air.

In those days the only "cures" available were large, fat tablets coated with bright pink gelatine. They had a faint, unpleasant smell and an even worse taste, and - in any case - struggling to force one down nearly always made me retch, so they really didn't work for me. Even now, though I only feel carsick if the road is particularly winding (and *never* if I'm doing the driving), I dislike the smell of leather intensely and am relieved that the range of cars I currently ride in are upholstered in fabric and other man-made materials. So I was quite happy that for several years our main holidays were Friday-night-to-Sunday-night breaks spent in Keyingham with either Grandpa and Grandma Taylor or with Auntie Annie and Uncle Will Wright.

Our week in Easington was spent with Kitty and her four-year-old daughter, Hilary, in a sparsely furnished, wooden chalet. It was almost as large as a Village Hall and its outer walls were painted a forbidding, matt black. It had just a single storey and was divided into six separate rooms by plywood screens. Kitty was my mother's cousin, and sharing the chalet's rent and food costs made it possible for both families to get away fairly cheaply. My father was with us for two or three days, which was fine, and Granny and Grandpa Langdale came over for one night, but the rest of the time the two women shopped at the little village store, chatted, made up packed lunches, cooked simple evening meals, and took us down to the beach whenever the sun shone. If it rained they knitted jumpers for the winter, played board games with me, or read little stories to Hilary. Most of the time, though, the sun beat down relentlessly, which made the trek down the long, dusty lane to the shore quite an ordeal, and sitting on the bare sands with no breakwaters to lean against, and no shade except our own umbrellas, soon became uncomfortable. We were often the only people there. The North Sea remains cold even in the height of summer, and the only ships to be seen were usually no nearer than the distant horizon, so I was always glad to get back to the cool, echoing hut and a good book. I missed my friends and I missed the wireless, and I soon discovered that I had to ration my reading; I hadn't been able to bring nearly enough books and, though I normally enjoy re-reading my favourites from time to time, to read them twice in one week is not particularly satisfying.

One thing, however, gave me great pleasure: the visit to the Museum. "Our" chalet was in the garden of this museum - indeed, we were actually renting it from the two elderly spinsters who owned the whole property - and they rather grudgingly let my mother persuade them to show us round it. I'd already heard about this museum from Grandma Taylor and, if I hadn't known that she was invariably truthful and very unlikely to make up a story just to entertain or tease, I would never have believed her account of what it contained. As it was I couldn't wait to inspect its marvels.

The museum had been set up by a relative of the two women (father or uncle, perhaps) in three rooms of his large Victorian house. It had probably started as a collection of curios found on the shore or acquired from local sailors returning with unwanted souvenirs from foreign parts, but gradually he'd begun to make things himself to add to its charms. He made artificial flowers from unusual materials and, to protect them from dust and damage, he arranged them under large glass domes – the kind which used to be a fashionable feature of many Victorian drawing-rooms. He set up country scenes with crudely painted backgrounds, dried grasses and sandy soil, then added small animals and birds - inexpertly stuffed, and arranged in awkward, unnatural attitudes - in an attempt to imitate reality. I suppose none of this was particularly unusual but, for the last thirty years of his life, the materials he used were more than strange - they were bizarre. He took to saving his own hair, finger and toe nail clippings and incorporating them into his flower pictures and miniature models. I found the exhibits fascinating and repellent in equal measure, and I've often wondered what became of them when the old ladies died.

'Who on earth would want to give them house room nowadays?' my mother remarked quietly to Kitty, when we got back to our chalet. "Or pay to see them? They gave me the shudders.'

Our week in Bridlington was very different. We had sometimes visited the town for a few hours on a Saturday or Sunday; some old friends my parents were very fond of had recently moved there to live, so we occasionally went over to enjoy their company and catch up on their news. On one of these visits it was suggested that we might like to take lodgings in the town for a week's holiday and be able to spend more time together. There were other advantages, too, to this arrangement. Their son, Brian, was only three months older than me and I'd known him all my life, so it was pointed out that I would have someone to play with at least part of the time. Of course, it didn't work out like that. He was at an age when it was embarrassing for him to be seen by his friends dragging a mere girl around with him, and I was certainly not interested in fishing from the pier or playing French cricket on the beach - his current preoccupations. But I was very happy making my own temporary friends on the sands, building complicated castles, pottering in and out of the shallows at the sea's edge, or just spending time with my mother and father. The other main advantage was that it was cheap.

In those days a town like Bridlington offered visitors hotels, guest houses, bed and breakfast places, and rooms which were advertised in Yorkshire-based newspapers in a section headed Holiday Accommodation. To most local people the distinctions between these various places were clear and precise, and the differences in cost were very significant. The terms under which such "Accommodation" was let were well-known and always the same : rent was paid for the bedrooms booked, and basic breakfast food was provided - bread, butter, milk, tea and sugar - but the main items needed for that and all other meals of the day had to be bought and brought in by the guests themselves. The landlady would then cook and serve them. This meant that - if you were rich enough - you could, for example, choose to have steak, chicken, or plaice for your main meal with expensive vegetables, but if money was tight some scrag-end of mutton and a few onions, carrots and potatoes could be stretched to feed the family for a couple of days, especially if followed with suet pudding and treacle. Oddly though, guests were almost always charged extra for an item listed on the bill as "Use of cruet". Some people found this comical, but many felt it was ridiculous and resented it.

Of course the mother still had to plan the days' menus and work to her usual budget, but at least she was freed from the kitchen and routine household chores, and no one was faced with tripe or tapioca pudding unless they chose to be! Obviously there could be drawbacks. The landlady's cooking might be a bit hit and miss, she wasn't always too pleased with the type of food brought in, she might grudge any extra trouble involved in some of the dishes requested, and there might well be some very restrictive house rules which the family didn't expect. Trailing sand into the hall, or bringing back seaweed or little buckets of sea creatures, would naturally be frowned on and any exuberant galloping up and down the stairs could lead to some extremely acid comments but, with a bit of give and take, good relations could usually be restored. Bed linen was always provided and one smallish towel each, but beach towels were always guests' own responsibility. Few landladies offered the use of any kind of sitting-room, which meant that guests were expected to leave the house after breakfast and not return until just before a mealtime. This presented quite a serious problem for a family if the weather was wet or cold and windy. The front door was generally locked at half past ten or eleven every night and guests were rarely given a key, so evening jaunts had to be very carefully timed. We, however, were lucky. Our reasonably comfortable accommodation was chosen by Delia, the family friend, and it was run by someone she knew well. And I think that we must have been quite popular with our landlady because we ate out several times at Delia and Jim's house or at a cafe they recommended.

Our days tended to follow the same pattern. Rather unexpectedly, as soon as we arrived in Bridlington, my father surprised us by announcing that he intended to get up at seven o'clock every day for an early swim - and he hoped I would go with him! Reluctantly I agreed, and the next morning I left my warm bed when he called me and we trotted down through a grey sea mist to the chilly beach, our coats over our swimming costumes and rolled-up towels tucked under our arms. Bridlington has wide stretches of beautiful golden sands sweeping round a large, smoothly-curved bay, but they held little appeal for me when shrouded in a damp sea-roke. We left our coats and towels near some steps and my father quickly ran to plunge into the water and swim rather clumsily up and down, parallel to the shore.

'It's wonderful!' he yelled, as those hardy souls who jump in first always do. 'Come on in!'

I teetered on the foam's edge, already shivering violently with cold and full of dread: the waves seemed enormous and the water swirling round my feet was icy. He knew I couldn't swim and I knew he wanted to teach me and be able to boast about his tough little girl's courage and determination to learn. But I also knew that I wasn't tough. I was a coward, and energetic, physical exercise was not my idea of fun - in fact, I didn't care for it at all. After about five minutes of misery I did manage to force myself to walk forward at a stupidly slow pace and let the water inch its freezing way up to my thighs, but by then my father was beginning to tire of waiting and he forced the pace by splashing quantities of water at me. I gasped with shock and was unable to resist when he tipped me swiftly on to my back and proceeded to hold me up and shout instructions about how to float, relaxed, with gentle arm and leg movements. I then remembered how, over a year ago, he had taught me to ride a bike - at first supporting me by holding on to the saddle and running alongside as I pedalled, then secretly letting go when he felt I could manage alone. That trick had worked well, but I was sure that if he tried a similar technique in water I would flounder disastrously. I found relaxing impossible. After a few minutes we were both so cold and frustrated that he gave up and we ran up the beach to try to towel ourselves dry before struggling back into our clammy coats.

I'm not sure if it was because breakfast tasted so good after we'd finally got ourselves into dry clothes and begun to feel warm again, or because he was determined to prove that he was, at heart, a robust, outdoor type of man but - whatever the reason - we continued to force ourselves into the chilly water around seven o'clock for the next three mornings. I went because I couldn't bear to disappoint him, and I think I managed to put up a fairly convincing show of unselfishness by insisting that I would be fine playing around in the shallows while he enjoyed himself having what he called "a really good swim" without bothering about me.

At first I felt that the only way I could bear the next fifteen minutes or so was to force myself to jump up and down in the waves and pretend to be trying to swim while faking enthusiastic pleasure in the experience, but I soon realised that I might just as well make a genuine attempt to keep afloat on my front and strike out with a kind of breast-stroke - cum - dog-paddle. To my surprise I found it exhilarating and by the end of the third day I was able to make about five clumsy strokes towards the shore before collapsing with my knees scraping the sand. Nevertheless, I was still relieved each day when my father called that it was time to come out - and even more so when, with no comment or explanation, he decided we'd give it a miss for the rest of the week.

Usually, by about ten o'clock, the sun would come out and we were able to spend time on the beach. My mother seemed to enjoy visiting unfamiliar shops to buy the food for the day, and my father and I would hire two deck chairs and set them up in our favourite spot so that, when she'd delivered her carrier-bags to the landlady, she could sit in reasonable comfort and appreciate the tray of tea he would fetch from the nearby stall for them to share. She'd read and knit, and look forward to long chats with Delia, who joined us whenever she could. My father also read a good deal of the time but he always seemed glad to give up his deck chair when Delia arrived, and go for lengthy strolls around the bay with his trouser legs rolled up to his calves and the little waves lapping round his ankles. Occasionally, he would try a bit of line-fishing or join in some of the impromptu games of beach cricket, football or quoits which groups of youths and other young fathers might organise. For a man who generally worked hard, and for such long hours, being able to potter around in the sunshine at his own pace was a welcome change. Every so often he would take me from my sand and water-play on the pretext of buying me an ice-cream, or a bunch of brightly coloured, tissue-paper flags for the current sandcastle, and he'd treat me to a donkey ride. Or we'd go to see if the Punch and Judy show had started. However, after seeing it once or twice, we agreed that neither of us cared much for Punch or Judy: a leisurely walk along the promenade, window-shopping, was far more interesting.

It was on the first of these trips that I discovered the joys of the Amusement Arcade. The prizes looked so tempting under the brilliant lights, and the brassy music - mixed with the harsh, mechanical sounds of the laughing sailor, the dancing skeletons and the pinball bells - seemed so enticing that I found the Arcade increasingly irresistible. I invariably managed to persuade my father into it at least once a day and I'd willingly have spent all my carefully saved up holiday money there in the first few visits. As we neared the open doors I could feel my mouth going dry with excitement and, ever since then, I have had some understanding and real sympathy with compulsive gamblers. Luckily, I never won anything and, wisely, my father gave me the freedom to realise for myself that the prizes were tawdry and the chances of taking any of them home were minimal. More than any of the other attractions, it was probably the imitation crane or "grabber" which - coupled with my inborn Yorkshire canniness - finally convinced me that it was all just a money trap. These impressive glass cases were filled, at children's eye-level, with a most attractive selection of toys and a quantity of luxury knick-knacks which would appeal to adults. By means of the multi-directional steering-wheel, attached to the outside of the display case, it was fairly easy to guide the arms of the crane so that they hovered over the chosen item. It was not too difficult either to lower them to grab the desired prize and start to carry it to the hole in the centre where it could then be released into the chute leading to the player's hands. But, of course, there were complications. All the tempting articles were shiny and inconveniently shaped, and they slipped from the grabber's claws as soon as the crane began to edge sideways, and - just to remove the slightest chance of success - the whole operation was timed so that it was not possible to work at it with slow care. All the manoeuvres had to be completed before the bell rang and the crane's action stopped. We never saw anyone win.

By midweek I had transferred my interest to the evening performances of the Concert Party we visited twice, and took home some very happy memories of the (to me) glamorous dancer who wore flame-coloured, silk-georgette dresses, and the handsome young tenor who sang "Just a Song at Twilight" with such romantic fervour. I was convinced they must be in love with each other.

WELCOME BREAKS

I was lucky! Because the village was only about eighteen miles from our house I was able to spend a few days of my Easter holidays and part of every summer with relatives in Keyingham. From the age of nine I was allowed to travel alone into the centre of Hull on a number 15 bus and catch an East Riding double-decker out to Keyingham. I suppose it was fairly unusual, even in those days, for a young child to be given so much freedom - especially an only child - but my parents wanted to give me plenty of opportunities to develop self-confidence and gain a sense of responsible independence. I was quietly proud of their trust in me but I must admit that, the first two or three times I did it, I had slightly confused dreams the night before I left and I was always quite relieved when I had negotiated the short journey from the local bus terminus to the Withernsea bus stop. This involved crossing busy Paragon Square, skirting the war memorial in the centre, and heading for the corner shops which had, on their upper façade, a large clock face surrounded - even in broad daylight - by flashing, red electric lights assuring everyone that GUINESS IS GOOD FOR YOU. Or was it ANY TIME IS GUINESS TIME? I can't be sure now.

 I came to know the road to Keyingham very well: the slow drive through the traffic of the town centre, speeding up slightly through the rather more pleasant suburbs, stopping occasionally for more people to get on, and then joining the rather dreary stretch of major road which ran parallel with the Hull Docks. For the first few trips I didn't dare risk going to sit upstairs in case the conductor forgot I'd asked to be put off at Keyingham Hill Top - I might not get down the stairs at the right time and would have a long walk back to Church Lane – so I had no chance of catching sight of the ships, large and small, anchored beyond the high walls bordering the hidden docks. A glimpse of the imposing doors of Hull Prison was the most I could look forward to before we came to the boring acres of neatly stacked pit props, weathering just beyond the road's grass verge. Once past Hedon - apart from two small villages and several clusters of houses - there was little to interest me in the flat fields of sugar beet and other, unidentified, vegetation, so it's not surprising that I always had a breathless feeling of pleasurable anticipation when the bus rounded a final sweeping bend, the village came into view, and I caught my first sight of Auntie Annie's house on the brow of the gently rising hill ahead.

By the time I started making these solo trips, Grandpa and Grandma Taylor had left East Mount for the new bungalow he'd designed and had had built on the far side of the village. But before they moved I was taken to spend four or five weeks with them. I can't remember the details, but for some reason the Parrys had sent my father to work in London for a few months. Apparently the firm was somehow involved in the building of Bush House there, and something had gone wrong. My father was sent to act as a kind of Clerk of Works (maybe to watch over the Parrys' interests - I just don't know) and he was living near the site - inadequately funded, of course - in digs where only breakfast was provided. He was working very long hours and it was a highly stressful job. He was a family man who loved his own home and it was an added strain that he could not get back to be with us more than once a month. After three months or so my mother began to worry. His letters home had become skimpy and somewhat disjointed; there was no humour in them. So she left me with Auntie Mirrie and went up to London to stay with him for a weekend.

She found him pale, noticeably thinner, and uncharacteristically nervy and irritable, and she realised that part of the problem was that he was not eating properly. It seems that every day he ate at the same grubby café, chosen because it was near the site and he could spread his papers out on the table and continue to work at them throughout every rushed meal. Tactful questioning of the friendly waitress led to my mother finding out that he almost always ordered fried or scrambled eggs on toast. They were the easiest to eat and he couldn't be bothered to think of or fuss with anything else. When she came back she immediately arranged for me to go to stay with Grandpa and Grandma Taylor while she returned to London to look after my father until he'd finished the job.

Naturally I had to attend the village school. I quickly made friends there and soon felt that Keyingham was my second home. There wasn't time to feel homesick, and going to the school where my father, Uncle Harry, Auntie Florrie and Olive Watson had been pupils was quite exciting - particularly as it was still run by the same headmaster. He taught the top junior class plus all the seniors who didn't get a scholarship to higher education in Hull. Miss Middleton managed the infants with gentle firmness, and his wife was still in charge of the sevens to tens. Not surprisingly their methods and approaches were very different from those in my Hull school - they may have been considered progressive in the early 1900s but they'd hardly progressed any further since. The infants were cramped into their own cosy little quarters, the rest were in one large room with the Head at one end and his wife at the other. There was a sliding screen, but it was never drawn across so I was able to see and hear all that went on in his class as well as hers.

In her way Mrs Jefferson was very kind but far too gushing for my comfort. For some reason she was unnecessarily impressed by what I was able to read and write, and she covered all my too simple sums with flamboyant capital Rs in red ink. I cringe even now when I recall the time she read something I had written and swept me up in her arms in full view of all the classes.

'You quaint little thing.' she crowed. 'That's lovely . . . *Lovely!*'

I was red with embarrassment for the rest of the afternoon and ran back to East Mount for my tea before any of my new friends could waylay and tease me. They'd forgotten by morning - or were so used to Mrs Jeff's ways that they hadn't noticed anything worth mentioning.

The headmaster, though, was positively frightening. I had never come across anyone like him. I learned much later that he was an intellectual - well-read and in many ways an original thinker - so it may be that his occasional outbursts of vociferous temper stemmed from frustration at the limited personal opportunities his post in such a small school offered. True, he had to control a number of awkward thirteen- and fourteen-year-old farm boys, none of whom wanted to be in a classroom learning what they probably considered useless information, but he was much taller and stronger than any of them and could use his powerful voice effectively to subdue any pupil if he wished. When roused he would rampage up and down the aisles between the seniors' desks shaking a nasty-looking cane, and sometimes using it on one or two alleged culprits. It was my first experience of violence in any shape or form.

As it turned out, he was the only male teacher I came across throughout my years of schooling and I just might have been emotionally scarred by this encounter if I hadn't overheard a conversation between Grandma and Nora which made me see another side to him. It seems that, whenever he and his wife went to one of the Jacksons' rather select tennis teas, their contribution to the buffet table loaded with other guests' choice items was a packet of Marmite sandwiches, thickly cut. Yet, apparently, the Jeffs always chose to eat from the plates of dainty salmon sandwiches, fancy trifles, or home-baked cakes, and their offering was always left for someone to dispose of, surreptitiously, later. I'm not sure why this made me feel better, but it did - though I still kept my head well down if he raised his voice at all threateningly.

When my father came home he thoroughly enjoyed recalling incidents from his time in the school and discovering similarities between our experiences.

'Does Mrs Jeff still send you out to play early if you've finished your sums and got them all right? And does she still make every child come to her desk when they've done five, so that she can draw a line below them in red ink? And woe betide anyone who smudges it?'

'Yes. And if any boy finishes his work early, *he* sends him to water the plants in the schoolhouse garden or pull up twenty-five weeds. It's called a Reward!'

Nevertheless, despite the drawbacks, I was glad I'd been to that school, if only because I made several friends who always made me welcome whenever I arrived to spend a few days in the village. And it certainly made me appreciate the joys of my Bricknell Avenue school even more.

About a year later Grandma and Grandpa Taylor moved to their new bungalow. Maynor (they'd saved the name-plate from the Robin Hood's Bay cottage when it was sold), was on the main road at the far side of the village. It was a typical example of the ribbon development popular all over the country at that time, but strongly condemned in later years. I loved it. It was largish, modern, and very different from Auntie Annie's West View in its conveniences, furnishings and general atmosphere, but I loved them both and I was happy to be staying in either house. It was always necessary, though, to be sure - when I stayed at one place – that I paid at least one visit to the other, or there would be some unpleasantly edged remarks to my mother the next time she was around. I think she must have found it quite difficult to explain why I had lived a while at East Mount rather than with

Auntie Annie and Uncle Will. Perhaps she made the excuse that it was nearer for me to walk to the school (though it couldn't have made more than five minutes difference) or that I wouldn't have to cross the main Hull to Withernsea road.

At West View, of course, I very much enjoyed being made a fuss of. I could do no wrong there and, if I was staying there on my own, I always slept in the richly-furnished guest bedroom. I was given choices of what I wanted to eat, I wasn't expected to help clear the table, tidy my room, or be sent on messages, and I could roam the big garden or sit around indoors and read for as long as I liked. My books, toys, paint-box and crayons were kept in a special, low cupboard and Olive was always happy for me to follow her around if I wished, chattering to her as she worked and "helping" her with the baking or the strawberry picking. For much of the time, though, I chose to entertain myself, and imaginative play kept me very contented. The rather impressive staircase with its scarlet and blue carpet, gleaming white-painted edges and highly polished brass rods seemed wonderful to me and I revelled in sweeping down it in a fringed silk shawl of Auntie's, imagining I was Lady Twistleton-Mansfield going to a ball. The heavy green plush curtains which hung at the long dining-room's bay window were just ideal for my pretend theatre-play, and the pointed arches of the slender windows at either side of the marble fireplace were like the pictures of castles in my old fairy-tale books. I easily could be a princess waiting for a handsome prince to rescue me.

Eventually, of course, these solitary occupations palled but Auntie would play Ludo or Snakes and Ladders with me on demand, and when I grew a little older we progressed, via Nine Men's Morris, Happy Families and Strip Jack Naked, to the more sophisticated pleasures of Lexicon and a simple version of Rummy. Eventually she even taught me to play two-pack Bezique. Not surprisingly, when I got home from such a visit, I gather that my mother had to bring me down to earth pretty sharply.

'It's easy to tell where she's been, isn't it?' I once heard her mutter to my father. 'I think I've got a bit of siding-up to do over the next few days - *as* usual. . .' I had no idea what she meant.

Life at Maynor, on the other hand, was not geared around me. Grandma still had help in the house three or four days a week but she was always busy. She took her responsibilities as president of the village W.I. and her work on several committees very seriously. She held meetings at the house, enjoyed entertaining and exchanging visits with a number of local friends, and was justifiably proud of her homemaking and cooking skills. She saw no need to entertain me but I was usually able to choose whatever I wanted to do - as long as I played quietly (I was never a noisy child, anyway) and went to bed at the set time! There were lots of books of all kinds to read, I could walk down to the village shop if I wanted to, go to play with a friend, or visit Nora, Shirley and baby Michael in their pleasant little house just a few hundred yards beyond Uncle Will's paddock. If Grandpa was not using his elderly typewriter I was allowed to spend as long as I liked typing experimentally on the coloured sheets of spare paper he brought for me from the printing works.

Naturally, Auntie Nora and the children spent a fair amount of time at Maynor. She could at times be rather alarmingly short-tempered and irritable (understandable, considering she was in her late twenties, virtually a single-parent family, and must have missed her young husband dreadfully) but she was usually fun to be with. She could play the piano in a pleasantly slapdash way, knew lots of comic songs and slightly cheeky versions of hymns, and she had a great deal of physical energy - rather more than I (used to my mother's slower pace and the limitations her weight imposed upon her) could sometimes cope with. Often after, say, a brisk walk in cold drizzle to the far side of Ottrinham and back, pushing the pram with Shirley sitting most of the way at Baby Michael's feet, we'd sing a few verses of "Oh my Darling Clementine" and the whole of "Ten Green Bottles", plus Gracie Fields' "The Biggest Aspidistra in the World". We might even dash down to the shop for a bag of acid drops before going home and then take advantage of any bit of clearer weather by chasing Shirley round the garden with me handicapped by having to skip with a rope instead of running. Hardly my favourite activity! But when the children were in bed Auntie Nora would read me chunks of Uncle Bill's fascinating letters, then start her ironing and spend the next hour chatting with me as if I were an adult and listening with apparent interest to anything I had to say. I learned a lot from my times with her. Little wonder that, next to home, Keyingham was my favourite place.

VISITS AND VISITORS

There were, of course, other friends and relations we enjoyed visiting from time to time but I rarely stayed with any of them. After all, most of them lived in Hull or within an easy bus or car ride. We exchanged one or two weekend visits every year with Harry and Florrie, of course – they were always thought of as my parents' greatest friends – and Broomfleet, the tiny village where Harry was headmaster for several years, was only a few miles from Hull. Until their daughter Juliet was born (when I was about seven) Florrie worked as a supply teacher in nearby village schools which she had to travel to on a motor bike. I quite enjoyed staying in the old school house, having free run of the playground and access to some of the empty classrooms' equipment, but I was always aware that I was on the outer edge of their reunion party. They were obviously very happy to be together again. The men talked cricket and other shared hobbies, and the women were so keen to exchange any recent, personal news and catch up on Keyingham gossip that it quickly became clear that I was more or less forgotten. So, generally, I was very happy to fade into the background and absorb – and learn from – a fair amount of the adults' conversation, particularly the slightly risqué stories the two men swapped.

Uncle Harry had an attractive voice and a talent for imitating – and probably exaggerating – the broad Yorkshire dialect of the local area. He had a fund of entertaining anecdotes about his pupils. Though I was too young to realise it then, his teaching methods were fairly unconventional. It could be said that he was a determined innovator, constantly trying to find more interesting and effective ways of involving children in their learning than he had experienced in *his* schooldays. Within the limitations imposed by the traditional curriculum, he wanted to make school more relevant to their daily lives. I remember his account of how, when trying to get some boys to show how well they understood the Shelley poem which begins "Hail to thee, blithe spirit / Bird thou never wert" by getting them to put it into their own words, one lad came up with 'Whotcheer , skylark / Thoo nivver wos a bod'! And how, having asked the class to label their diagrams of a cross-sectioned flower with a description of its various parts, he found the base of one neatly designated as "some sticky stuff called clart". Of course, I realise now that these stories were probably apocryphal but, at the time, I believed every word.

Harry and my father were both interested in puzzles and they each had a book of problems which they could discuss when they met and try to solve. They both enjoyed the logical and mathematical ones but my father specialised in the hands-on, mechanical type while Harry's main interest was in the quirky, practical posers. I remember very clearly the weekend when my father turned up with a classical Chinese puzzle he had made from a diagram in his book, using pieces of scrap metal and heavy wire. It was a complicated arrangement consisting of an oblong plate connected to a series of thick curtain rings by a hairpin–shaped device securely slotted through them. He and Harry spent several frustrating hours working out how to free this sealed "hairpin" before they were successful. Not surprisingly it was a while before I saw any fun in this kind of activity but, when I finally managed – with help - to release two of the rings, and grasped the principle of how to continue the procedure, I began to appreciate its charm.

But I very quickly saw the fun in Harry's choice of puzzle – and so did my mother and Florrie. For more than an hour one Saturday evening the two men struggled to answer the question: is it possible to take your waistcoat off without removing your jacket? It may sound stupid nowadays, but we literally cried with laughter watching the contortions of two grown men struggling to slot a reluctant waistcoat, worn by one of them, up the back, down a sleeve, and every whichway, out of his tweed jacket. Utterly absurd, of course, but I can definitely state it *is* possible – though there's some danger that, in the process, you might well ruin a waistcoat, slip a disc, or be left with a semi-permanent resemblance to the Notre Dame bell-ringer. A somewhat unusual illustration of the dogmatic statement, so often made by those born before radio and television became a commonplace, time-consuming part of many people's lives: that we used to make our own entertainment and were none the worse for it.

One of my favourite evening visits was to my mother's cousin, Ann Peacock. She was a few years older than my mother, striking-looking, very intelligent and well able to express her thoughtful opinions with confidence and a good deal of wit. Her father had been a talented music teacher who had a fierce temper and treated Ann and her brother Mark with unnecessary harshness. I've been told that Annie, his timid wife, was so overawed by him that even after he became seriously ill and bedridden, if she did something to displease him, she would obediently fetch the walking-stick he demanded and stand meekly at his side while he beat her with it. He died, fairly young, before I was born and his wife had to return to work in the family firm to earn her living. He may have left little or no money but Ann, at least, had inherited his musical abilities; she became an accomplished pianist, passionately interested in classical music and opera. Music held no attraction for Mark Peacock – a pleasant enough man with few memorable characteristics – but there'd never been any need for their father to drive Ann to regular keyboard practice, and for the rest of her life (except for the last two years of the 1914-18 War) she always spent more than an hour every day at the piano, playing for her own pleasure and striving to improve her skill. She had a strong contralto voice and a large repertoire of songs which varied from "Dido's Lament" to "The Floral Dance". Although some of the pieces she played or sang were way beyond me, I loved going with my parents to spend an evening at their house and I'm always grateful for the musical grounding I gained there. It balanced, very successfully, the simple diet I enjoyed with Uncle Tom and his vamped accompaniment to popular songs.

As soon as she was old enough Ann joined the WAACs (the Women's Army Auxiliary Corps – a forerunner of the ATS – which was created during World War 1) and, among other things, she drove a truck for some months in France in 1918. At the end of the war, back in England at the same time as many thousands of men from the Forces, she had to take the first job she was offered: cashier in Boyes, a flourishing shop on Hessle Road which catered mainly for the fishing community centred around there. It sold practically everything for the home except furniture and food. The merchandise was cheap but good value and, perhaps because it was a family firm, the employees were well treated. Ann stayed there all her working life. She was very capable and was quickly given more and more responsibility until she became one of the firm's mainstays.

We visited Boyes once or twice and I was able to see her at work. She spent a lot of her time, with one or two assistants, in a large cage-like arrangement set on a high platform in the centre of the ground floor and there she was able (and expected) to keep an eye on every part of the shop. The rectangular, open counters, loaded with goods, were laid out in rows and every one had a salesman or woman standing on guard nearby. Each counter was linked to the 'cage' by a stout overhead wire which had a round, metal container with a short chain hanging from it. When a purchase was complete the assistant wrote out a bill, put it and the money into the container, screwed it into the holder on the wire, and pulled the chain sharply down. It then whizzed at great speed across to the cage where a receipt was processed and, with any change, was sent back to the assistant – again at a dashing speed – to give to the customer. Like most children (and many adults) I found this operation quite fascinating to watch, especially as the lines were usually very busy and the little bells, which rang each time the containers were used, added to the general atmosphere of excitement.

There were two managers there, each in charge of different sections: a Mr Laycock and a Mr Boocock. One day my father rang the shop with a message for Ann from my mother and he recognised her voice when the phone was answered.

'Can I speak to one of the Cocks?' he said.

'Pea, Boo, or Lay?' replied Ann smoothly. Typical of both of them – but this time she was the one who'd scored.

Soon after she left the WAACs and was back home in Hull, she met Joe and they were immediately attracted. They found they enjoyed the same books and plays, and shared many interests, including their political views. Joe even played the violin a little and had a very pleasant tenor voice. Within a few months they decided to get engaged. Joe had a warm, friendly personality and he was made very welcome by the Taylor family but, unfortunately, soon after they got engaged (and Ann had collected most of the clothes for a conventional trousseau) her brother Mark got married and it became clear that their mother didn't have anything like enough money to live comfortably on her own.

'And anyway,' Annie pathetically maintained, "I couldn't possibly face living on my own. No one would expect me to at my age."

It seemed the only way Ann and Joe could marry was for him to move into her mother's house – not a prospect a man like Joe could relish. He was just coming to terms with the idea when his elderly, widower father had a serious accident and lost both his legs. Joe was his only child and it was obviously his responsibility to care for him. There was now little chance of their marrying in the near future. With his father increasingly depressed and vile-tempered, and Annie so nervous and obstinately clinging, it was clear that the two could never live happily in the same house. Ann resignedly took her trousseau clothes into general use.

When we returned from Grantham to live in Hull, Ann and Joe became even closer friends of my parents and, though they turned up often to spend the evening with us, we only occasionally visited Ann's house. This may have been because the four of them found Annie's company a little inhibiting, but I preferred it when we did go there because then, instead of having to leave them all half way through the evening to go to bed, I was part of the gathering till late. I could enjoy the music – we didn't have a piano at home as none of us could play – and there was always a little supper before we went home. But even more important to me was Ann's collection of copies of "The Readers' Digest", which was added to every month. They were kept on the lowest shelf of her open bookcase and whenever I began to lose interest in the talk or the music I was able to drift over and sit on the floor beside it and read and read until we went home. I generally ignored the drastically abridged book at the end of the magazine but I loved the funny anecdotes and the Increase Your Word Power sections, and I found most of the main articles quite fascinating. Some of them may have been fairly unsuitable reading for an eight or nine-year-old but they certainly did me no harm and the general knowledge incidentally absorbed from them was invaluable. At school I seemed to know a great deal more about the world than most of my class – though my pronunciation of some of the words I acquired via these articles (without ever hearing them spoken) could be embarrassing. I remember once asking to be taken to a "gymnacker" and – another time – if we had a record of songs from the "Mick-a-doo". Perhaps it would have been better if I'd followed Uncle Bill's playful advice. He said that, whenever he came across a strange word he couldn't pronounce, he always read it to himself as "bumblebees".

After Ann and Joe had been engaged for about six years, Joe's father became seriously ill and Ann unobtrusively began to get another trousseau together.

'I'm very glad,' my father muttered privately to my mother. 'If they don't manage to get married soon they'll forget what they're going for."

But it wasn't to be. The man recovered and was increasingly disagreeable, and Ann's mother seemed to become even more frail and dependent on Ann's company and care. The second trousseau was taken into everyday use.

Early in 1935 the firm Joe worked for closed down and he found it impossible to get another job. Though he was willing to take on anything offered, nothing was offered and he was on the dole for many months. One night when he and Ann came to see us, my father suggested Joe might start a window-cleaning round.

'I would, like a shot,' said Joe, 'but so many men have thought of it that anyone who can afford to have their windows cleaned has got someone already.'

My parents exchanged grins. 'Not in the villages,' said my father.

'I've been asking round Keyingham, for example,' my mother reported, 'and I can give you five addresses this minute where they would be glad of a cleaner to go at least once a month. And it must be the same in many other villages between here and Withernsea.'

'But the problem is how do I get there? I've nothing but a bike.' Joe looked miserably frustrated. '*And* I'd have to pull a heavy ladder and a bucket on some sort of trailer behind me, wouldn't I?'

'We've thought of that! If we let you have our old Morgan on long loan that would solve both those problems. It doesn't use much petrol and with the hood down it would be easy to slope a ladder into the passenger seat, and still have room for buckets etc. We only ever use the car on a Sunday or for an occasional evening trip, and you wouldn't need it then anyway . . . So what do you think?'

Joe didn't need to consider it for more than sixty seconds and, by the end of that cheerful evening, plans had been made for Ann and Joe to spend the next weekend or two touring nearby Holderness villages calling on any likely-looking houses to offer his services. Within a few weeks Joe had built up quite a sizeable round which earned him almost a pound more than the dole he'd had to rely on before. Their fortunes weren't exactly made but things were certainly looking up.

Nearly a year later, having successfully survived the inevitable slackening of demand during a wet winter, Joe sold his round for a few pounds. He'd managed to get a job driving a delivery lorry for a local soft-drinks firm and this was the first step of a slow but sure climb up their promotion ladder. When he died he was a manager, based in the factory.

In 1938 his father died and, after being engaged for eighteen years, Ann and Joe were married and he moved in with Ann and her mother. There were only about twenty of us at the wedding. The bride's mother gave her away, my father was best man and my mother was the matron of honour. I remember it as a thoroughly joyous occasion and the bride looked wonderful in the glamorous wedding dress she had somewhat surprisingly chosen. They deserved their fourteen years of happiness. Ann's mother lived until 1943 and, sadly, Joe died painfully of lung cancer in 1952.

We'd been to a very different type of family wedding just a few months before Ann's – but a similarly happy one. Auntie Mirrie's son, Albert, had married Madge and I'd been asked to be one of the five bridesmaids: two of us children, two young women friends, and her married sister as matron of honour. Madge'n'Albert (my father and I couldn't decide why their names were always put in this order; my mother was sure this was a typical example of the dominant one being named first) had long been accepted as a single unit by the time we moved back to Hull and were regular, very welcome visitors to our house. While a young boy Albert had shown considerable talent as a footballer and to his great delight he was offered a trial with the city's leading team. For reasons no one in the family could understand, Uncle Tom refused to let his stepson take up the chance and – presumably because Tom had been financially responsible for her son for the last ten years – Mirrie apparently didn't try to fight the decision.

Understandably Albert always felt very bitter about this. He and Tom had never liked each other much, anyway, and – although when he left school he'd had to agree to work in the transport business Tom had set up in the thirties, with capital earned from selling coal – Albert had left home to live in lodgings as soon as he could. It's possible – even likely –that Mirrie gave him money to help him do this. She was a thrifty woman and I suspect that managing Tom's books provided plenty of opportunities for salting a little away each week into her personal savings account. Or, maybe, Tom was very generous with the housekeeping money.

Madge and Albert had met when in their teens but it had taken him several years of patient courting, as it was then termed, before he was able to persuade Madge to look on him as her permanent boy-friend. She was a trained dressmaker with a good job at one of the leading dress shops in the city and what she lacked in the way of prettiness she more than made up for with her lively personality and smart clothes. She was very thin – the boyish-figure look, much admired in the Bright Young Things era – and her job, coupled with her dressmaking skills, meant that she was well aware of the latest styles and could run up copies of them for herself very cheaply. She was easily the most fashionable young woman I knew and I was always captivated by what I thought of as her sophistication, her heavy make-up and bright nail varnish. The Taylor family were somewhat critical of her lack of interest in anything much beyond her own appearance and the latest film stars' antics as reported in cheap magazines, but they admitted she had a kind heart and, after she eventually agreed to accept Albert's engagement ring, they were appreciative of her energising effect upon all aspects of his life. He had an impish sense of humour with a real talent for making his observations of everyday life into funny stories, and Madge gradually began to share his (and our) pleasure in unexpected incidents and people's curious foibles.

However, Madge wouldn't think of marrying until they had saved enough for a wedding to be proud of and a reasonably well-furnished house of their own. She saved for these things as determinedly as he did and, just before they reached their thirties, they were able to name the day. I was thrilled to be asked to be a bridesmaid and loved the pale green crepe de chine dresses Madge made for us, but I was disappointed in the flat pancakes of frilled fabric she designed to serve as our hats. They were made of material left over from the dresses and were tied onto the side of our heads with streamers of broad satin ribbon. I thought they looked ridiculous on top of our short, fringed bobs and it was particularly galling that the grown-up attendants were given flattering confections of delicate pink organza with large, romantic brims. Only the prospect of being allowed to keep the dress and the posy of sweet peas and wispy fern stopped me from refusing to take part. As soon as the wedding photographs had been taken I deliberately "lost" the hat and somehow it was never seen again.

Like the rest of our family friends, Madge'n'Albert often turned up at our house for the evening but occasionally we went to their new house. They were always very hospitable, though Madge rarely got home before six o'clock in the evening. Like Ann, Madge never had any children and both worked long hours, full-time, until they retired at sixty-five. This was fairly unusual for married women of their generation but Madge, at least, was conventional enough to do all the housework, shopping etc. and expected no help from her husband. Her house was always immaculate.

'Polished to death!' claimed her mother-in-law, Mirrie. "But *so* chilly. And there's never a bit of home-baking on the table. She fries chips every night to go with their first course and it's always bought cakes or biscuits for pudding."

I wasn't surprised at Madge's fussy cleanliness. She had once taken me to see her mother in *her* sparkling house and I'd been highly embarrassed when I dropped a couple of almost invisible crumbs from the biscuit Madge had insisted I should be given. Immediately her mother rushed to fetch a dustpan and brush and swept the carpet all round my feet with an irritable flourish. I wasn't taken there again.

Albert may have missed his mother's home-cooking but he was clearly proud of his spotless home and his energetic, stylish wife. And he always looked sleek and well-fed to me.

PLEASURES

It may be true that, for some only children, time passes slowly and hangs heavily - and I think it's likely that, for all youngsters, time seems to stretch out far more lingeringly than for older people. But there was so much happening most of the time in my life that I was almost never bored; in fact there was rarely enough time to do all that I wanted to do. Quite often, of course, what I wanted to do was to sit and read or dawdle around with a friend - hardly particularly energetic occupations - but I also had interests which took me out of the house on a regular basis, and these were sources of great pleasure.

After my spell in hospital with scarlet fever Auntie Mirrie decided that I was knock-kneed and she was worried that this might lessen my chances of finding fame and fortune on the stage. My eagerness to learn the monologues Stanley Holloway was making famous at the time, and the panache with which I "performed" them for long-suffering relatives' entertainment, convinced her afresh that the fortune teller's predictions for my future were false - I was definitely heading for international theatrical success. I must therefore begin correcting any physical shortcomings as soon as possible. She insisted on enrolling me in Tommy Foster's Saturday morning dance class immediately. His classes were the most prestigious in Hull at that time - and the most expensive - and it was understood that she and Uncle Tom would pay for them. It was to be considered as a birthday present. They also provided, quite unexpectedly, a pair of bronze leather dance pumps and a black mock-leather case to keep and carry them in. I was, of course, delighted.

I attended the classes regularly for over a year and enjoyed every one but, in the end-of-year presentation of a musical version of "The Pied Piper of Hamelin", I only featured as one of the little boys who skipped away after the Piper - and apparently she could see no improvement in the shape of my knees. Auntie Mirrie began to have second thoughts. I'd already guessed, from watching some of the older girls in the class with wistful admiration, that ballet was not really my forte, so I was more than happy when she suggested I should leave and join a late afternoon class run by a young woman who specialised in Greek and Modern Interpretative Dancing. This was held in a room over a shop and was a bit of a come down from the Fosters' large hall with its well-polished dance floor, but - although I had to catch two local buses to get to it, rather than just one - I enjoyed it even more. I was just beginning to shape up pretty well (though my knees, apparently, weren't) when, unfortunately for me, the teacher became pregnant and abruptly gave up the class. Auntie, reflecting on my interest in singing and my ability to hold a tune, then began to search around for a class which might cultivate *this* talent. To my great pleasure she happened on one which, in addition to a little singing and elocution training, offered some opportunities to gain acting experience. I began to shed my slight Hull accent, with its ugly glottal stop, and to realise I must never say "I aren't" . . .

These activities were a real pleasure but, to some extent, I was pushed into them. Nobody, though, pushed me into going to the Regal Cinema. As soon as I was free of Tommy Foster's Saturday class I began to spend most of my pocket-money on going to the Mickey Mouse Club. This was held every Saturday morning in the biggest cinema in Hull - handily right by the main bus station. Hundreds of children joined this club and were regular attenders and, though my first visit was with Gillian, for some reason which I can't remember, she never went again. Luckily I was quite happy to go alone and sit among crowds of children I didn't know. We were each given a lacquered metal badge - white with a black and red Mickey Mouse pictured on it - and we all wore them proudly. I think it cost threepence to get in, which – with the necessary bus fares - was quite a lot to find in those days, but the Regal was a fairly recently-built, upmarket cinema and this price meant that the children lucky enough to be able to afford it tended to be fairly well-behaved. Any rowdy behaviour was dealt with swiftly - the culprits found themselves firmly removed for the rest of the session by one of the four men stationed strategically around the place so, although there were no other adults with us, there were few real problems. The restlessness and understandable noise, which inevitably developed between our being let into the auditorium and the start of the programme, ceased as soon as the lights dimmed, the impressive curtains swished open, and the first film titles came up on the screen.

We were shown cartoons, slapstick comedy, and a selection of old Westerns, with a sprinkling of B-rated dramas considered suitable for children. There was never any attempt to educate us and we all thought it was very good value. The Chief

Mouse - I think he must have been the cinema manager - was the Club's figurehead and he spoke to us from time to time, illuminated by a spotlight, from the front of the stage. One Saturday he announced that it had been decided that the Club should have a Committee chosen from the members. They would help select the films to be shown and would decide on Club rules and plan other possible activities: would anyone who wanted to volunteer please leave their name and address at the pay desk after the show. This sounded good to me so I gave my name in and got a postcard a few days later to say I'd been chosen as a member. The first meeting was to be held half an hour before the doors opened on the next Saturday. Of course, it was really just a publicity stunt but I naturally found it very exciting, especially as the eight children involved met in the impressively plush committee room normally used by the cinema chain's executives. As far as I know we only met three times after that first day: once to talk about which kinds of film we liked best, once to be given instructions for joining a parade at the War Memorial on November 11th, and once (in the words of our chairman, the Chief Mouse) "to discuss the plight of the Basque children". We never did have an opportunity to see and select films - at least not during my time in office!

However, the November 11th event was exciting enough; we were to be part of the Remembrance Ceremony at Hull's Cenotaph. The cinema was at one corner of Paragon Square and in the centre of that square there, to commemorate the 1914-1918 War, is an imposing, quite dramatic statue of two soldiers. After representatives of the armed forces, veterans, and important dignitaries had laid their poppy wreaths, and local organisations - Scouts, Guides and Boys' Brigade etc. - had paraded past, our committee, with Chief Mouse in solicitous attendance, led a large group of Club members across from the cinema to stand round the Memorial for a minute or two. Before we set off I had been given a bunch of flowers to lay at its base on behalf of the Club and, as we paused, several photographs were taken by the press. When the report was published later in the Hull Daily Mail, the photograph which accompanied it showed me standing in the central position and, because I was holding the flowers, it gave the impression that I was the leader of the whole crowd. No wonder the girl next to me looked depressed. No one at home seemed impressed, though; in fact it was barely mentioned. Little chance of my becoming undeservedly swelled headed. It wasn't until years later that I found a glossy copy of the print tucked away in an old cardboard box of family documents.

I was, however, justifiably featured strongly in the committee's next venture. At our final meeting the Chief Mouse suggested that the Club should consider doing something (a collection?) for some of the Basque children who were being brought over to Hull as refugees, fleeing from the desperate situation in Spain at that time. It seems, from the account of this meeting reported in the Hull Daily Mail, that Jean Langdale had a great deal to say in support of this proposal and the motion was carried. Again this was, I suspect, very good publicity for the cinema chain and, again, it received scant attention at home, but I'm not sure how much was actually achieved and, in any case, my circumstances soon changed and I had to move on. I therefore lost touch with any possible developments.

But not all my activities were so formalised and not all were unmixed pleasures. Until Gillian passed her scholarship to Newland High School and the pressures of homework meant we spent far less time together, we became accepted as honorary members of a boys' gang. These three were about our age. They lived close by, and for most of one year we all met regularly on the ten-foot behind our houses to roller-skate, play ball games and generally hang around together. At one time, when the boys were around, Gillian took to referring to me as Pie-face which I found intensely irritating, and my attempt to retaliate by calling her Pudding-face fell dismally flat. However, I became especially popular when I invented a particularly piercing call-sign which we could all use as a signal that we were ready to meet to play. And when my father made me a stout and stylish pair of wooden stilts which I was happy to lend to anyone who wanted to try them, I was definitely a welcome member of the gang. She got her own back, though. When we played anything which required us to take on an imaginative role, Gillian was always Ginger Rogers and I had to be Lily Pons.

'She's a famous film star who sings,' she told me firmly, when I objected. 'You should be proud!'

I'd never heard of her, and nor had the rest of the gang, but Gillian's forceful personality won the day. I was stuck with Lily, just as I generally seemed to be stuck in the tent looking after the baby when we played Cowboys and Indians, while she got to gallop around on horseback with one side or the other. Surely it can't still rankle, can it?

Not that I was all that keen on galloping around. Though I was thin and wiry, I was never physically very energetic. After our early morning activities during our Bridlington holiday, my father tried taking me every Friday evening to the open air swimming pool on Albert Avenue, but I really wasn't keen. I didn't like the fact that the water was dark greyish-brown and I couldn't see the bottom. And even the very real thrill of riding there and back on the pillion of his motor bike didn't compensate for the discomfort of trying to dry and dress myself in a cramped wooden cabin where the walls, seat and floor were wringing wet with unidentifiable moisture. I tried not to be a pain, and I was very careful not to complain, but it must have been clear that I was very luke-warm about our trips and we soon stopped going. I was happy to have more time to spend with the gang, even if sometimes now I had to be a rancher's daughter (Gillian's idea, of course) tied to a tree, with the Indian contingent (including Big Chief Gillian Scarlet Feather) dancing round me with bloodcurdling cries and brandishing tomahawks. In fact, it made quite a nice change.

Considering the amount of freedom we children were given, it is perhaps surprising that we didn't get up to some really serious mischief but - apart from doing a few stupid things like daring one another to jump off high walls - our parents' confidence in our good sense was largely justified. Except, I'm afraid, for one thing. Unbeknown to them, during some light summer evenings when they thought we were in the field behind our houses or in one another's gardens, we spent a lot of the time playing on and around the building sites towards the end of our road. We couldn't, by today's standards, be called vandals but piles of sand were more or less demolished as we leapt over and around them, one or two bags of plaster got split and scattered, and we thought it quite fun to scrape quantities of the still damp putty from the edges of newly installed window panes. Fortunately, as far as I know, no glass ever fell out of the frames - perhaps because we were only able to take the putty from one side: the outside. We just enjoyed seeing how large a lump of the stuff we could collect and play about with. I'm ashamed to say I simply didn't think about the consequences, or to consider that we were undoing men's careful work and actually stealing material from the builders. I even came home one night so proud of the quantity I'd harvested that I showed it to my father.

'You can have this if you think you can use it for anything!' I said, with condescending generosity.

He was so shocked that it must have been at least thirty seconds before he was able to speak. I prefer to forget what he said to me, *and* the way he said it - and I hated it that he seemed so bitterly disappointed in me. It was forcibly pointed out that, apart from its being a criminal activity, it was extremely dangerous to play around building sites and I was not only never to go near them again but, to drive the lesson home, I was forbidden to play with the gang, or even outside our garden, for the next two weeks. The lesson was learned. This was the last criminal activity I've ever been involved in, unless we count occasionally exceeding the speed limit slightly, and even that was sheer carelessness - I think.

After the putty episode the gang began to disintegrate, mainly I expect because we were all entering the next phase of growing up. We remained friendly but tended to mix mostly with our own sex. I was persuaded, at one point, to join a Brownie Pack (I think my father imagined this might encourage me to become interested in more constructive outdoor pursuits, practical skills and even camping!) but I left after two sessions. The appeal of wearing a brown uniform and collecting brightly coloured badges faded quickly when I found I had to walk a mile to get to the meeting hall and then sit uncomfortably on the floor round a painted cardboard toadstool for much of the time. Putting one or two pennies into a slot in the top of the shaky toadstool – for some unexplained reason – seemed both foolish and pointless to me, and Brown Owl wasn't particularly attractive or inspiring as a leader. Perhaps it was not a well-run Pack, or – more likely – there was something lacking in me, but I remember feeling I knew far more interesting ways of spending an evening.

I sensed that both my parents were proud of my achievements at school but I think I was unconsciously aware that my father sometimes wished I could have shown at least a little enthusiasm for some of his more masculine interests like fishing, model-making, cars, trains and aeroplanes, and outdoor pursuits. I tried, of course, but it must have been obvious they were not really for me. I never knew - and never asked - why they didn't have more children (it may have been largely a financial decision) and, in any case, the possibility of another child joining our close threesome simply never occurred to me. But now I think my father would have enjoyed having a son to share his interests and learn some of his skills.

So when, the next winter, there was a lengthy period of heavy snow and he suggested I might like a sledge, I put on a delighted smile and asked when it would arrive.

'I'll be making it, of course,' he said. 'I'll get the wood tomorrow.'

For the last few weeks he had been making a one-string fiddle like the one he'd seen a comedian play on the Tivoli theatre stage, and he was trying to think of a way to make a bow to play it with. He had no intention of wasting money by buying one. So he was happy to leave the problem to one side and concentrate on the simpler task of making a toboggan. At the beginning of the winter he had turned our little box room into a workshop and was able to pursue his hobbies in relative warmth and comfort, and the next Saturday I was presented with a sledge. It was a bitterly cold, grey day but we set off for the open country, prepared to spend two or three hours skimming down any slopes we could find. These were few and far between but I did my best to show enthusiasm, longing all the time for home, a roaring fire and my latest library book. Luckily, it soon began to snow again, the afternoon light faded rapidly, and we had to trudge home, dragging the heavy sledge, as best we could. The memory of the acute pain in my fingers when I unwisely held them close to the roaring fire is distressingly vivid but at least I'd learned one lesson from that experience – how not to deal with chilblains. By the next day only dirty slush remained and my father was able to return, undaunted, to solving the problem of the fiddle's bow.

He'd already managed to make a slender, wooden frame and - though somewhat more substantial and rigid than a bought one would have been - it was quite adequate for its task on a one-string fiddle. The difficulty was finding some fine but strong hair to complete it. A few nights later, just as I was drifting off to sleep, I heard my father creeping into my bedroom.

'I'm just borrowing your little black chair for a few minutes,' he whispered. 'I'll bring it back soon.'

I was too tired to ask what he wanted it for. This little wooden chair had been made for my mother when she was a three-year-old and when it was given to me as a baby my father had noticed that its stuffed seat had become very lumpy and the fabric cover was threadbare. So he'd taken it apart, made a cover from some black leatherette and stuffed it with the horsehair he'd cut as a memento from the tail of Auntie Annie's pony, White Wings, when it died. The cover was then nailed into place with decorative nails; it was a very professional job and I was very fond of that little chair. When I got up the next morning my chair was in its usual place and the fiddle bow painstakingly strung with silky greyish hair. The chair's seat, though, was now lopsided and never quite the same again. Incidentally, though my father had great fun working out and marking the guide positions for the fingers to press on the "stem" of the fiddle, it was not really successful as a musical instrument. He never managed to play it very well and the tone left a lot to be desired but, in any case, his real interest had been in the making of it and the challenges it provided. Still, it was beautifully crafted - a work of art - so my mother stood it in the corner near the window and for several years it made a great conversation piece.

PROBLEMS

Most of my problems were very minor ones. I was happy at Bricknell Avenue Elementary School and, though in my last twelve months there I began to see far less of Gillian, I had plenty of friends from my own class. There still wasn't much money to spare in our house but we were a great deal better off than many families at that time, partly because my mother was such an excellent manager. She and my father were both willing to live quite frugally and, because I was always aware of how economical we had to be to stay out of debt, I did not expect them to spend a lot on me either. Nevertheless I was very fortunate to have so many childless relatives to help fill my Christmas pillowcase with modest presents and to have dance classes etc. paid for by Auntie Mirrie. Granny Langdale, too, being a trained and - in many ways - talented dressmaker and tailoress, was very willing to save us money by making some of my clothes. But, to some extent, this was one of my minor problems.

I don't think my mother ever forgot that when I was about four Granny had asked me if I would like her to make me a dress for Christmas.

'What colour would you like? You choose any colour you fancy,' she said expansively.

'Could you manage two colours?' I asked, no doubt knowing she would like to give me what I wanted.

'Of course I could. . . And what kind of material do you want?'

'Shiny please. And pink and yellow,' I replied.

It arrived late, of course. Her garments were never ready on time but, when it finally came, pink it most certainly was: pale salmon pink satin with bright yellow ribbon, plaited, to trim the round neck and to make a sash. It was lucky that it came by post rather than when she next visited because I really didn't like it; I could see it was a big mistake and that my mother was dismayed. I didn't even want to try it on and I never asked to wear it. But it was worn once - when Granny came over for the day to see us and my mother insisted I put it on. After that the dress simply disappeared and I've no idea what happened to it. I've thought since, though, that at least she'd kept her promise. Though I'm sure she must have deplored my taste, Granny had made me the dress I'd chosen, and I know my mother would have made quite sure I thanked her properly.

I definitely didn't choose the coat, though. This arrived unexpectedly one morning when I was about eight, and when I first opened the parcel it looked very attractive. Apparently Granny had had some material left over when she'd made herself a winter coat and had decided to make it into one for me. It was a very dark green - a somewhat unusual colour for a young child at that time - and the note inside explained that it was generously cut so that I could "grow into" it over the next couple of years. The style she had designed was somehow vaguely Russian, with a full skirt and high stand-up, military-type collar. This might have been just acceptable but Grannie seemed to have developed delusions of grandeur, for she had trimmed the hemline, the collar and cuffs with glossy black fur - probably only dyed rabbit, but still far too sophisticated for a skinny eight-year-old.

'For heaven's sake! When and where does she think she can wear that?' was my mother's immediate reaction. 'She'd be laughed at in school and be teased as a show-off at dance class . . . And I can just see the reactions of the neighbours if I sent her to the shops for a bag of potatoes wearing that!' She paused to take a deep breath. 'Grandma Taylor would have a fit if Jean got off the bus in the village looking like a lost Cossack . . . And Grandpa would just chuckle and tell her to be sure to wipe the snow off her boots before she came into the house.'

I was equally reluctant to wear it, of course, but one cold, dark night we were going on a rare trip to the Pictures and I was persuaded to put it on; then at least I could say I'd actually worn it. Afterwards it was put away at the back of my wardrobe. This was a pity because we were on a tight budget, and buying reasonable quality clothes for a family in the thirties - even when the father was in work - could be quite a problem.

The next winter it was raked out and I was told to try it on again. It was still a little too large and still embarrassingly unsuitable. My mother waited until Bonfire Night and then suggested I wore it to go into the garden to watch the little firework display my father had arranged around our bonfire.

Somehow the coat got stained with a dollop of tomato ketchup from a baked potato I was chewing, a sparkler singed one of the sleeves and the skirt suffered quite a lot of damage when I managed to sit down in some mud. It couldn't possibly be worn again, of course, but - as I expected - I wasn't scolded. In fact I seem to remember I was given several extra roast chestnuts to console me.

Still, we were very grateful for Granny's help over the next few years. When she offered to make two summer dresses for me to wear at school (one to wear and one in the wash) my mother, herself, bought some pretty material and a suitable pattern, and I always felt comfortable in them. She then made two pleated skirts from soft tweed remnants and I wore them all winter with jumpers and cardigans knitted by my mother. Cheap, but stylish!

My mother enjoyed knitting but, for me, it was a problem. In our last year at primary school Miss Murray, who took the girls for Needlework while our class teacher took the boys for lessons with the grand title of Technical Drawing, told several of us that we could begin knitting something we could actually wear. This was a reward for doing good work with our sewing - or maybe, once we'd finished our cross-stitch mats, hemmed aprons and embroidered recipe book covers, she'd run out of ideas. Anyway, we were all proudly enthusiastic. The plan was that as soon as our mothers bought some wool, needles and a jumper or cardigan pattern, we could start. Finding the cash at short notice to buy the wool may have been difficult for some of the parents, especially after having recently paid for the recipe book cover, so it's not surprising that only one girl turned up the next week fully equipped to knit. Dorothy, usually a pleasant little girl, was understandably rather smug as she took several balls of soft yellow wool and some new needles out of a paper bag, then produced the necessary pattern with a proud flourish. On the front was a most attractive, coloured photograph of a smiling girl wearing a short cardigan, and the rest of us gazed at it enviously. By the end of the lesson Dorothy had finished an inch of the back's welt and I expect, like me, the rest of the group couldn't get home fast enough to start urgent negotiations with their mothers.

When I got home from school a few days later I was slightly daunted to find that my mother had been to the local wool-shop and bought several hanks of thinnish crepe yarn (I can't wear wool - I always find it unbearably itchy) in a dull maroon colour. The smart little carrier bag also held a pair of thin needles and a pattern leaflet for a long, straight cardigan - very serviceable and totally uninspiring. I'm still puzzled as to why she had chosen these particular materials: it was so unlike her usual taste and thoughtfulness. Even winding the stuff into balls was depressing and, because the yarn and the needles were fairly thin, just casting on the large number of stitches for the back took me over half a lesson. Meanwhile Dorothy finished another two inches of hers - including three lines of fancy stitches. From then on my cardigan became a very real problem: it never seemed to grow any longer even though I sneakily pulled it hard whenever no one was looking. We were encouraged to take our knitting home and work on it between sessions but, as I had other, far more interesting things to do, it languished untouched in its smart little carrier from one Wednesday to the next. But it haunted me and, when the end of the term came and Dorothy and one or two others had already worn their garments several times, I was still struggling to finish the back of mine. I left the school at the end of the year with one front and two sleeves unstarted. My mother had never offered to help.

'Everybody knits at a different tension, so it would make it look very uneven,' she said when I once tried dropping hints.

I knew that my knitting looked very uneven anyway, so how could it matter? I didn't try again. I just got more worried over the waste of money and drearily pressed on with knit a row, purl a row. It's quite surprising that, even for the sake of economy, my mother never seemed to consider taking over from me but, eventually, the whole carrierful drifted into a cupboard and was forgotten. I think it probably disappeared the next time we moved house but the memory of the problem hung around at the back of my mind for a long time - and it wasn't until I was engaged to be married, and rashly offered to make a pullover for my boyfriend, that I ventured to take up knitting again.

In an undemonstrative way my mother and I were very close and, as children often are, I was always sensitive to what and how she was feeling. One result of this was that, if I began to misbehave in some way, start to show-off, or speak tactlessly, she had only to look at me warningly or give an almost imperceptible shake of the head and I would change my mind. She didn't need to speak - and she certainly never needed to raise her voice - I just became aware of her displeasure and would do my best to regain her good opinion. This may sound too idyllic to be true but this is how it was. There were drawbacks, though. For one thing, because our sense of humour and our appreciation of the ridiculous were more or less identical, there were many occasions, when other people were involved, when we dare not even glance at one another for fear of collapsing with laughter. And there was another, darker side to our shared empathy - at least as far as I was concerned.

My mother, quite frequently, suffered severe attacks of migraine and, in those days, there seemed to be little that doctors could do to help. There was no obvious pattern in the timing of when they occurred, and we could never identify what triggered an attack. The violent headaches would come on suddenly, with no warning, and almost immediately she would feel (and perhaps be) very sick. The attack could sometimes last up to three or four hours and the only way she could get any relief would be to go to lie down in a darkened room, with a cloth soaked in Florida Water over her forehead. My father and I would keep as quiet as possible and, eventually she would be able to come back downstairs and gradually regain her normal colour and energy. She always preferred us to ignore what had happened and she discouraged any fussy inquiries about how she felt, but it must have been a serious problem for her.

To a lesser degree it was a very real problem for me, too. In a strange way I seemed to share some of the pain as her normally cheerful face darkened, and I watched her miserable withdrawal upstairs with a mixture of relief and distress. Afterwards the fear of its happening again hung over me like a black cloud until the reassuring effect of several days' return to her usual, equable self allowed me to forget about it. Yet always, at the back of my mind, a tiny shadow of anxiety and unease remained.

Because of the way I was brought up - except for a slight, unadmitted fear of the dark - I was generally comfortable being on my own and I enjoyed being self-reliant. By the time I was about ten my mother would never worry if I was a bit late getting home from school; she rightly assumed that I had come round the long way and was staying to play for a little while with my schoolfriend Sandra. Late one afternoon I set off from her back garden to go home for tea. It was a fine, sunny day and I quite looked forward to walking across the huge, bare field that lay between Sandra's and the outskirts of the little estate where I lived. There had been plans to extend "our" estate on to this field and a loop road had been completed a year or two before, linking it to Bricknell Avenue. The scheme had been temporarily abandoned because of financial cut-backs, and the road was useless: deserted. I waved goodbye to Sandra, watched her go into her house, and set off for home. I reached this road in five or six minutes but, as I started to cross it - probably deep in imagining I was trekking across the Sahara or strolling in my crimson crinoline in the gardens of a palace with Queen Elizabeth I - there was a screech of brakes and a bicycle pulled up beside me.

'What do you mean by cheeking me!?!' It was a big, ugly-looking boy wearing a blue and white striped apron and he was obviously very angry. 'I haven't,' I said nervously. 'I don't know what you're talking about.' 'You're a liar,' he sneered and, laying his bike down at the kerbside, he took hold of my wrist and dragged me a few yards on to the grass.

He flopped heavily to the ground, forcing me face downwards across his knees, and efficiently pulled down my knickers.

'I'll show you! I'll smack you till you cry. Cry! Cry! Cry!'

But of course I didn't . . . partly, I think, because I was so shocked. The only time I'd ever been smacked in my life I'd deserved it. I had just got home from staying, on my own with Auntie Annie at West View, and I'd objected to being asked to go upstairs to fetch something for my mother by saying wearily, 'Ooh, I'm always having to do things in this house!' My father had swiftly pushed up my sleeve and smacked my arm – hard.

The main reason I now refused to cry, though, was because of a sudden, vivid memory of my admired teacher, Miss Davis, and the story she'd told us when I was at my previous school. She had been so brave when she pretended she wasn't frightened of those bullying girls that they had been shamed into leaving her alone. I would do the same! And, stupidly, I forced myself to keep silent, screwing up my eyes so as not to cry. I'll never know if he would have stopped if I had wept (or, perhaps, said I was sorry for whatever he was accusing me of?) but I didn't, and he became even more angry and increased the force of his blows. Suddenly he pushed me roughly onto the grass and scrambled up. As he ran to grab his bike I thought I could hear someone shouting and I crouched down, fearful of what might be happening. When I dared to look up I saw he was frantically pedalling away down the road, and I realised that a man on a bicycle was now chasing him, waving one arm and shouting something I couldn't understand.

I didn't wait. I staggered up, managed to pull on my knickers, and set off, grimly trying to swallow down any sobs and force my shaking legs carry me home. Oddly enough, I saw no one until I stumbled into my mother's arms and the tears finally came. I felt her trembling as she held me but she remained quite calm as she tried to understand my muddled account of what had happened, and I found this - and her non-committal reaction when she looked at my bottom - very comforting. She quickly made me a hot, drink of sweet cocoa and fetched our kindly next-door neighbour to talk to me as I stood in the kitchen with my mug, while she went into the other room to ring my father at work. My memory of the rest of that day is uncertain and rather muddled. Presumably - for the sake of speed and to save my hearing what was said - my father must have phoned the police before he dashed home, because the detective constable who lived near the end of our road arrived to talk to me in what seemed to me to be within a few minutes. I remember trying, not very successfully, to describe what the boy looked like and saying that I thought he must be a butcher's boy because of his striped apron. At some point, our family doctor came and took me upstairs to examine me, gently, making little jokes about my tummy and the need to find a really soft cushion to sit on when I had my tea. And that was it.

Everything was kept very low-key and matter-of-fact and, luckily, there was no school next morning. It was Saturday so I had my usual little lie-in, which was very good for my tender bottom. On Monday, mid-morning, my mother came to school with me, carrying a soft cushion, and I waited outside the headmistress's office while she went in alone for a few minutes. At playtime the Head herself took me into the classroom, saying she just wanted to explain to my teacher that it didn't matter that I was late for once, and I went to sit on my usual chair at the back. When the class came in no one noticed the cushion and, as I chose not to say anything to anyone about my experience, I don't think any of the children got to know about it. It was reported in the paper, quite sensationally and very inaccurately of course, and it mentioned that three other girls had recently been attacked in a similar way. We learned from our detective that the man I'd seen chasing the boy had been working in his garden next door to Sandra's and had become worried when he - to quote – 'saw something puzzling happening in the distance'. He'd set off on his bike to investigate and was very distressed by the fact that, because he was elderly and had a weak heart, he 'hadn't been able to catch the lout'. But it wasn't until some years later that my mother told me that, for a fortnight after it happened, my father and Ann's husband Joe had roamed the neighbourhood on bicycles every night looking for the boy until it was dusk.

'And I was glad Joe went with him,' she said, 'because heaven knows what your father intended to do to him if he'd found him. Your poor bottom looked like a piece of liver and, as the bruises faded, you could actually see the outline of the brute's hand in places. I was just thankful you couldn't see it for yourself.'

Understandably, I never again walked across that field on my own but I didn't avoid it, and - because of the sensible way my parents seemed to react to what had happened - I suffered no lasting mental or emotional harm. For several weeks afterwards though, if I happened to be walking alone to or from school and there was no woman in sight, I became slightly alarmed, and if I saw a youth or a man coming towards me I would hover close to the nearest gate prepared - if necessary - to rush up the path and knock for help. But the need to do this soon faded and my normal confidence returned.

Then, one Saturday morning some months later, I went to the local shops for my mother and I saw the boy again - still wearing a butcher's apron - coming out of the barber's shop on the corner. He cycled off up Hall Road. I felt a bit sick and my legs suddenly felt strangely shaky, but I managed to get home fairly quickly to tell my mother what I'd seen and she was able to contact our detective immediately. Luckily, even though the boy lived about a mile away, the barber knew who he was and a few weeks later we had to attend a Juvenile Court. He was bound over for twelve months - which my usually humane, compassionate father thought was far too lenient. And I know that it always rankled with my mother - who had taken great pains to ensure I would be confident when answering questions in Court, and had insisted I wore my best clothes - that one lady magistrate said, in a distinctly patronising tone, 'She looks fine to me. Perhaps not much harm was done.'

Perhaps, if I'd looked more pathetic and waif like . . .

I now understand that it could have been a much more serious type of assault, and this may be why my parents responded politely, rather than rancorously, to the boy's father when he managed to catch up with us as we came out into the pale sunshine. This elderly little man was visibly nervous and distressed but he was determined to face us and to apologise for his son's behaviour.

'His mother and me can't think what got into him,' he added, his mouth trembling. 'She'd have come today if she could . . . She wanted to see if the little girl was all right . . . But she's crippled - in a wheel chair - and . . . ' He turned away and, shaking his head, made his way back into the building.

I expect my parents realised that his problems were far greater than any I had suffered.

THE SCHOLARSHIP YEAR

In the thirties all children in Hull's Elementary schools had to take the Scholarship examination just before Easter, in their Standard IV year, and - according to the results they achieved - they were then allocated a place for September in an appropriate school. Our school was in a fairly affluent suburb and, because most of the parents' occupations were professional or skilled, their ambitions and expectations were high. In many cases, therefore, their children were under some pressure to aim for Grammar Schools and High Schools or, at least, one of the Technical Colleges. My parents, however, rarely mentioned it. They bought me the book of practice tests the school suggested, casually went through it with me, then – apparently – assumed I would do well. In most schools, the "best" teacher was given the scholarship class and he or she had the daunting responsibility of preparing the children thoroughly without making them too anxious to do themselves justice when they came to take the tests. We had Miss Simpson - and we were lucky.

She was a plain-looking woman of about thirty-five who invariably wore grey or dun-coloured jumpers and skirts, and whose hair was trimmed uncompromisingly into an Eton crop. She took her work and herself very seriously. None of us was actually afraid of her but, as far as I can remember, it was very rare for anyone one in our class of over fifty children to dare to step out of line - an enviable type of disciplinarian. I imagine she recognised and valued the solid grounding we had been given by our earlier teachers because she built on their work with smooth competence. She certainly couldn't be described as a barrel of laughs - in fact I don't think there were many laughs - but her calm predictability was almost as comforting as Miss Murray's cosiness had been. And, in addition to all the basic skills we needed for the coming exams, she managed to fit in a surprising amount of interesting extras.

True, we only had one art lesson in the whole year - and what a palaver that was! It involved giving out to each of the twenty-six double desks: a white china palette, two jars of water, two paint brushes, two newly-sharpened pencils, one rubber, one pair of compasses, two rulers, and two sheets of drawing paper. We had been asked to bring a bit of rag to wipe our brushes on but, of course, some had to be torn up to provide for the forgetful ones. Miss Simpson then explained the principles and techniques to be used when we drew and coloured the patterns we were going to design, and ten minutes later she came round to put generous blobs of red, blue and yellow paint into the three sections of our shared palettes. We were off! From start to finish this lesson took up the whole of one afternoon and, though it yielded great satisfaction (the children's) and a decorative wall display (Miss Simpson's), the operation was never repeated. And, with so many to control and cater for in one furniture-filled classroom, plus all the subsequent collecting, washing out and clearing up of equipment to be organized, who can blame her?

We had a somewhat similar experience when we went on a Nature Study expedition. It was a fine, sunny afternoon and when we got back from our dinners Miss Simpson was waiting to give each of us either a jam jar, a little white net on the end of a bamboo stick, or a paper bag. She lined us up at the patio door in pairs with Colin - a stolid, dependable boy - at the front.

'We are going to walk across the playing field to the drain by the hedge and when you get there you MUST stand and wait until I tell you to spread out along the edge. I shall then want those of you with jars or nets to look for anything swimming or floating around. Half fill your jam jar with water first then try to scoop what you have found into the net and, very gently, transfer it into the jar without hurting it. Those of you with the bags are going to look for interesting things on the banks - flowers, pebbles and so on. Put them carefully into your bag so that we can look at them properly when we get back. Lead off, Colin, and NO TALKING, please, till we get to the ditch!'

We set off sedately enough but the unaccustomed sense of freedom stirred by the open field was too much for most of us. We broke ranks, started to run, and overtook reliable Colin at a cracking pace. Jars were dropped, nets and sticks became entangled causing several children to trip over them, and bags escaped from careless hands and blew off in the breeze. Miss Simpson's whistle shrilled and we stopped to turn and face her icy anger. A very subdued class was marched smartly back into the classroom, jars , nets and bags were collected, and that was the end of any practical Nature Study for Standard IV.

In other areas of the curriculum, though, she was inspirational. She had high expectations of our ability to enjoy good literature, and to take a real interest in accounts of historical events. In addition to such books as "Wind in the Willows", "Treasure Island" and "Puck of Pook's Hill", she introduced us to the plots of suitable Shakespearean plays and read us impressive extracts from them. I must admit I found Beowolf hard going, but the boys revelled in it. We learned a piece of poetry every week - sometimes our own, individual choice from a children's anthology, and occasionally something such as "Full fathom five my father lies / Of his bones are coral made . . . ".

I can't claim to have made sense of all of it, but the sound of the words enchanted me and lingered at the back of my mind until I was old enough to appreciate them with more understanding. They felt like old friends when I later had to study them at a higher level.

She set high standards for us to work towards and I think most of us glowed at her none too frequent praise. I usually got high marks for my compositions, as we called our essays, and I almost always found a brief, complimentary comment at the bottom. It was a shock, therefore, to be summoned quietly to her desk one day and privately told that she was disappointed in my last piece of writing. I don't remember the actual subject we had been set but it must have been something about imagining our future lives; I do remember, though, that it was a piece I was particularly proud of and that, when she called me out, I certainly wasn't expecting any disapproval. She pointed to the paragraph where I described visiting a cafe in the evening with friends. I had included a description of what I was wearing and I'd drawn upon various details of an outfit of Madge's which I regarded as the height of sophistication.

'I am sorry to think your main ambition is to acquire expensive clothes and spend all your spare time chatting in smart cafes,' she said sadly. 'I'd like you to remember that there is a lot more to life than cocktail hats, diamond rings and scarlet nails.'

I was devastated - though I'm sure she would have objected to my using such a strong word in that type of context. I felt she had misunderstood the reasons for my writing about the imaginary incident; it was really just a childish attempt to produce a light-hearted picture of the kind of adult woman I'd seen on films, rather than any serious hopes for my own future. Nevertheless I was upset about having disappointed her and ashamed that I'd thought it clever to write about such trivialities. Her warning was, perhaps, timely though - and I not only heeded it at that point but it made a lasting impression on me. I've seldom been drawn towards superficial signs of success and I've certainly never lusted after a really frivolous hat - cocktail or otherwise. It turns out I haven't the face for one and, in any case, I'm not sure I would recognise a cocktail hat if I saw one.

Our class had to sit the scholarship exams at Hall Road School and I think it was a straight exchange: they came to ours. I found the thought of unfamiliar surroundings a little daunting and most of us were afraid that we might not get to the school on time, but I was reasonably confident about the tests themselves. After all, in the Christmas exams I'd managed, by just one mark, to wrest the top-of-class seat from my friendly rival, Jean Limon. Still, we all felt more confident when we learned that the Head and Miss Simpson would take us to Hall Road one afternoon in the previous week and that we'd be shown the classroom where we'd be taking the exams. Once the exams were over, and we knew the results were not due until early July, we more or less forgot about them and settled back comfortably into our usual school routines.

In June I had what I considered to be a brilliant idea. I'd suddenly realised that in a few weeks time we would be leaving Bricknell Avenue School for good and that, because most of us had been very happy there, we ought to think of a way of saying thank you to our teachers. In those days it was not the custom to give them presents when you finally left their class. I got a group of girls together one playtime and, after a few hesitations, they agreed that we should ask the headmistress if we could put on a little concert for the three top junior classes at the end of the term - all our own work. This was a pretty unusual request but she took a risk and said we could stay behind for half an hour any afternoon we liked and practise, unsupervised, in the school hall. Because the school had only been opened five or six years and had been built to impress, the hall was large enough to hold up to two hundred children and it had a substantial stage at one end.

So the eight of us set about planning a suitable "scene" for each of the three teachers and the girls were kind enough to let me be in charge of the whole venture. They put up with my inevitable bossiness very patiently and, surprisingly, we were still good friends at the end. Somehow we managed to keep it all secret from the rest of the school - maybe they just weren't interested in what a few girls were getting up to - but I've wondered since whether any of the Staff sneaked an occasional look at what we were doing and, maybe, someone kept a watchful eye upon us without our realising they were around. In either case, I expect they had a good laugh.

Despite being very brief and pathetically amateurish (Drama was not a school subject in the thirties) the actual concert seemed to be a success. We'd invented our own country dance as a tribute to Miss Wilkins and it might have been quite impressive but for the fact that, lacking any other means of providing music to accompany it, we had to produce our own: we simply sang all the verses of "The Lincolnshire Poacher" as we danced. An odd choice but someone had remembered that Miss Wilkins had once said she came from Lincolnshire! Naturally this left us all rather breathless which was a little unfortunate as our next tribute was to Miss Murray and, inevitably, this involved a song. We'd chosen one of our favourites: the round "Fie, nay prithee John". It's a fairly long and complicated one, and has to be sung at speed, but we managed to sing it twice through without its collapsing into a disastrous muddle. I doubt whether there was much recognisable tune left by the time we got to the end - all gasping desperately for air - but we did triumphantly finish at the same time.

However, it's the item we'd planned for Miss Simpson that

embarrasses me to think of now - though, at the time, I was extremely proud of it and had no doubt whatever about its suitability and charm for her. We had all agreed that she would enjoy seeing something from one of Shakespeare's plays and I had personally chosen the Tomb scene from "Romeo and Juliet", as most of us had been taken to see the famous film which starred Norma Shearer and Leslie Howard and been thrilled by it. Of course I was to play Juliet, and Dorothy (of the yellow cardigan fame) would be Romeo. We took it very seriously, delivering our lines with intense feeling and dramatic gestures, and we'd made a real effort to devise some form of costumes etc. But, to adults, it must have been either hilarious or hideous to watch - or maybe a mixture of both. At the end there was some uncertain clapping, then the eight of us were thanked, very briefly, by a smiling but distinctly red-faced headmistress. I didn't see the other teachers' reactions - they were extra busy marshalling their classes out of the Hall and had their backs to me - but I was smugly confident they'd enjoyed it and were deeply flattered by our efforts! Perhaps someone should have told me . . .

Towards the end of June my mother and father developed an extremely irritating habit of occasionally exchanging muttered remarks in a form of dog-Latin which I couldn't even begin to understand. They must have practised the skill when they were children for they were expert at using the language and, whatever the subject was, it seemed to afford them a great deal of amusement and satisfaction. Once or twice I was able to pick up a kind of recurring phrase which sounded like "ickibo in edshay" but it made no sense to me. One morning in July I woke to hear my mother calling over the back fence to Mrs Slide next door but I couldn't hear what was being said: there just seemed to be an unusual amount of excited activity down there. When I went down for breakfast there was an open letter by my plate. I'd passed the Scholarship Examination and was to go to the hoped-for Newland High School in September.

My parents kissed me quietly and managed to look fairly casual about the news as my father said offhandedly, 'We knew you'd get it, of course.' But the impression they were trying to create crumbled as they started to laugh, pulling me out of the chair and into the back garden. There, leaning against the fence, was the one thing I'd been longing for ever since I'd outgrown my little fairy cycle four years ago: a bicycle. It was only a second-hand sit-up-and-beg bike (old-fashioned even for the thirties) but I didn't care. It was a bike of my own and I wouldn't need to beg rides from other, luckier girls ever again. When I was told that it had been waiting for today's news, hidden in Mr Slide's shed, the "ickibo in edshay" began to make sense.

Leaving Bricknell Avenue School was not difficult now. Several of my eight friends had passed for Newland, too, and we were all pleasurably excited at the prospect of learning French and Science, buying a hockey stick and a special Reeves paint box, and wearing the prestigious uniform. In addition, there were the summer holidays, equipped with my new bicycle, to look forward to. A week before we left, Grandpa Taylor gave me a beautiful autograph album for my birthday. He was colour-blind - a slightly awkward handicap for a printer - and this meant that he had to limit his undoubted talent for drawing rural scenery, houses and churches, to simple pencil or pen-and-ink sketches. Of course I was delighted to find an attractive little picture of Robin Hood's Bay which he had drawn on the first page of the album and, using this as an excuse for showing it to Miss Simpson, I plucked up the courage to ask if she would sign a page for me. She asked if she might take the book home for the night, and returned it to me the next day with seven lines from "Julius Caesar" above her signature, beginning :

"There is a tide in the affairs of men which, taken at the flood, leads on to fortune . . ."

Once again, I didn't really understand the extract's meaning for several years but I very much appreciated the time she had taken to choose those lines and copy them out so beautifully, just for me.

I can't remember now whether our interview with the Newland headmistress was at the end of the summer term or just before the autumn term began, but I have a very clear recollection of my mother and me walking down the long drive which led to the imposing-looking school buildings.

'She's bound to ask what you want to be when you grow up,' said my mother, slightly nervously. 'What are you going to say?'
I had no doubts. 'An author!' I said.

'You can't say that.'

She was quite definite; job security and a reasonable pension to look forward to must have been her overriding ambitions for me. We were living through hard times and she knew it.

'She'll think you are showing off ! Better say a secretary . . . Or say you want to get into the Civil Service.'

I shuddered. I didn't want to be a secretary, and I had no idea what the Civil Service was, but I was willing to go along with her advice. She clearly felt strongly about this. When our turn came to go into the Head's pleasant, oak-panelled office I think my mother was more nervous than I was; her lack of experience of any kind of higher education made her unnecessarily unsure of her own abilities and she may also have been wondering how I would respond to this formidable lady. As it happened, the interview was very brief and I got the distinct impression that the lady lost interest in me when I told her I wanted to be a secretary. In fact, looking back, it was hardly worth changing into our best clothes - or walking the mile for. I'm not sure why there had to be an interview anyway.

*

Two days after I left Bricknell, when we had just returned home from buying one or two items of uniform from the High School's long list of requirements, the bad news broke. Harry Parry had died unexpectedly of a heart attack. He was in London on business at the time and my father - who was so distressed that he found it difficult to tell us on the phone what had happened - came home immediately to pack an overnight bag and drive Lola and her husband to the London hospital to make the necessary arrangements for bringing Harry's body back to Hull. It was a difficult time for them all and my mother was surprised at how upset my father was and how much he missed his former boss during the next few weeks. Naturally, he attended the funeral and I remember he was somewhat taken aback to find that, although Lola was the only blood relative there, because she was a woman she didn't seem to be involved in the ceremony. Apparently Jewish custom dictated that she must remain on the fringe of the proceedings.

'She stood about twenty yards away from us all, so I walked over to stand with her,' he said, and his voice sounded strange - a mixture of surprise and amusement. 'And I suddenly realised she was leaning, quite casually, against her own tombstone. Apparently you buy a plot and a headstone as soon as you have the money, so that they're there ready when you need them.' He paused, bemused, for a few seconds. 'It gave me a very odd feeling to see her name on that stone.'

Although my main preoccupation that holiday was the practical preparations for the adventure of the new school, even I noticed my father's unhappiness. I thought at first it might be due to there being some difficulty in finding the money to pay for all the new clothes etc. I had to have, but my mother explained that she had been saving for this expense for quite some time and, though we weren't going for the dearest options where there was a choice, there was no real problem. His unhappiness seemed to be linked with his work and, as I could do nothing to help there, I pushed it to the back of my mind.

As the beginning of term drew near, two simple thoughts recurred constantly throughout each day:

'Newland High School, here I come!' and 'Shall I be able to cope?'

NEWLAND HIGH SCHOOL

On the first morning of term I was escorted to Newland High School for Girls by Gillian, who was revelling in her superior knowledge of the school and its routines.

'I shan't be taking you every morning,' she said condescendingly. 'As soon as you can manage on your own I shall have to go back to my own friends. We second years have too much to do, you know, to have time to be bothered with the little ones.'

Little ones! Manage! I seethed, and promised myself that I would set off ten minutes earlier next morning and avoid being called for and "taken" ever again. Nevertheless, I was grateful (even if I didn't show it) to be shown this first day where to stand to wait to be told where to hang my coat and where my classroom was. There seemed to be hundreds of new girls chattering excitedly in couples or small groups, but I couldn't see any of my old classmates around - none of them lived anywhere near me and all would have come from a different direction. At nine o'clock we were lined up ready to go into the building and an officious-looking young woman wearing a Prefect's badge was stationed at the entrance collecting something from each girl before she went in. I was puzzled.

'Where's your certificate?' the prefect demanded, when I reached the entrance. I didn't know what she meant, and I certainly didn't have one.

'You can't come in without a certificate,' she said impatiently. 'You'd better go to the end of the queue and wait.'

I was hot with shame and bewilderment and I slunk to the back, feeling as if my bright world had suddenly collapsed around me. When all the girls but me had gone in, the prefect told me to wait outside while she went to fetch the school secretary, who explained that I should have brought a form, signed by one of my parents, which stated that I had not had (or been in contact with) any infectious diseases during the past four weeks.

'You were sent this form with the list of uniform requirements, and we cannot allow you to come in until you produce it,' she declared, then added with weary irritation. 'Wait there until Vera fetches you another one in case you've lost it, then go home and get it signed.' And she strode off with the prefect reluctantly in tow.

Panic-stricken, I raced home and shouted to my mother with what little breath I had left, 'You forgot the form! You didn't give me a form! And they've started without me now.' Then the tears came.

My mother must have been startled to see me so distraught but, when she managed to make sense of what I was saying, she insisted that we'd never had such a form and, knowing how meticulously methodical she always was, I realised this was probably true. As she began to mop me up and calm me down, my father arrived for his breakfast; he'd been called out at five o'clock that morning to repair some machinery urgently. So, once the form was signed, he rushed me back to the school on the back of his motor bike. I stood at the main entrance for a minute, watching him zoom away and feeling very forlorn. I didn't know where to go or to whom I should take the form, so I trailed miserably round the empty foyer for several minutes before the secretary came out of her room and told me to wait until she had time to look up which class and which form teacher I'd been assigned to. It seemed a worryingly long time before she came back to me and, even then, I had to wait till she found someone who could take me to the right room.

My memories of the next few weeks are very hazy. It's almost as if I never fully recovered from that unfortunate first day. I felt I never really caught up with the rest of the class, always sensing that I'd been robbed of a proper introduction to the school, that I'd missed out on some vital instructions or information. Although it soon became obvious why our form teacher was known throughout the school as the kindest and most interesting member of the Year 1 team, I found it hard to get used to seeing her, at most, only twice a day - for registration and for English. The others were so impersonal that I never felt they saw us as individuals, only as a class unit, and the fact that there was only Jean Limon from our old school in the same class as me meant there was really no one I knew well enough to discuss my reactions with. And to make matters even worse, I found I *hated* hockey.

It's hardly surprising, therefore, that when - towards the end of September - my parents sat me down one evening and asked how I'd feel if my father took another job and we moved to another town, I said I wouldn't mind. It sounded like quite an adventure. They explained that, since Harry Parry died, the job at Metal Box had become uncomfortable. Cutting costs drastically meant that all the workmen were to be paid less. There were no payments for overtime however many extra hours had to be worked, and it was still expected that my father would happily rush to help Lola and Joss with any minor domestic problem at any hour of the day or night - even at weekends - in addition to his forty-two hour week at the factory. There had rarely been any extra financial rewards but Harry had always been appreciative. *They* simply took his good-will services as their automatic right.

I was told there had been an unexpected telephone call from Archie Carter who was the husband of a cousin of my mother's - Cathy Taylor. We'd almost never met up with this couple but we knew he was an area salesman for a motor oil company and, judging by the size of his car and their stylish house, a very successful one. Apparently he'd been asked to find a suitable rep. to open up a new connection in Norfolk. He'd rung to ask if my father would be interested.

'I'm not sure I can see myself as a commercial traveller,' was my father's considered reaction, 'and I don't know that I've got the confidence to go, "cold", to try persuading people to change their supplier and go over to an unknown brand . . . But it's a tempting offer.'

It certainly was. We discussed it, on and off, for days - and I was included most of the time as a matter of course. I don't know whether I had any real power of veto - there was little disagreement at any time - but I was always given the impression that my opinions and wishes were of equal value to any of theirs. And I never had the feeling that I was being persuaded into agreeing with a previously arrived at decision. The advantages of this move were clear: a small rise in salary, a good car provided, some commission paid on successful orders, a higher level of independence for my father, and much easier working hours. A newly-built house had already been bought for the salesman to rent, and he was assured that the actual removal expenses would be paid by the firm. Any reluctance he might have about giving up the more practical engineering side of his work which he so much enjoyed, was overcome when it was pointed out that it was his knowledge and experience as an engineer which made him such an attractive proposition to the oil company. He could meet customers on their own level, speak with some authority, and give them useful advice if needed.

There were several significant drawbacks to the move though. We would again lose the pleasures and comfort of close contact with our family and friends, considerable expense would be involved in kitting me out with a new school uniform and buying several items of the more formal clothing my father would need for his new role, and - most important of all - there was a risk that, if he was not successful at opening up a new area and making sufficient sales to justify the company's financial backing, the venture would fail. He'd have to look for another job and we'd have to move again to yet another new place. It was not an easy decision to make - and it had to be made quickly. But, within a week it was decided: we'd go.

My father left for Norwich three weeks later. He'd been to Bradford for a day to meet his new boss and have a crash course on the various types of oils he'd be selling, and the business routines he needed to be familiar with. He came back impressed with the quality of both the man and the product.

'It makes me feel so much happier about urging people to buy, now that I'm confident it's really good stuff,' he told us when he returned, and he set off for Norwich with Archie to be shown – he was assured - how to become a salesman in four easy lessons.

We had an excited call from him telling us that the house was almost ready, the plaster had now dried out, and would May please let him know tomorrow what colour she wanted the painters to distemper the walls. He'd found time to go to the city Education Office to make enquiries about transferring my scholarship and had been given advice about which High School to choose for me.

'You can pay the last rent up to November 7th,' he said with a touch of triumph in his voice, 'and arrange for the removal men to start packing our goods and chattels on the 4th. We're moving that week.'

Norwich

A NEW HOUSE AND A NEW SCHOOL

We arrived in our shiny black Morris Minor nearly an hour before the removal van, and so were able to wander round the new house at our leisure. It didn't take long. It was in a block of four and seemed very narrow compared to the one we'd just left. It had two quite small rooms leading off the long entrance hall; there was a pleasant front room, with a rather inadequate-looking electric fire, and a living-cum-dining-room with an open fireplace and a French window leading out to a small back garden. At the end of the hall were the kitchen and the back door.

'Lovely to have two separate rooms,' gloated my mother, but she was somewhat shocked to find that the kitchen, though reasonably long, was only the width of the hall and the stairs which ran up its left-hand side.

'We'll have to get Bill to come and give me some advice on how a ship's cook copes with the lack of space in his galley - especially if he's anything like my size. And I don't believe there's going to be enough room for me to stand between the oven and the cupboard under the sink, if I open either of the doors.' She was right. There wasn't. 'I'd best tackle it side-saddle, I think.' It worked - just.

My father looked really worried - he clearly hadn't realised its limitations - so she made no mention of the problems which would arise from there being no pantry and little space for our kitchen cabinet (now vital as a food store,) and she hurriedly went on to praise the agreeable effect of having smooth magnolia walls throughout the house and the advantages of having just a small front garden. This prompted my father to go out to test the quality of the soil and start planning how to level the tussocky ground for a lawn, while we went upstairs to see the two bedrooms, the bathroom, and the miniscule box-room. Largely, I think, because we'd be using the living-room most of the time and the noise from the wireless might disturb me if I slept in the room directly above it, it was decided there and then that I should have the front bedroom - much the more desirable I thought, especially as it had a pretty little fireplace. This, from my point of view, was a decision I later very much regretted, though its drawback did not become apparent for many months.

By bedtime we were almost straight, but when I settled down - desperately tired - in my new room I soon became very alarmed. Our road branched off one of the main roads out of Norwich. It looped round a large circle of empty grassland and - like our old house in Hull - the rest of the houses planned for this suburb had yet to be built. Once again there were views from my bedroom of open fields with just a few houses to be seen in the far distance and, while there was still some afternoon light, I revelled in this. But as soon as I turned off the light and got into bed I heard a frightening noise. Not far away I could hear children screaming and shouting threateningly and a faint orange light gleamed through my thick curtains. Either we had come to live in a very rough area, full of menacing children who would make my life extremely difficult, or we were surrounded by fields full of dangerous gipsies who would be equally intimidating to an eleven year-old girl from Yorkshire!

I turned my back to the window and pulled the eiderdown up to my ears, but it was a long time before I managed to get to sleep and, even then, the noise hadn't entirely died down.

There was so much to do the next day that I forgot about this problem most of the time and I didn't mention it to my parents - I felt they had enough to worry about - but that night I waited anxiously for the noise to begin again . . . There was nothing. And I not only never heard it again but I didn't see any sign of gangs of rough children or hordes of alarming gipsies either. It was a complete mystery.

But, years later, I heard my mother say to a friend, 'It was very cold the day we moved to Norwich, but at least it wasn't wet. And we could have expected it because, after all, we moved in on Bonfire Night.' How could I have missed it?

After various adjustments and compromises were made, the house turned out to be very comfortable. There were shops and a well-stocked public library on the main road less than five minutes walk away. There is no doubt it was a very pleasant area to live - despite the fact that, once again, we had to put up with the slight disruption of other houses being built around us - and our neighbours were quiet and highly respectable. So quiet and respectable in fact that I have no recollection whatsoever of those whose hallway wall we shared, and very few memories of the family of four on our other side, except that he was manager of a shoe shop and that their name, intriguingly, was Bruin - a surname I hadn't come across before or since.

'I wish we'd known them before they had their second child,' said my father, gazing out of our window at the two small children playing in their garden. 'I would have liked to tell people I lived next door to Daddy Bear, Mummy Bear and Baby Bear.'

Much more interesting were the people who lived in the bungalow next to the Bruins. After a few weeks of exchanging greetings and remarks about the weather with my mother whenever they met, the somewhat faded-looking woman who lived there confessed that her husband was a plain-clothes policeman. He was a cheerful, rotund man of about thirty-five who apparently tried to keep his profession secret for as long as possible. There was nothing unusual about that - policemen are often not popular in the area where they live - but it was unusual that, as there was no question in those days of their knowing my parents well enough to be on first name terms, neither he nor his wife told them their surname. 'Mrs . . . er . . . um . . .' soon sounded very awkward. We got to know the reason purely by chance. One day the postman asked my mother if she would take in a parcel for 'Mrs . . . er. . . um at number 48, and the name was above the address. It was Bastard.

'Poor devil! And for a policeman, too . . .' was my father's immediate reaction.

I was bewildered. As I hadn't heard the word before in any context, I couldn't understand the underlying amusement in his voice or the odd expression on my mother's face as she said sympathetically, 'No wonder they don't have any children. Why on earth haven't they changed it?'

Over the years, whenever I've heard or read it in its more common contexts, I've wondered that too.

A day or two after we moved, my mother and I went to see my new school and meet the headmistress. Both were a little unusual. I knew that my father had chosen this particular girls' school (almost all High Schools at this time were single sex) because he had been told that it had a good reputation for sound academic results but that it was not as conventional as the prestigious Norwich High School. It was built in 1929 by the Local Education Authority on land from the Sewell estate, and was noted for its modern architecture and progressive methods. Its motto was an indicator of its singularity. No worthy Latin aphorism for Blyth High School: the motto was "Be a blithe spirit and spell it with a Y".

The Head's study was comfortably conventional but its occupant was definitely not. For one thing, Mrs Whittaker apparently had a husband and a young son - this at a time when women were not normally allowed to continue teaching after they married. And, in any profession, women with children were expected to stay at home to look after them. For another thing, she seemed more like an actress giving a bravura performance as a slightly eccentric Duchess than a Head in her own school. She was tall and full-bodied, and her academic gown, draped over a well-cut suit, floated elegantly behind her as she showed us around the school. So did wisps of her greying hair which was piled untidily on top of her head. I didn't find her exactly intimidating, but to me she was very much an unknown - and therefore unpredictable - quantity. I was glad, throughout my time at that school, that I had almost no personal contact with her though, with hindsight, I now think of her with some admiration and respect.

The buildings we saw that afternoon surprised us. Apart from the two-tiered entrance block which contained her study, the secretary's office, and the Staff Room, the school was single storey. The juniors were separated from the senior girls by an imposing, central assembly hall. Both departments' rooms were built around a large rose garden, with a roofed walkway running round it to protect anyone walking to a classroom or the Hall in bad weather. Even in late autumn the unusual layout looked quite charmingly domestic – even cosy. But then we realised that all the classrooms had six, glass-panelled doors and these were folded back in pairs so that the whole of the side facing inwards onto the walkway and the garden was open and, therefore, exposed to the weather. And it was November . . . windy and cold, very cold.

'This is like the Open Air School for tubercular children that we have in Hull,' said my baffled mother. 'How does everyone keep warm? And are these doors kept open all the time?'

'All the time,' said Mrs Whittaker serenely. She beckoned to a girl who was clearly on her way to the hockey field. 'And now I'm going to hand you over to one of my senior girls. She will explain anything you need to know and then take you to see Jean's classroom. Room four please, Sylvia.' And she stepped onto a nearby gravel path and sailed off round the rose beds, the sleeves of her gown billowing behind her like two black wings.

Sylvia was very happy to explain that the doors were never closed unless rain was beating in or snow was drifting on to the walkway and, even then, teachers had to wait for written permission from the Head to be sent round. When we got to the classroom we could see that all the girls were wearing thick blazers and most had on red knitted mittens. The teacher had a thin overcoat under her black gown and she too wore woollen mittens. Yet they all looked quite comfortable and there was such a pleasant working atmosphere that I began to feel comfortable as well. Before she left us Sylvia told me that, if I chose to cycle to school, I could leave my bicycle in the building near the house at the far end of the school grounds. She said that this house was part of the school. Midday dinners were cooked and served there and there were several rooms used for small group tuition and individual music lessons.

'It belonged to the Sewell family and Anna Sewell used to live there,' she said. 'You'll actually be leaving your bike in Black Beauty's stable.' I could hardly wait for Monday to come.

The Head had told us that I could wear my Newland uniform until Christmas and we were glad of this for the list of items to be replaced was worryingly complicated. I looked forward to wearing the regulation, pleated gymslip. I hoped it might transform me into the sort of girl I'd seen pictured on the covers of popular stories of life in expensive boarding schools – "Sylvia goes to Mallory Towers", "Jill Saves the Day!" - but when I got it home, I realised its black material was quite rough and heavy, and the sash to go round the waist felt coarse rather than silky. Still, I guessed that I'd be glad of its warmth and that of the thick, pillar-box red jumpers which were to be worn underneath it instead of the blouses and ties I was used to. But I didn't much like their square necklines, or the embroidered shields which had to be sewn onto their centres, and when I tried one on I found that the wool was so harsh that I quickly started to develop an irritating rash.

'There's only one thing to do,' said my mother. 'I'll post one tomorrow to Granny and ask if she can make some kind of thin blouses for you to wear as invisible liners. And that reminds me - we're going to have to ask her to help with these as well. . .' She pointed to the second page of the list. 'It says you need three pairs of regulation knickers . . .'

'What on earth are regulation knickers?' my father interrupted. He grinned wickedly. 'Though, come to think of it, I'd quite fancy seeing some irregular ones.'

My mother raised her eyebrows then pointedly ignored him. '. . . and six pairs of white muslin liners,' she went on.

We found that the knickers could only be bought from the shop nominated by the school as they had to be made of sturdy black sateen, with a four-inch square pocket on the right leg. The pocket flap had to have three rubber buttons to keep any money we might carry absolutely secure. Later I learned that, from time to time, there was a snap inspection to make sure that our knickers and their pockets were correct. I've often wondered since how the girls who travelled to school by public transport managed to negotiate those awkward buttons to get at their fare money, if they stuck religiously to the school rules. But at least I never mislaid any cash while I was at Blyth or had any pinched.

My mother ordered the obligatory Cash's name tapes and knitted me three pairs of red mittens – 'What a palaver,' was my father's scornful reaction – and, when Granny came just before Christmas to see our new house, she sewed all the liners for me. She also took home a length of cheap white rayon to make the required "evening" dress - but the ample knickers with their buttoned pocket defeated her. We had to buy those.

As soon as I was fully equipped and looked the same as the rest of the class, I really felt I was part of the school and could start enjoying the life there. I was put to sit in the centre of the room - a comparatively warm spot. I soon got used to the regulation thick, black stockings held up by elastic garters, to wearing warm mittens which left my fingers bare whenever I needed to do any writing, and to working with cool fresh air blowing around me all day. At least this regime left us all pretty healthy for I cannot recall ever having a cold while I was at that school.

Some of the school's policies and routines were rather

different from the ones I'd experienced in Hull and from what I'd heard of in other schools. Perhaps the most unusual was that there was almost no homework until the beginning of the School Certificate course - that is until most of us were fourteen. Each girl was given the name of a well-known painter and told this was not to be divulged to anyone. Every week each class was given the title or subject of the painting to be submitted by the next Monday, labelled only with one's pseudonym. This was our only homework and, presumably, was checked against the art teachers' lists. The best pictures were displayed on the walls of the Hall and Art Rooms, and this was - in effect - the only feedback we got. The art lessons themselves were also strange. We were again just given a title or an object and left to work on it as we pleased while the teacher changed the wall displays or wandered round to look over a few shoulders, occasionally murmuring an encouraging comment. I found this bewildering. To begin with, I was used to struggling with one and a half hours' home work nearly every night at Newland, and I'd never been asked to paint pictures as part of it. I was no artist; in two years I managed to get just one picture on display and, for once, I'd had a little help from my father with that. I felt I could have done with some help in class, or at least a hint or two as to what I was doing wrong. In addition, I hated my pseudonym. It was Bizet and we only knew him as a composer of music. As my father failed to track down any artist of this name at the local library we decided that the teacher must have run out of well-known names by the time I had arrived in November.

Apparently, the intention of the art department's methods was to give us ample opportunities for free self-expression and this meant that our anonymity had to be preserved and our creative talents left unhampered. Mine refused to flourish. The idea behind the decision not to start giving homework too early was that pupils needed the time and freedom to enjoy life outside school and develop their own interests and activities. On the whole I think this was true. We were generally worked very hard in lesson time and it was acknowledged by the local education authority that the Certificate and Higher Certificate exam. results, and the proportion of university places awarded, were at least equal to those of the other High Schools in the area.

Most other subjects were taught conventionally. I remember very clearly that we had a considerable amount of formal grammar, spelling and correct pronunciation drilled into us. Most of us found this very boring at the time, but - despite its leaving me uncomfortably pedantic - I've been grateful for this useful grounding ever since. However, our history lessons were an interesting mixture of chunks of information delivered by an enthusiast, and an opportunity to compile personal notebooks summarising the facts we'd learned, illustrated with miniature, coloured-in drawings we culled from attractive wall charts and picture books. We followed the development of houses, then costume, then transport etc. and related them to the date-line which was stuck as a pull-out feature at the end of the notebook. It really made sense to me and I certainly didn't mind that, by the time I joined the class, they'd arrived at the Tudor house - which was the period we'd spent all our time covering at my previous school. I even asked if I could work at home to fill in the first few pages of my book with pictures of caves, cruck houses etc.

I liked it that we remained in our own classrooms most of the time. The teachers moved round to us, and this meant that, instead of having to lug heavy satchels of books from one room to another, we could keep most of what we needed in our own desks. It may have had some drawbacks for the teachers - no easy access to any materials they needed for each lesson, for instance - but it did make for a peaceful building, which was especially important in a school with rooms open to the corridors. We learned to move around quietly when necessary and to have consideration for others and, in any case, the school had large quantities of text books which could be housed in the classrooms' ample cupboards or in pupils' own desks.

Geography, though, was one of the few exceptions. We all loved our one-a-week geography lessons but I'm not sure that anyone actually learned anything. For some unfathomable reason the teacher was expected to take two classes together in an upstairs room in the admin. block, directly above the headmistress's study. This meant that we had to crush into unsuitable desks, with at least a quarter of us perched at the back on makeshift tables. The room was more or less permanently blacked out and the whole period was devoted to a slide show of photographs of different parts of the world, with the teacher giving an illuminating running commentary. She was a young and popular teacher who clearly knew and liked her subject, but none of it made much impression on us. We saw it as an enjoyable, relaxing time when no demands were made upon us, plus a welcome opportunity to munch quietly through the chocolate bars we'd bought at the Tuck

Shop at Recreation - just like a visit to the cinema.

*

On the whole my parents and I very much enjoyed living in Norwich. We liked the house - though it was not really big enough to have more than one visitor to stay at any one time - and Norwich was a beautiful, lively city with many fascinating historical buildings to visit and excellent shops to browse round. Having a car was a godsend to all of us. We were able to explore the countryside at weekends and, despite the much quoted criticism by a character in one of Noel Coward's plays of Norfolk's lack of undulation, we found it very attractive - especially, of course, the Broads. My father was able to take up fishing again and my mother would sit in the folding chair we always carried in the car boot, content to read or knit and enjoy the fresh air and the riverside scenery. I either sat reading on a tartan blanket by her side or roamed the banks with Paddy, watching the small cabin cruisers bustling past or the sailing dinghies tacking from one side of the river to the other. Just occasionally I would get my father to fix me up with his spare rod and try to become enthusiastic about fishing, but I found it a bit pointless. Any fish he caught (there were never very many) were always transferred to the keep-net until it was time to go home and then released back into the river, and if I caught one - this happened twice I think, in two years - I couldn't bear to take it off the hook, or replace the bait.

The type of work my father was doing and the fact that it

involved a car made a great deal of difference to my mother's life. Not only was he home every evening and able to rely on having uninterrupted weekends but, at least once a week, he would take her with him to the farms and small firms he was visiting and she would wait happily in the car with our dog curled up on the seat beside her. Paddy was so mad keen on the car that he would jump into it enthusiastically even when one of us just went to fetch something from it in the evening, then look pathetically reproachful when he had to be dragged out. I always took a house key to school with me so that my mother could decide to go whenever she felt like it and, although I secretly was always disappointed when I got home and found that she was out, it was obvious how much she and my father revelled in having this time on their own together. There was always a tasty cold lunch left for me, of course, but I missed having her there to welcome me and listen to my prattling on about the morning's events. I missed Paddy too but there was an upside: I could read a book all the time I was eating. I realise now that, compared with some of today's latchkey children, I had absolutely nothing to grumble about.

There was, however, a downside to the job for my father. He didn't really have the temperament for a thrusting salesman. He was a very likeable man and popular wherever he went, but he found it difficult to steamroller prospective customers into changing their established suppliers, especially as Miller's Oil was slightly more expensive. And, although he had a wicked - at times fairly bawdy - sense of humour, he couldn't trot out the conventional commercial travellers' flow of smutty stories which many customers seemed to expect. There's no doubt that he was reasonably successful in building many new connections and the powers that be at Head Office were pleased with his progress, but he was never entirely comfortable in the job and he heartily disliked writing the report which he was required to complete and post off every night.

A year or so before we left Hull - probably to make up for the loss of Polly Parrot, he had bought a pair of pretty green budgerigars and, after several distressing failures, had managed to breed from them. It had been decided, as soon as we knew we would be moving, that he would keep just one very young bird and sell off all the rest. He knew that, if he isolated Micky as we called him, there was a good chance that he might be trained to talk - a hobby which my father would enjoy. It worked. Mickey soon became very tame and, if you used a bit of imagination, he could be heard to say 'Mickey Dripping! Mickey Dripping!' quite often. He normally lived in our living-room in a smart wooden cage which my father had made for him but every evening, while my father wrote his dreaded report, he was let out to fly round the room for exercise. Mickey was very much attached to my father and, after circling the room a few times, he would land on his shoulder companionably chattering unintelligible messages into his ear most of the time.

When he got bored with this he would flutter down to the table and pick at the edge of the embroidered runner or try to rearrange the cigarette ends in my father's ash tray. To stop him doing this my father took to putting a half-open box of matches for him to play with and the little bird would spend the next few minutes struggling to pull one or two out and lay them in a line on the table. He was a pleasure to watch and no doubt this helped to ease the minor misery of the report writing.

Nevertheless I can still hear my father's regular complaint, 'I'm sick of writing "I had a long talk with Mr So-and-so at Such-and-such motor repair firm or farm or factory . . ." and the Office must be just as sick of reading the same old phrases day after day!' Finding any variation was almost impossible.

But at least he had more time now for his hobbies and, for a while he became engrossed in making quite sizeable model gliders and, later, equally large model aircraft with intricate balsa wood frames covered in a special kind of tissue paper which became tautly rigid when coated with a watery glue. Their propellers were powered by thick rubber bands which had to be wound up tightly before being released. For some weeks we spent every fine Sunday driving miles to a bracken-covered hill to launch, first, the graceful gliders and, later, an impressive but fragile plane. Eventually, of course, the thrill of seeing them fly and making delicate adjustments to improve their performance was somewhat outweighed by a fair proportion of failures - veering wildly off course in response to a sudden gust of wind or plummeting nose first into distant bracken - and repairing the resultant damage became a burden rather than a pleasure. For me, toiling up and down the hill searching for a lost glider or plane had palled long ago but my father persisted until he had more or less perfected his model-making skills and had real success in flying them.

EASTER 1938

By the spring of 1938, Hitler's impact on the international situation was causing deep anxiety in Britain and many people became increasingly preoccupied by the need to prepare for what seemed to be inevitable, despite the efforts and optimism of Ramsay Macdonald and his diplomats: WAR.

My father volunteered to join the Observer Corps and, though he quietly refused to tell us anything at all about what its purpose was and what it involved, we recognised that it was an important commitment. He was training two evenings a week somewhere in the centre of Norwich and he told us he'd had to sign the Official Secrets Act and be thoroughly vetted before he was allowed to join. After the war we learned that he'd been working in the underground centre which received and coordinated reports of incoming aircraft from the many, widespread East Anglian observation posts. Later, of course, they were able to use the recently-developed radar to help to detect and track them as they flew towards the coast – quite some time before they came into sight. A short while after the war ended we were particularly interested to read in the national press that three or four scientists had been awarded significant sums of money for their work in the late 1930s on the invention and development of radar and that one of them was a first cousin of my mother's. We'd rarely heard any mention of him and, in any case – because of the earlier problem with the Friendly Society funds – we had more or less lost contact with that branch of the family, but it was still quite gratifying to think that my father had been involved too, albeit in such a very minor way.

Soon after our first Christmas in Norwich we began to look forward to spending Easter at Maynor. We were sorry that Grandpa Taylor would not be there to greet us. As the village ARP (air raid precautions) organiser he had to attend an area meeting in Withernsea that evening, but it was good to know that Nora, Shirley and Michael were going to be there with us over the weekend. As we drove up to Yorkshire my parents swapped stories of things Grandpa had said and done which had made them laugh or made them proud, for my father was almost as fond of him as my mother was.

'I can't wait to see him again. I really miss his regular Wednesday visits to Linkfield Road for a plate of corned beef hash,' she said.

After one of Grandma's lavish high teas I helped put Shirley and Michael to bed, then Nora set off for some sort of village meeting and the rest of us settled down to listen to a Rob Wilton comedy show on the wireless. We heard the 9.45 bus arrive at the stop a hundred yards or so down the road and, as it pulled away, I saw my mother begin to smile, anticipating the pleasure to come. Grandma turned down the volume on the wireless so that we could be ready to welcome Grandpa if he'd been lucky enough to catch that bus. A minute or two later we heard the sound of a car engine being revved repeatedly. It was refusing to start.

'I'd better go and see what's the matter,' my father said. 'I think that driver needs some help.' And, grabbing the torch kept in the hallstand drawer, he hurried out into the night.

We sat quietly waiting. Suddenly my father appeared and called my mother into the hall.

'Stay here with Grandma, Jean,' he ordered.

Grandma sat immobile, as if frozen to her chair, and - faintly - we could still hear the audience laughing as Rob Wilton continued his hilarious monologue. We had no idea what was happening but, somehow, we sensed something was very wrong and I went over and turned the wireless off. I didn't know what to say to Grandma and could only mumble that everything was going to be all right, but she shook her head impatiently and said nothing. After what seemed hours of awkward silence we heard someone crying hysterically and my mother came in, supporting a distraught Nora.

'I was walking home . . .' Nora sobbed. 'I saw there was an accident . . . I went up to somebody . . . I said I lived at the next house up the road . . . Could I help . . . Could I fetch anything . . . They said . . . They said . . . A man's been killed. And then I saw Frank . . .' and, struggling with her own tears, my mother tried to put her collapsing sister into a chair.

We could hear my father talking quietly on the phone in the hall and then he came in and knelt down in front of Grandma. I'm afraid it's Will,' he said. 'He's . . .'

'I know,' she interrupted, stony-faced. 'He's dead. You've no need to tell me.'

There were no tears, no signs of emotion, not then or - as far as we knew - at any other time.

Apparently, when Grandpa got off the bus he had started to walk across the road and a car heading towards Hull had knocked him down. No one on the bus had been aware that anything untoward had happened so it had simply driven off, but the car driver had obviously felt the impact, and his car had stalled. He had then tried, unsuccessfully, to start up again - which is the sound we'd all heard. When my father got to the car, the confused driver told him he thought he'd knocked someone down but he couldn't see anything on the road so he was trying to get the car started so that he could drive on. When my father shone the torch around he saw some scattered debris and he was, by now, joined in his search by two men from nearby cottages who had also heard the car's madly-revving engine. They found Grandpa's body in the field on the far side of the road, and the fact that he had been flung over the hedge by the impact, indicated the high speed at which the car must have been travelling. His death had been instantaneous. In the general confusion, made worse by the darkness and the local helpers' shock and distress, no tests were made by the village policeman when he arrived, but it is suspected that the driver had been drinking before the accident.

Two days later I went with Grandma into Hull and we toured the more expensive dress shops to find a black coat she felt was suitably appropriate to wear for the next few months of mourning: heavy lace lined with thick, black silk. It still surprises me that she had no intention of attending the funeral, and I was asked to stay with her at Maynor while Shirley and Michael spent the afternoon with Nora's friend and neighbour, the policeman's wife. Grandma waited in dignified silence in her high-backed chair for the family to return and I sat on a footstool nearby, ostensibly looking after her. It seemed a very long time indeed before the family appeared and people began to arrive to eat the sandwiches, cakes and pastries which my mother and Nora had prepared, and I was relieved of my uncomfortable responsibilities. But she seemed unmoved by it all and responded graciously to everyone who came over to pay their respects and offer their sympathy.

That night I slept on a camp bed in my parents' room and, when Nora brought them a tray of tea and thin bread and butter early next morning, I overheard them all quietly discussing Grandma's strange response to the last few days' tragic events. They must have assumed I was still asleep for they talked frankly of their being completely baffled by her unemotional attitude and apparent lack of distress. Nora, particularly, felt that - because she couldn't understand what her mother was feeling - she didn't know how best to help her through the next weeks and months.

'We must remember that she's not old, she's not yet sixty, so she has a lot of years to face alone,' said Nora.

'It must be shock,' said my mother. 'She'll suddenly suffer a reaction and it will hit her even harder for being delayed.'

But Grandma never did show any signs of shock or, indeed, of grief. She accepted all practical arrangements for her future comfort (Bill agreed to Nora's suggestion that she should give up their house as soon as possible and take the children to live permanently with her mother in Maynor) and Grandma continued exactly as before with all her village responsibilities and W.I. activities. She never mentioned Grandpa unless someone spoke of him first - and then only very briefly. But, although my father was only thirty-seven on that grim night, from then on his dark hair quickly became sprinkled with silver and my mother took a long time to recover her usual cheerfulness and sense of fun.

Selfishly, I am still sad that I was robbed of the opportunity - as an adult - to get to know my Grandfather better and to appreciate his rare qualities.

BLYTH SCHOOL

I continued to like school very much but there was one thing which puzzled me: although I soon made friends with girls in my class (and must have been reasonably popular, for I was elected as their Form Prefect for the last six weeks of my first summer term) I was never asked to any of their homes. In Hull we often went to play or at one another's houses and were sometimes invited to go for tea or to small birthday or Christmas parties. But in Norwich it not only didn't happen to me, but there was no sign that this kind of socialising was enjoyed by any of the others. In fact there were only two girls with whom I fairly regularly exchanged visits: Doris and Anne.

Anne was in a parallel class to mine and we became friendly after I'd been at the school a few months. It was a comfortable relationship because our parents almost immediately became friends too and, a year later, were able to help Anne's mother a good deal when her husband died of T.B.

Doris was in a class above me but, during my second term at Blyth, we often used to cycle together on our way back home for lunch or at the end of afternoon school. She lived about ten minutes ride beyond our house but, as time went on, we tended to linger quite some time before going home for tea and we became close friends. She was a reserved, very intelligent girl who combined a serious attitude to schoolwork with a willingness to discuss a wide range of interesting things - important or trivial - in satisfactory detail. This wasn't as solemn as it sounds, because she soon lost much of her reserve with me and we found we enjoyed laughing at the same things. She was always eager to hear about my family and home life but rarely mentioned hers so I knew little more than the fact that she had two sisters. But one day, looking slightly embarrassed, she said that "Mum" had told her she must ask me to go home with her for dinner the very next time that I knew my mother would be out with my father.

'She says she doesn't like to think of you on your own, so you've got to come and share with us,' Doris said, uncharacteristically avoiding my eyes as she spoke.

I couldn't help wondering if her apparent shyness was because she felt this invitation implied criticism of my mother, but I was so pleased with the idea of visiting her home that I could hardly wait to ask my parents' permission to go. I think my mother was equally pleased at this welcome sign of a breakthrough into Norfolk hospitality circles. She agreed that I could arrange to go in ten days' time. As we cycled home from school the afternoon before I was due to go, Doris said she had something to tell me and she sounded so serious that, by mutual consent, we got off our bikes in a quiet side road and went to sit under a tree. She told me that "Mum" wasn't her mother, but her foster-mother, and that she and her two younger sisters had been abandoned by (or taken from?) her natural parents some years ago and had lived at "Mum's" ever since. She didn't know - or didn't tell me - any other details, except that she thought she had an older brother somewhere.

'Two other things I have to tell you,' she said. 'Mum has two more girls as well - quite little ones - and . . .' She hesitated. 'One of my own sisters is very handicapped . . . You won't be frightened, will you?'

She looked at me, pathetically anxious. I felt like crying for her, but managed somehow to say, casually, 'Of course not.' I'm ashamed to admit, though, I was far from as sure as I sounded.

I was a little nervous on my first visit, but I soon began to feel comfortable. Her foster-mother - a maiden lady of unguessable age - was small, thin, and full of restless energy. She had sharp features, sharp eyes, and an abrupt way of speaking but her somewhat stern expression was occasionally softened by an unexpected bright smile and I immediately felt she was glad to see me. The little terrace house was sparsely furnished and so clean that everything gleamed softly despite the fact that the day was dull and the rooms dim and full of shadows. There was no fire in the polished grate and the shabby grey lino added to the general feeling of coldness in the house, but there was such warmth in the welcome I got from "Mum" and the girls that it simply didn't matter. We sat down at the kitchen table almost immediately to enjoy hot stew - a bit thin on meat, but thick with potatoes and carrots - followed by boiled suet pudding with a spoonful of treacle dribbled over everyone's helping.

We ate mainly in silence, partly I think because this was a house rule, but also because the little girls were shy at first and very much on their best behaviour. Their manners were impeccable but most of the time they watched me as if I were a new and curious experience and, as soon as we'd finished eating, they began to ask me all kinds of questions about my family and my home. They seemed to love hearing about my dog, our two goldfish, and Mickey Dripping's attempts at talking. Doris's handicapped sister was big and ungainly, with an unexpectedly large head. Her grunting speech was unintelligible to me but she insisted on sitting next to me at the table and turned her head constantly to watch me eat. We nodded and smiled at each other from time to time and I was relieved to find that we'd managed to establish some kind of link. Before Doris and I left to go back to school Miss Brown, as I now knew Mum was called, said I should come again if my mother was going to be out.

'It is good for the girls to see someone else here occasionally,' she said quietly, when Doris went to fetch our raincoats, and added as if we were conspirators, 'and Doris needs a friend from an ordinary family.' I felt flattered and very grown-up!

When I got home that night I described the visit in detail to my mother. She explained that it was quite likely that Miss Brown had taken on the task of providing a home and really caring for these five girls partly as a way of earning her living in her own house, but mainly because she wanted to devote her life and work to those who really needed her: youngsters who would benefit from having the comfort and support of a kind of family rather than having to live in an orphanage with - possibly - a frequently changing staff and a transient group of children. I understood even better when I found out later that she was a devout member of her local Chapel, strongly committed to bringing up her charges as good Christians.

'She'll get an allowance for each girl, her rent paid, and some sort of wage for herself, but there won't be much for extras. But from what you tell me, it sounds as if she'd be offended if we offered to pay for your dinner.' My mother hesitated, mulling over various possibilities. 'Do you think she'd let Doris come to spend the night here one weekend? Would you like that? Would Doris like that?'

And that's what we did. Every month or so I would go to Miss Brown's for my dinner and two or three weeks later Doris would come and stay Saturday night with us and we'd go out in the car somewhere for a picnic or visit a beauty spot. It was a happy arrangement for all of us.

I've always regretted that I have no means of knowing how Doris fared. Because she had always conscientiously taken on a variety of responsibilities for her sisters, and for many household chores, she was tied up at home most evenings and weekends, and when she started her School Certificate course, her fierce determination to do well meant that she had little time for anything other than school and homework. We gradually drifted apart and I'm ashamed to say that I cannot now remember her surname. But I shall always be glad to have known Miss Brown for a little while and grateful to have had a friend whose quiet, unselfish goodness and thoughtfulness for others in difficult circumstances made me more aware of my own good fortune. I hope she did well in her career - whatever it was - and found real happiness in her life.

*

By the end of my first winter at Blyth I had become more or less acclimatised to our classroom's spartan conditions, and always having to work rugged-up in several extra layers of clothing, but I certainly looked forward to summer with more than usual enthusiasm. It would be bliss to sit or move about freely in a cotton dress and ankle socks. So I was horrified to learn that our uniform remained more or less the same throughout the year; the only concession was that we could wear a white blouse under the heavy tunic instead of the scratchy red jumper. That summer was a particularly hot one and for weeks we sweltered under a blazing sun. The open classrooms were shady of course, and reasonably comfortable, but once outside - especially on our journeys to and from school - we were quickly drenched in sweat. The thick black stockings became minor instruments of torture and I stripped mine off the minute I got home, even at lunch time. This was foolish really because, even though my mother gave me fresh ones, dragging them on to my itchy, scarlet legs before setting off back to school was extremely uncomfortable. I'd looked forward, too, to seeing and smelling the massed roses blooming in the quadrangles but they soon began to wilt, despite their early morning dousing from the gardener's hosepipe. The headmistress - concerned about the threatened water-shortage - decided that, starting with the sixth form, each class in turn should be allowed to gather some so that every girl could take three or four home. Several lengthy downpours arrived before the lower classes got their share; a disappointment mixed with relief.

I can only assume that that summer's heat waves sparked off some vigorous protests from parents and the older pupils - or maybe the Head and her staff realised the seriousness of the problem - but it was announced in September that, next summer, we would be wearing cotton dresses and ankle socks and arrangements were being made to select their design. At the beginning of the spring term, notes were sent home outlining very sensible plans for these new dresses.

A good quality fabric, to be stocked only by the "best" (most expensive, of course) department store in Norwich, had been chosen and could now be ordered through the school bursar. Samples of the material were put on display in the Assembly Hall and to everyone's surprise it was white, prettily patterned with pastel-coloured flowers - pink, blue, yellow, orange or green. We could choose whatever colours we preferred and, as long as it was simple and had no frills, it could be made up into whatever style we liked! Going from one extreme to another, instead of looking like a crowd of Victorian charity-school girls, we were going to appear like a garden of flowers. We weren't too surprised, though, to be told that the winter uniform would remain unchanged.

However, for the Winter Concert, we were traditionally encouraged to transform ourselves into a gorgeous picture of feminine beauty - a sheer exaggeration, of course, but that is how it felt to us. I have no idea how many years this glorious occasion had been a regular feature of the school year (and, by arriving late in my first autumn term, I'd already missed it once) but it was definitely one of the highlights of the year for most of us. For weeks beforehand we learned and practised an ambitious programme of songs to insert between items of instrumental music and readings given by the most talented pupils. And, at last, I knew the justification for the required white "evening dress" Granny had had to make for me when I'd arrived the previous November. I also found out which shop stocked our school emblem - the imitation rowan berries worn, on this formal occasion, pinned on our right shoulders!

A week before the performance we were taken to the historic St. Andrew's Hall in the centre of Norwich for a full-blown rehearsal and shown the entrance to the crypt-like areas below it. This was where our parents were to bring us before they took their seats in the auditorium. We were all very excited about the concert but, oddly enough, I didn't hear anyone talking about their evening dress beforehand. So it was a great surprise to me to find, when we gathered with our class groups in the dim, chilly basement, that at least half the girls were wearing long dresses which were quite elaborate and obviously shop-bought. My knee-length, simple one of cheap rayon seemed very plain by comparison, but at least the corsage of vivid scarlet berries and dark green leaves gave it a touch of glamour - and I was far too interested in looking at the others' outfits to bother very much about my own. I was somewhat bewildered, though, when I noticed that some of the more expensive-looking dresses were worn by girls whom I knew came from the poorer areas of town. The doctors', solicitors' and various managers' daughters et al were mostly in less ostentatious ones.

At seven thirty precisely we filed very quietly into our assigned places on the semi-circle of tiers which rose behind the conductor's rostrum and sat, as instructed, with our hands clasped demurely in our laps. The effect, under the brilliant lights, was magical. We looked, to me, like a huge white anemone with our pale pink arms forming its hardly moving fronds, and our sprays of bright berries threading them together. A few minutes later, when we stood at our music teacher's signal and spiritedly launched into "Come and hasten to the dancing . . .", I sang " . . . How my heart up-bounds!" with real feeling.

I was truly proud and happy to be part of Blyth High!

MINOR PROBLEMS

There were just one or two flies in my fragrant ointment, of course, but nothing too serious. A few months after we'd arrived in Norwich Auntie Mirrie came to stay for a couple of weeks. She came by train as Uncle Tom felt he couldn't leave his newly established haulage business - two lorries (or wagons as he called them) which took mixed loads of goods from Hull to destinations throughout the country, picking up similar cargoes for delivery anywhere in the North of England on their way back home. He needed to be constantly on the phone, available to organise the drivers' schedules and their freight. Auntie settled comfortably into sharing my double bed and, throughout her stay, treated us all to many of her favourite little luxuries: cream cakes, trips to the cinema and a couple of lavish picnics on the banks of scenic Broads near Wroxham. She even presented my mother with a luxurious picnic case covered in a rich brown leatherette and fitted with a full tea service, matching cutlery, and a number of fancy Bakelite boxes with stylish chromium lids. It wouldn't have been out of place by the side of an upmarket shooting-brake at a Sandringham polo match but, for us, it turned out to be a time-consuming burden. It was finicky to fill, painfully heavy to carry, and an irritating nuisance to clean out when we got home. After Auntie left it was put up in the loft and only brought down when we eventually moved house, where a space in the new loft was immediately found for it. I can't ever remember seeing it again after that. Pity! It would probably already be worth a small fortune at an Antiques Fair.

Picnic case aside, we really enjoyed having her with us and, as usual, she was very good to me. She was obviously disappointed that I no longer went to a dance class but she seemed to think that I didn't need any more elocution lessons - apparently I now had no trace of a Hull accent and was in little danger of adopting the rather strange Norfolk one. All the staff at Blyth School not only set us excellent examples of good speech themselves, but were insistent on our maintaining similar high standards. In fact, during our first year, we were given thirty minutes speech training every week by a teacher from the English department. She was an Oxford graduate who proudly informed us in impressively plummy tones that she, herself, had "what is generally known as a Mayfair accent . . ."!

It seemed I'd also learned to avoid the more glaring grammatical errors so common in my native city, so Auntie cast around for something else to further her plans for developing my talents in preparation for my future career on the stage. She found it: piano lessons. Consequently, before she returned home she'd installed a second-hand piano in our front room and my mother was instructed to find a reputable teacher as soon as possible. Auntie Mirrie and Uncle Tom would pay - money no object - but my mother was a thrifty Yorkshire woman, born and bred. She asked around and discovered that a recently-graduated music student, who played the organ in a nearby church and ran a boys' choir, lived about thirty yards down the road from us. She persuaded him to take me on. I was his only pupil and I think he must have been very hard up, because his fee was ludicrously modest - but this might have been because he was acutely conscious of his total lack of teaching experience. He was a quiet, serious-minded young man, an only child who still lived with his parents, and he was probably very shy and uncertain about working with a twelve-year-old girl. Still, we got on pretty well and I managed to practise my scales and simple pieces for the required minimum - half an hour - most days. However, I cannot pretend that I was more than mildly enthusiastic. I would have enjoyed being able to play well but lacked the drive to work energetically towards becoming even moderately skilled. I have what many people in those days called "piano fingers" which meant they are long and slender and, even then, I could easily span just over an octave. I was flattered to be told this (it encouraged me to think I was effortlessly bound for musical success) but actually the idea that such fingers are a significant advantage is absurd. Many, probably most, accomplished pianists have strong - even stubby - fingers and, in addition to any natural talent, they possess a determined willingness to stick to a schedule of hard, regular practice.

My teacher - I don't think I ever called or referred to him by name, and I certainly can't recall now what it was - decided that my long, thin fingers needed strengthening, and he recommended that we should send away for a set of professionally-compiled exercises, specifically designed to produce this desirable effect. It consisted of a pack of shiny cards printed with a series of small, square photographs clearly showing how to control the movements of each finger, in turn and in isolation, into various difficult positions and with instructions as to how long each position should be held. Some of the movements were slightly painful but, because I was all too aware that the pack was very expensive, I persisted in trying to master each movement and reach the time-targets set. Practising scales and pieces now took second place, so I'm inclined to think that it was the exercises rather than over-long periods at the keyboard that were to blame for the uncomfortable and unsightly ganglions which began to develop on both slim wrists, and which have been a minor problem on and off ever since. Whatever the root cause, playing the piano made them worse and, after struggling on for several months after they appeared, it was decided that I should give up my lessons - at least temporarily. I never seriously returned to them and so can barely plough through the chords of a simple hymn tune – and, even then, only at a severely-retarded snail's pace. I've always regretted not being able to play but that lack was really no one's fault but my own.

I must confess that I also lacked any real interest in sport or any kind of energetic physical activity except dancing. At Primary School I quite enjoyed the occasional game of netball and was always happy doing what was then called Drill. This was the weekly lesson in the playground (if it was fine and reasonably warm weather) or the Hall (if it was not) when we stood in four lines and attempted to perform exercises simultaneously, obeying the teacher's shouted instructions like a platoon of soldiers.

"Arms up! Arms down! Arms out! Arms in! Up! Down! Out! In! One - Two - Three - Four!" and so on.

Not particularly exciting, and not very demanding I admit, but it seemed to me to be quite satisfying to be one of fifty children all trying to move in strictly synchronised unison. We got quite good at it. My only other sporting achievement was an unexpected talent for sack-racing. Opportunities for engaging in this activity were rare - they really only occurred round about the annual Sports Days - but it was discovered that, though almost all competitors in this race reached the finishing line by means of prolonged, energetic jumping, I could beat many of them by thrusting my feet into the lower corners of my sack and running furiously with tiny steps to the finishing post: inelegant and very tiring, but effective. It seems there were no rules about how you got there as long as you kept upright and your feet were always in the sack. Thinking it over since, I've come to the conclusion that my success in this field was due to my legendary long feet (aristocratic, I'd begun to maintain) and the fact that, because they are slender and rather pointed, they were eminently suitable for fitting into the corners of a sack! Anyway, in my last year at Bricknell I was proud to be chosen to go to the city's Junior Sports Day to represent my school - as Reserve. Not a very impressive record, I'm afraid.

At Blyth, in our second spring term, considerable emphasis was placed on our being able to swim so hockey was abandoned and, instead, we were taken by bus each week to the Samson and Hercules swimming baths in town. I think these must have been privately run rather than Council-owned. The entrance from the street to the foyer was most impressive with broad steps, flanked by two huge, biblical-looking figures - apparently carved from marble - straining to support the ornate portico. However, for us, there was no entrance fee; it was part of our education. We were taught by professional instructors and were all expected to be able to swim at least a width of the bath by half term. Most achieved this easily and those who were already good swimmers were encouraged to work towards much more ambitious targets. I found that the bad habits, acquired some years before through teaching myself a mongrel version of the dog-paddle-cum-breast-stroke in the cold waves of the North Sea at Bridlington, were difficult to shake off and they delayed my progress quite noticeably. I only just managed the width by the Easter holidays.

I did, though, manage to pick up several verrucae - presumably from the Samson and Hercules floor - and the effects of this were quite serious. To begin with, my complaints about the soles of my feet hurting when I walked were dismissed as trivial.

'Don't fuss, Jean. It's probably that you've got some grit in your shoes / the lining's wearing a bit thin / one or two of the little nails are starting to poke through . . . I'll get you some insoles next time I go into town . . .' etc.

But they got worse rather than better and eventually my mother had a really good look and thought she could see several small, hard corns under both my big toes and on the balls of my feet. So she took me to the Dr Scholls shop. There the somewhat off-hand assistant agreed they were tiny corns and proceeded to try to prise them out. Next day I could hardly walk but this soon improved and I continued to walk around as usual until, a couple of weeks later, the pain started up again and we found more "corns" had developed round the rapidly-returned original ones. A visit to the doctor was obviously needed.

'Pity you didn't come earlier,' he said accusingly. 'Walking on them has made them spread along under the skin. She now has eight verrucae on this foot and seven on this one, and it's too late to start painting them with a corrosive liquid. They need more drastic treatment, but there are so many that I'm afraid it's not possible for me to cut them out either. I'll arrange an immediate hospital appointment for you.'

And so began a five-week stint of hospital visits for sessions under an X-ray machine and, as the specialist promised, a week or two after the last session they began to dry up, shrink, and drop out. From then on there were no more problems but, for some time, time, my being unable to walk without considerable discomfort meant that my father had to plan his appointments around being free to drive me to the hospital as well as, daily, to and from school. It also meant that I couldn't take part in P.T. or Games lessons for most of a term, so I missed out on all the early, practical stages of learning to play tennis and never really caught up. I remained a discouraged "rabbit" for the rest of my life. If you don't play reasonably well you don't get chosen as a partner, so - unless you are so keen to improve that you insist on snatching any opportunity for a game regardless of others' reluctance to include you - you don't get much practice. It's a vicious circle but not, I must admit, one that distressed me very much.

What did distress me that year - at least a little - was a completely unexpected problem at home. I've always been ashamed of the fact that I have a horror of moths. Spiders I can tolerate (if they are not particularly oversized), mice, frogs, and bees I quite like, and – just to prove I'm not an out-and-out wimp - I really enjoy a good thunder storm. But moths give me the cold shudders. Even if I wear gloves and wrap a duster round my hand I can rarely force myself to pick up a dead one if it's larger than half a corn flake. And if it's alive and flying around I have to leave the room. It must be something innate rather than acquired, because my mother eventually told me that when I was just a few weeks, old and lying in my cot or pram, I would have a screaming fit if a fly flew anywhere near me.

One early summer evening we came in from a fishing trip and Paddy crouched down and began scratching at the carpet, snuffling, and shaking his head agitatedly so that his ears flapped like disorganised semaphore flags. I bent down to stroke and calm him and something from between his paws got caught round the middle finger of my right hand. I tried to flip it away but it clung on, and I couldn't even scrape it off onto the carpet. It looked like a large brown beetle with antennae shaped like horns, and its legs were wrapped round my finger so firmly that it was able to hang on until my father heard my frantic cries and came and prised it away. I was shaking with fright and disgust, so didn't notice that it then flew to the French window and got tangled in the net curtain. However, I knew it must still be somewhere in the room so I fled to the kitchen in panic and refused to go back until it was found and flung outside.

'There's no need to make such a fuss, girl,' said my father, comfortingly, and started to say 'It wasn't going to hurt . . .' but was interrupted by a sudden plop! As yet another of them dropped into the bare fire-grate. It buzzed madly across to the net curtain, and my mother and I collided painfully in the doorway as we raced for the kitchen. I decided it was time to do some piano practice in the other room and she thought it would be a good idea to bake a pie for tomorrow's tea, but after a while - as no more appeared - we drifted back into the living room to listen to a favourite wireless programme.

The next night I went to bed early, leaving my heavy curtains open so that I could read for a little while before settling to sleep, and - plop ! - then a fierce buzzing - and then, to my intense alarm, a huge beetle hurtled across the room and latched onto one of the white net curtains. Before I got to the top of the stairs I heard yet another one arrive, heading for the window. Thank heavens I had a fearless young father, willing to race up the stairs to rescue me from what he must have thought (from my hysterical shouts) was a raging fire, certain death - or at least a violent marauder! He efficiently disposed of the insects and, though we none of us understood what was happening, he patiently tried to persuade me back to bed. My more realistic mother quietly started to rig up a makeshift bed on the floor of the tiny box-room. Next morning he removed five more beetles from my bedroom nets and promised to find out where they came from, how they got there, and why. That evening he took me into the garden and pointed to our two chimneys, then to the chimney-pots of several of our neighbours' houses. We could just see small clouds of insects buzzing around them.

'I don't know why this happens,' he said, 'but it seems that at this time of the year, if you live very near large patches of grass, you are likely to have swarms of these insects circling around your chimney pots for an hour or so before dusk and, every so often, one falls in! Apparently it then makes for the light - in your case, your window. But they don't sting or anything, and they stop doing it after three or four weeks. So . . .'

'No!' I said. 'No! I'm not going back into that room until they've gone for good. No!' And I began to shake and feel sick.

'We don't want to change rooms with you. We can't move the furniture over just for a few weeks,' said my mother, reasonably. 'Anyway, Daddy has blocked your chimney, and the one in the living-room, with plywood sheets - so they won't be able to get into the rooms from now on.'

I still hated the idea. They still seriously frightened me even if they didn't sting, but I eventually agreed to move back into my own bed. I just didn't want my father to think I was a timid little female, prone to attacks of Victorian "vapours", so I managed to force myself to put up with the chilling, irregular sound of a heavy beetle crashing onto the backs of others seething on the thin wooden platform wedged above the grate. What I did find extremely difficult to cope with, though, was the continuous buzzing sound of the massed unfortunates as they jostled together, refusing to die. I had to accept that it would not be sensible to remove the plywood until complete silence proved they were all dead - they would fly to the window and be difficult to catch and collect - but this did not happen for over four weeks after they'd stopped flying round the chimney pots. I don't remember how many were taken from the downstairs plywood shelf, but there were a hundred and twenty-seven on mine.

The plywood was replaced, of course, ready for the next year but, by then, houses were being built on the grassland opposite and the beetles must have moved elsewhere. I now had only the occasional stray moth to contend with in the summer but, by keeping all windows closed if the lights were on, I could usually manage to keep the house pretty moth-free. My father grumbled a bit about the resultant stuffiness but, now I come to think about it, I don't remember my mother objecting much.

WAR BREAKS OUT

Far more serious, though, than any personal problems was the international situation. Like many of those born in the Twenties, I'd thought of the 1914-18 War as just another chapter of history: hardly more relevant than the Battle of Hastings. But now it seemed we were in danger of having to fight yet another war with Germany and people's fears for the future were growing.

When I was younger, Auntie Mirrie had often told me - in considerable dramatic detail - lots of interesting anecdotes about our family, friends and neighbours, and I would listen eagerly, fascinated by her tales of what some of the people I knew had done before I was born. Sometimes, inevitably, these stories involved things which had happened during the War. One Sunday, when I was about eight and staying at Auntie's for the weekend, I curled up cosily in bed beside her while she drank her early morning tea and I asked why she didn't take sugar in it. Instead of referring to her diabetes, she told me about the poor substitute that people had had to use during wartime.

'Turned the tea purple, you know! I just couldn't stomach it, so I had to get used to drinking tea without.'

This must have reminded her of other, greater horrors and, because at this time that conflict was still regarded as the war to end all wars, she obviously saw no reason why I shouldn't hear about the terrible Zeppelin raids on Hull and how local people had suffered. She told me how hundreds were so terrified that whole families trekked every night into the surrounding countryside to escape the bombs which they knew would rain down on the city. She explained the possible death, injuries and destruction faced by those who had to stay behind. I wish she hadn't. Auntie Mirrie could bring any stories vividly alive for me and these particular ones, illustrated with personal details, made a deep and lasting impression. So it could be said that, at thirteen, I was uncomfortably well-prepared to face that Sunday morning in September when Chamberlain announced on the wireless that we were now at war with Germany.

It was scarcely unexpected. Apart from the vital decisions being made about rearming and the organisation of voluntary civilian defence teams, many practical preparations involving the whole population had been set up in Britain over the previous few months. As war became increasingly likely, Government leaflets had been distributed giving householders advice about air raid precautions etc. and, like all other families, we'd been fitted with gas masks and made blackout arrangements for every window. We'd stocked up on torches, candles, matches, and as many tinned goods and non-perishable groceries as we could afford.

Several weeks before that momentous Sunday broadcast, my father had begun to dig a large, rectangular pit in our back garden. It looked worryingly like a grave but it was, of course, the first stage of building a small air raid shelter. As soon as the Prime Minister finished speaking, my father gave my mother a solemn, comforting hug and went out to start work on lining the shelter with the thin wooden laths he'd stacked nearby under an old rubber sheet. Many people remember that morning as one of bright sunshine; in Norwich it was suitably dull and grey, with drearily overcast skies. But at least it was dry and already I could make sense of the compact shape he'd designed and imagine how bunks could be fitted in. Mr Bruin next door and the man over the back fence came out too.

'I know what I'd like to do with that piece of paper Chamberlain kept waving about last year,' my father shouted to the other two, 'only it wouldn't be clean enough then to preserve in the archives, I'm afraid!'

'And I know what *I'd* like to do to Hitler!' The normally mild and gentlemanly Mr Bruin slammed his spade into the bottom of his half-dug pit with vicious emphasis. 'I'd like to throw him into this hole, pile your planks on top of him, jump up and down on them till he stopped squealing, shovel all this ruddy pile of soil on top . . . and walk away!'

The man over the back fence leaned on his spade and nodded enviously towards our completed hole.

'Well, I know the missus won't give me any peace in *my* time till I've caught up with you two, so I'd better get on with it sharpish.'

And all three of them set about their jobs with grim energy.

Less than an hour later the air raid sirens went off. There was no mistaking those loud, wailing notes or the responding up and down sensation they caused in your stomach - we'd already been treated to several rehearsals in the past few weeks - but there had always been official announcements beforehand which warned us of the day and precise time the practice would occur. This alarm was a shock and yet exactly what most of us had nervously foreseen and dreaded. It was very frightening and, though the all-clear siren was sounded after a few minutes, I think most people still feared that squadrons of German planes were heading towards the vulnerable Norfolk coast, loaded with bombs. My father was on duty that evening in the Observer Corps control centre and my mother and I stayed nervously downstairs until he returned just after midnight. He was able to tell us he'd learned that it had been a false alarm, sparked off by an unidentified aircraft flying over the coast, but we didn't find this particularly reassuring. So for many nights to come I lay in bed, in the pitch darkness produced by the temporary, but efficient, blackout arrangements made by my mother, with nightmarish pictures of people being injured and homes being destroyed racing through my mind.

But, just like the lad with sore eyes is supposed to have said, you can get used to anything, given time and we had plenty of time to get used to being at war. Surprisingly, things at first moved slowly and it was some months before the "real" war began. I was given a fat notebook with a glossy black cover and the intention was that I should keep a diary of important events and how they affected the Langdale trio but, long before the pleasure of being the first to write on its smooth, snow-white pages had faded, I became bored with searching for something worth writing about. Over the next few weeks my immediate fears faded into the background and, although the air raid shelter was quickly completed and fitted out to make it passably comfortable, it was only used once or twice - and even then the alarms were brief and proved to be mistakes. Many people, indulging in wishful thinking (or perhaps trying to bolster up one another's hopes and courage) had, from the very beginning, gone along with the optimistic view that it would all be over by Christmas. They had forgotten - or chose to ignore - the fact that exactly the same had been said at the start of the 1914-18 war: and that one had lasted over four years. I don't think any of us seriously believed that this war would be over so quickly or with little or no fighting, but these fairly uneventful months lulled us into the dangerous feeling that we were reasonably safe and that our lives could go on more or less normally, at least for the time being.

There were several pressing, unavoidable anxieties, though, for our family. Bill had been made captain of a sizeable merchant ship which usually sailed the Atlantic routes. It was clear that these were particularly vulnerable to attack and it was known that the Germans had a worrying number of modern U-boats. It was also probable that Hull would again be an obvious target for enemy bombing raids; its important docks and easily identifiable location so close to the Continent made it an attractive proposition for the German Air Force. On a purely personal level it might seem that *we* were in a more fortunate position. My father was born in 1901, so he had been too young to fight in the 14-18 war. He was now thirty-eight and a married man with a child so, unless this war went on for many years, he would be unlikely to be called up. His present job, however, was swiftly coming to an end. There would be no point in employing salesmen to persuade people to buy Miller's oil - all petroleum products not needed by the armed forces, the factories or defence services would be strictly rationed in the very near future. He needed to start applying for a new job immediately, and we must be prepared to move once again.

Within a fortnight of his sending off his first applications he was asked to go for interview for the post of assistant engineer at Wolverhampton's Waterworks. Sensibly, my mother suggested we should go with him so that, if he was offered the job, we could look round that day for a house to rent. Moving house would be expensive enough anyway, without having to make yet another journey across country and spend yet another night in the area just to find somewhere to live. So we all three went and, for me at least, it was an adventure. It was quite a journey. There was no easy way to travel by train from Norwich to Wolverhampton, and almost impossible by bus. I don't remember the details or how many changes we had to make, but I do know that we had to go round by London and Birmingham, and that – although we set off in the early morning - it was quite late in the evening when we arrived. The trains and all the stations were dreary, lit only by dim bulbs because of the blackout regulations which had been in force since the war began. I slept some of the time but wakened when we were a few miles from London to see a huge, empty area of grassland flooded with softly glowing light. It was an odd experience and we never heard it mentioned or explained - even after the war - but we assumed it was intended as a decoy for enemy bombers. Perhaps it was hoped they would think it was part of London, insufficiently blacked out? Or a large factory?

We had to put up at a dingy hotel close to the station; it was too late to search for anywhere else and we felt we were lucky to find one with vacant rooms. It was the first hotel I'd stayed in, and I'd been thrilled with the idea when the plans were explained to me, but I can't say I was very impressed. There was an unidentifiable, stale smell in the entrance hall (it was too poky to be called a foyer) and it seemed to follow us up to our bedrooms where it lingered throughout our stay. And breakfast was somewhat meagre, even though food rationing hadn't yet started.

He got the job, of course. My mother and I had spent the morning exploring the town centre's shops and facilities; the sun was shining and we were quite favourably impressed with what we saw. By the time my father met us with the good news, my mother had - "just in case" - found a suitable letting agent and, after a snack lunch, he whisked us round in his car to look at three possible places to rent. Surprisingly, the Waterworks site was in Tettenhall - an attractive village on the outskirts of Wolverhampton. Over the past fifty years or so the town had expanded considerably and, by the nineteen thirties, it had reached the foot of the Rock, a steep road leading up to the plateau on which the village was built. This effectively separated the town, and its many industrial areas, from Tettenhall and enhanced the feeling of superiority the village population undoubtedly enjoyed. It had a pleasant village green surrounded by broad paths, trees and a number of small shops. Several Victorian houses of grey stone - built in the style of a cathedral close or Oxbridge college - flanked the high wall of a small, minor public school. In the three or four little streets leading from the green, the houses were an interesting mix of ages, styles and sizes but, just beyond them, a number of fairly recently-built roads spread out into the open countryside. The houses bordering these roads were all individually-designed - stockbroker Tudor was the most popular choice - and each was surrounded by well laid-out gardens, many with a curved drive leading up to the impressive front door. Successful business men and the upper management staff of Wolverhampton's many industries clearly preferred to live near their work, but well out of the sight, sound and smoke of its factories.

'Tettenhall is where you should live,' said the agent, waving his hand dramatically towards a cluster of these houses. But even I knew he couldn't possibly mean in one of those. 'And, if you could persuade them to accept your daughter, the High School would be the best place for her to go. It's only about half a mile from the bottom of the Rock. '

That sounded more achievable - though, from the tone of his voice, it seemed he thought I had only an outside chance of going there. My mother stiffened slightly and exchanged a meaningful look with my father, and I knew that they were now determined that that was the school for me. But he was an astute salesman. Before taking us up to Tettenhall he'd shown us round a house on the main road, below the Rock. It was much too big for us and my father said firmly that the rent was quite a bit more than we could afford. The second house was apparently well within our price range but it was shabby and inconvenient. So, after taking us on the informative tour of Tettenhall, when he drew up outside an interesting-looking house in a quiet, leafy side-road, we were all very ready to be charmed.

It was semi-detached, with a very small front garden, and its shallow bay window had diamond panes which I found enchanting and my mother regarded with justifiable doubt. She knew they would be the devil to clean and that the lead strips separating them allow the window to curve dangerously if they are cleaned with a too vigorous pressure. But she was prepared to accept this problem when she saw how good the two houses looked, linked by a wide, open porch. This had a polished red-tiled floor, and a pretty, little window through which we could see a hall and the first few steps of a staircase before it took a right-angled turn to the upper floor. The wooden pillars which supported the ceiling of the porch were black oak and so were the strips of wood set in the cream plaster facade of the long room above it.

'Just a *touch* of mock-Tudor,' muttered my father.

'H-m-m - and yet more leaded panes,' she grumbled, but I could see she liked what she saw.

We were just as pleased with what we found inside. The tiled hall was light and roomy, with a useful cloakroom tucked under the stairs. The sitting-room at the front was smallish but cosy and the dining-room behind it was nearly its mirror-image, but it had a door leading into the high-hedged garden. Both rooms had coal fires set in attractive fire-places and the dining-room had an oak plate-rack round its upper walls. The square kitchen at the back of the hall, though rather dark, was quite large and it had a coke-fired range, similar to a small Aga, standing against the wall shared with the neighbours. There were three decent-sized bedrooms, and the bathroom was long and narrow; it stretched above the porch. I held my breath when my father asked what the rent for this house was, hoping desperately that it wouldn't be too high for our family to afford.

The agent was a little vague, even slightly shifty. It was really a high-class area: there was another pair of similar houses next door, plus a larger one of the same type of design on the corner - all owner-occupied: the next three houses which lay the other way were even larger and more superior: the view from the front window was really desirable - there were no other houses there, just a long evergreen hedge: it was a really high-class . . . My father stopped him.

'There's a BUT, though, isn't there? So let's have it,' he said, with uncharacteristic sharpness.

"W-e-l-l . . . It's the council houses - and the ladies!"

We hadn't noticed the council houses. Because of the trees which lined the road we hadn't realised that most of the rest of the houses - though agreeably nondescript - were council built. My parents grinned at each other, no doubt recalling our Grantham house and the fleas in the back bedroom. Where was the problem for us?

'It doesn't go down too well with those looking for a bit of class, you see,' the agent explained.

'So what's this about the ladies?' My mother sounded really anxious - we needed to get this settled today if possible.

The answer was unexpected. Apparently the house belonged to two maiden ladies - elderly sisters, who had reluctantly decided to move back to the safety of their old family home in the country. They had loved this house and hated the thought of anyone living there who wouldn't look after it properly and - even worse - who might "disgrace" the area. So any prospective tenants would have to be inspected for suitability by their solicitor. The result of these factors meant that the asking rent was reasonably moderate - that is, according to the agent. It would be a bit of a struggle for us, but we were used to economising. We would see the solicitor the next morning.

We were back in Norwich by early evening with keys to our new home tucked safely in my mother's handbag, along with a note asking my headmistress to send the High School Head a detailed report of my academic standards and general acceptability. The next morning my mother started making packing lists and arranging a date with a removal firm.

'So I suppose we're in for another period of panicky kerfuffle . . . once again!' she said cheerfully.

Of course, we'd all be sorry to leave Norwich and the Norfolk countryside but, as usual, we were undismayed. We enjoyed a challenge.

TETTENHALL

OUR NEW HOME

Once again it was winter when we moved - just in time for Christmas - and, because it had stood empty for many weeks, the house took some time to warm up. Nevertheless, I immediately felt it was home, and I loved my new bedroom. It was fairly large and had a long sash window which overlooked the back garden. For a couple of weeks there were problems with fitting effective blackout curtains - securing the downstairs windows had to be seen to first, of course - but I still managed some bedtime reading by huddling under the bedclothes with a torch, so I was happy.

Though it didn't occur to me at the time, I think my father probably had some difficulty in adjusting to his new job. In Norwich he had been virtually his own boss with complete autonomy over how he organised his time. He'd had a decent car, which he was allowed to use for his own purposes if he paid for the petrol, and he'd spent his days in a smart business suit. At the Waterworks, as the assistant engineer, he was at the beck and call of a rather moody man (whom he always referred to as Mr J.) who was less well-qualified, and far less experienced, than he was. He had to supervise a small gang of workmen but was not in overall charge of them, as Mr J. constantly made very clear. But there were compensations: my father could become a practical engineer again with problems to solve, things to make, and satisfying, tangible results to contemplate at the end of the day. It was no hardship for him to bike to work, to wear overalls and to get his hands dirty, so - apart from a few remarks to my mother about the unpredictable sullenness of his boss - he never grumbled or lost his cheerful, humorous approach to life. I know he missed his Observer Corps duties and the comradeship of the others on his shifts, but he was very much aware that he was not suffering the dangers and hardships the members of the Forces were facing - and would face increasingly as the war situation worsened.

My mother seemed to settle in quite quickly. Though the house was a good ten minutes walk (quite a problem for someone of her weight) from the village shops and the regular bus service into town, there were still convenient delivery vans for bread, milk, vegetables, and laundry, and a good grocery shop in Wolverhampton which sent an elderly man round every Thursday to take down her order to arrive the next day. She was somewhat taken aback though, when she set out about ten o'clock on our first morning to explore the local shops, to see our middle-aged neighbour vigorously sweeping her side of the porch wearing high-heeled mules and a pale blue satin negligee trimmed with white swansdown.

'Morning!' she called out and added, in what my mother later described as a cut-glass accent, 'Hope you've settled in successfully.' And without waiting for a reply, she whisked through her front door and slammed it smartly shut.

From then on the two of them would meet on the porch occasionally as they swept, mopped, or polished their half with Cardinal Red, or as they took in the milk. My mother would be fully dressed, of course, and wearing a sensible apron, while the neighbour would be swanning about in either a luxurious dressing-gown or a smart corded-silk housecoat. They never exchanged more than a single, polite sentence and we rarely saw her husband. He left every weekday morning around nine with a briefcase, a rolled umbrella, and ultra-conventional striped trousers showing below his smart grey overcoat; he always nodded graciously if he caught sight of one of us. Most days, wearing well-cut tweeds and a rather dashing felt hat, *she* left – presumably off for lunch - around eleven thirty and we almost never saw either of them return. My father delighted in inventing weird scenarios about what they were up to during the day. I remember they included spying for the Germans, robbing banks, running a high-class second-hand clothes shop, and organising the Wolverhampton branch of the white-slave trade. But whatever it was, it must have been financially worthwhile for, most Saturdays, they loaded suitcases and two bags of golf clubs into their sports car and disappeared until Sunday evening. It was clear that we were not their sort - and they definitely weren't ours.

We enjoyed a quietly cordial relationship with our other immediate neighbours but, as far as we could tell, the couple who lived next to them were determined to keep everyone at a respectable distance. They had exchanged the diamond panes in their bay window for plain glass and placed an oval dining table into its curve so that anyone passing by could see (and admire ?) its highly polished surface and be impressed by the fact that - whatever the time of day - it was always elegantly set for dinner for two. There were intricate lace mats, silver cutlery, crystal wine glasses and tall red candles in silver holders, and - quite often - a centrepiece of fresh flowers floating in a bowl of ruby glass. I must admit that I was impressed, but when my mother pointed out that the arrangement never changed and that we never saw them eating there (though the curtains were always open no matter what time of day or evening it was) I was inclined to wonder if the implied sophisticated lifestyle was just an attempt to appear grander than they actually were. Perhaps, as my father mischievously suggested, they really ate fish and chips out of newspaper at the kitchen table and drank beer or tea out of enamel mugs.

Happily for us, the families in the two houses beyond that of the golfing couple more than made up for the others' shortcomings. Mr and Mrs James were welcoming and their daughter, June, quickly became a valued friend. She was about thirty, unmarried, and pleasantly gossipy and her work in one of the leading hairdressing salons in the centre of Wolverhampton provided masses of interesting material for discussion. I found her carefully-chosen clothes and impeccable, delicate make-up an inspiring example of good taste. Although she was a really attractive-looking woman there was no man in her life and, apparently, there never had been. She seemed completely content to spend most of her leisure time at home with her quiet-living parents, helping with the housework, renewing her nail varnish, planning her next co-ordinated outfits (with make-up to match!) and knitting twin-sets which would harmonize with those she already had. Perhaps she had already begun to realize that the war would soon force changes into everyone's lives. There would be shortages (inevitably clothes and make-up, must become less important - even to a hairdresser) and, if it went on for some years, unattached young women might well be called up. So, whatever the reason, she began to spend a fair amount of time with us and to take an interest in the books my mother was reading; she was now eager to swap a pile of the shop's glossy magazines for some of my parents' old favourites. Though, come to think of it, I really enjoyed those slightly tatty magazines and so did my mother. We weren't sniffy.

Lucy Dixon was a very different proposition. She lived next door to the Jameses and it was several months before my parents made friends with her. I think she took her time making up her mind about our family (and we found her rather morose-looking face and preoccupied manner a little forbidding) but, when she did eventually decide to stop and talk as she walked her scruffy little dog, it quickly became obvious to the three of them that they were kindred spirits. Her detached house was more recently built than ours and its design more modern. It was beautifully furnished - mainly with items from her old home, I think - and the downstairs rooms were lined with shelves of books. Her mother lived with her and I was fascinated by Mrs Dixon: she looked just like a little old lady in a Victorian portrait, and I'd never seen one in real life before - or since.

At this time Lucy must have been about forty-five, so I would think her mother was in her late seventies. She was thin and frail-looking and, as far as we could see, she spent all day sitting gracefully in a high-backed chair with her blue-veined hands folded in her lap. She invariably wore very old-fashioned clothes: an ankle-length dress of stiff black silk with narrow white lace at her wrists, and a pearl-edged cameo brooch pinned onto a black velvet ribbon round her neck. Her sparse white hair was coiled into a severe bun and this added to her aura of genteel dignity; only her sweet expression and frequent gentle smiles prevented me from feeling shy of her. We had to assume that Lucy fitted all the cooking, shopping and cleaning around her own working hours but, though my mother and I spent a fair amount of time with her at our house or theirs, we saw no sign of this. Maybe the old lady was more active than we gave her credit for. Maybe, as soon as she was alone, she grabbed a duster and a tin of polish and whipped round the house at breakneck speed, or dashed into the kitchen to concoct a three-course meal, but it was highly unlikely - and not something you could ask Lucy about.

Lucy had worked for the last twenty years as a receptionist and dispenser for the village doctors. It wasn't a full-time job and she was not a fully-qualified pharmacist, but she'd had some formal training and passed exams which entitled her to work under a doctor's supervision. She was a very intelligent, well-read woman and had been educated at a good boarding school. As my father commented to my mother it was surprising she hadn't trained for a more rewarding career.

'Dispensing certainly won't pay very much, yet they live very well. I think there must still be family money, don't you, Frank?'

My mother's interest was kindly. She was fond of Lucy and concerned that her friend might find her spinster life constricting or disappointing.

'Did I tell you that, when her father died, she was only eighteen and felt she had to take a job? Well, Lady Somebody-or-other asked if she would go and live with her family, as her companion - and Lucy stayed with her until her own mother needed her. So, really, circumstances meant she had to give up any chance of going to college.'

'Pity,' said my father. 'She's highly intelligent and very strong-minded. She'd have made a great teacher, an excellent university librarian, or perhaps a hospital Matron. Anyway, as it turns out, she does a lot for John, and that must give her a great deal of private satisfaction.'

John was her divorced sister's son and he lived with Lucy and his grandmother almost all the time. His mother had a demanding career working long hours as the catering manageress in a large factory in Cheshire, and would have found it difficult to give John the supportive home-life he deserved. Apparently, once he had passed his scholarship at eleven, Lucy had wisely insisted he came to live with her. This, my mother eventually gathered, gave Lucy's sister the freedom to enjoy the rich social life she'd been hankering for, and gave John a stable - if somewhat narrow - background. As a valuable bonus, it meant he was able to attend the local Grammar School: an independent foundation with a reputation for providing a very high-standard academic education. John, who was a year older than me, was extremely bright and deeply interested in Maths and Science. He'd already set his sights on a Cambridge scholarship (and in due course he became a Cantab. Ph. D.) and found it easy to study under Lucy's care. As a thirteen-year-old with no experience of teen-age boys, I found his gruff, reserved manner rather intimidating, but I soon began to appreciate his occasional witty remarks and off-key sense of humour - and to feel that his dark hair and pale face were quite attractive.

Of course, it took several months for these early encounters to develop into close friendships but they helped my parents feel, very quickly, that Tettenhall was a good place to live. And I had my new school to settle into and to provide me with new interests and new friends.

WOLVERHAMPTON GIRLS' HIGH SCHOOL

Once again I was allowed to continue wearing my old uniform for a few weeks but, when I saw the others' elegant clothes, I felt embarrassed by the clumsiness of mine. My harsh, red jumper and bulkily-pleated gymslip, topped by a thick, black woollen blazer, made me stand out from the rest like a Rupert Annual on a shelf of leather-bound classics. Waiting to get new clothes was difficult but so was finding the money for replacing my uniform yet again. This was a fee-paying independent school; its pupils had to pass an Entrance Examination and even those of us who went in on a scholarship were billed according to our father's income. So my father had to pay four guineas a year (which was well over half a week's wages) and buy all my books, too. It was a relief to find that, at first, I needed very few and that, next year, I would be able to get most of them from the sale the Prefects set up every July.

Not surprisingly, the regulation uniform list was long and, apart from the grey stockings and the three types of shoes required, it could only be bought from one shop - the most expensive outfitters in Wolverhampton, of course.

'What the blazes are ward shoes?' muttered my father. 'And what on earth is the romper suit for? She's thirteen, for God's sake!'

The ward shoes were granny-type, soft-soled shoes to wear indoors. They were hardly stylish but the romper suits were blush-making; thank heavens no one saw us in them except the gym-mistress. They were made of stiff, sky-blue linen; they were round-necked, sleeveless, and the lower half ended in brief, baggy pants elasticised like knickers. In fact, just like the old-fashioned rompers babies used to wear! We had to strip off our stockings and tunic, and wear the "suit" over our blouses and knickers - but you can get used to anything, given time!

Luckily, the rest of the uniform was flattering, even to plump adolescent girls: a simple, well-cut pinafore dress made of smooth, light navy gabardine, a pale blue poplin blouse, a discreetly striped tie, and a broad belt of brown leather. The navy blazer was of similarly fine quality and we could wear a smart cardigan indoors if the weather was really cold. I loved it all, especially the pearl grey stockings - fine wool or lisle, or even silk if you were a sixth-former. They seemed the height of desirability to me but I soon realised that the cheaper versions, which some of us had to wear, soon turned a sickly pinkish-grey after being washed a couple of times. They had to be darned fairly frequently too, and - as wartime shortages developed and clothes rationing by means of coupons was brought in - they became quite difficult to replace. I decided not to ask about the summer uniform.

On my first morning I was introduced into a class which had already started a lesson. I can't remember which teacher was taking it, or what the subject was, but I know it was in a large room and - for once - the girls were clustered into an informal circle, away from the desks. This caused me some embarrassment because it meant that my arrival caused a lengthy interruption. A chair had to be found and a space had to be made for me and, when at last I was seated, almost every girl could stare at me and take stock of my relatively unattractive uniform. I would have been happier sitting in a desk at the back of the class, but my discomfort is not the only reason why I remember the scene so clearly. After a few minutes of keeping my eyes shyly on my lap, I looked up to see that one of the girls opposite, just visible behind two others in the inner circle, was looking at me fixedly and, as our eyes met, she gave me a warm, friendly smile. I smiled back gratefully. The rest of the lesson period was easier for me. At the end, Marjorie came over and offered to take me to our next class, and though - because we lived an inconvenient distance from each other and initially had different interests and preoccupations - we didn't become more than companionable members of the same class for quite a while, her kindly gesture was the beginning of a close, lifelong friendship which we have both come to value very much.

W.G.H.S. was superficially very different from Blyth High School, though they both provided an excellent education. The school building, three storeys high, looked like a large, country hotel set in pleasant grounds; it had high ceilings, tasteful pictures on its oak-panelled walls and - praise be! - it was warm. Both schools had adopted the public school system (which was logically based on where the pupils boarded) of dividing us into "Houses". This device was useful. It supported firm discipline strategies and gave some point to various competitive events which, presumably, was why all the House Mistresses worked hard to foster their girls' enthusiastic loyalty and commitment. But there was little similarity in the way the two schools organised their working day. At W.G.H.S., and at Newland High, the routines were conventional. Registration in a "home" room with our class teacher was followed by Assembly in the Hall, then we returned to collect our heavy satchels crammed with the morning's books, and moved from subject room to subject room while the teachers stayed put. Lugging books around and making time-wasting treks along corridors crowded with girls hurrying from one classroom to another, almost identical one, seemed stupid to me after the relative calm of Blyth, though it made obvious sense to have dedicated Art and Science rooms.

On a lighter note, I was completely baffled by the school song which I had to learn almost as soon as I arrived. I'd already learned one for Newland and one for Blyth, and cannot now recall them, but I'm pretty sure they were about loyalty to one another and to the respective Alma Mater's ideals. So what in heaven's name, was this one about?

'Forty years on getting older and older, shorter in wind but in memory long . . . ' I chanted grimly as I washed up the tea things that night.

My father put down his newspaper and came into the kitchen to listen. I was flattered, until I saw he was struggling to stifle his laughter and - when I got to "Till the field rings again and again, with the tramp of the twenty-two men!" - I wasn't able to manage the final rousing chorus of "Follow up! Follow up! Follow up!" because, by then, he'd collapsed onto a stool and looked in danger of laughing himself off-balance any minute.

'Why have you learned the Harrow School song?' he demanded.

I was annoyed. 'It's *our* school song . . . and even if I can't make much sense of it, I've got to practise it for Friday. Apparently we sing it twice a term at Assembly.'

'I'm not surprised you can't make much sense of it.' My father was grinning and shaking his head in bewilderment. 'It's all to do with the manly comradeship of the Harrow football team!'

It sounded unlikely - surely rugby was the game the "posh" schools favoured? - but he explained that Harrow did play football, too: under their own rules, of course !

Now, I can understand why boys' Grammar Schools (even though they were largely day rather than boarding-schools) chose to imitate the organisations, methods, and traditions of famous, much admired Public Schools and I can see why, when the importance of higher education for girls was finally recognised and schools were founded especially for them, it was perhaps inevitable that most of them should follow these existing examples. What I can't understand, though, is why any of them should adopt a boys' school song. What reflected glory could possibly be gained? Nevertheless, at Friday's Assembly I certainly understood - and very much enjoyed - hearing the whispers of some of the older girls behind me after we'd sung the words about the twenty-two men tramping the field.

'Oh, if only! If only!' they moaned.

There were, however, two unpleasant shocks for me in my first week at this new school. The first was that I was now expected to do at least ninety minutes homework every night, and even more at the weekend. The second blow was that my class had begun their Latin course well over a year ago. At Blyth I'd only had a term of it and, I regret to say, I never really caught up. My father, whose Technical College course had included a little German (and no other language), had been intrigued by my Latin textbook and was always willing to test me with on the lists of new words I was given to learn and to help untangle the mysteries of case and tense. I think he appreciated the logic involved in the rules of its grammar, and he so revelled in the sound of its words that, before long, Paddy acquired an extra name.

For some years he'd been addressed at times as Dog. We would often say, 'Come on, Dog! Let's put your lead on!' This had gradually developed into a double-barrelled name - Pog-Dog - but as we grew more familiar with Latin endings this was changed to Pogus (pronounced as in "bogus"), which was soon elevated to Pogus Pogastibus. And, after my father had read Robert Graves' "I, Claudius", Paddy was awarded - on really serious occasions - the ceremonial title of Pogus Pogastibus, Prefect of Rome. My mother said she was worried that, if we weren't careful, the dog would be getting above himself and start demanding gourmet food and more luxurious bedding but, thankfully, Paddy didn't let it go to his head and modestly refused to answer to his new name.

Art lessons, as might be expected, were unlike those I had been used to at Blyth and they generated no homework. I had hoped they would include some element of helpful instruction so that I might, at last have some success ; but I was disappointed - the class had finished the skills-based part of the course and moved on to greater things . So when, three months after I arrived, we had to choose either Art or Music as one of our eight or nine subjects for School Certificate, I was told I had to take Music - which meant all my subjects would be academic. It was pointed out that only seven girls that year were being allowed to take Music: it was an honour! But I've always suspected that the art mistress had been involved in the unusually arbitrary directive. However, taking Music did help me reach one of my goals.

During the daily Assembly the school choir sat in the balcony at the back of the Hall and often sang impressive descants to our morning hymns. I longed to join them but when I tried to volunteer I was told, 'You have to wait to be asked - and no one is asked until they are at least in the fourth form.' So no descants for me, at least not yet . . . But then, what if nobody asked me? It made me think of unmarried girls' traditional dread of "being left on the shelf" (when, ironically, that was where I was aching to sit every morning!) and I couldn't help recalling Gracie Fields singing dolefully about taking her harp to a party, ". . . and nobody asked me to play . . ."

Then it dawned on me that it was the choir mistress who taught the School Cert. Music Course and, as the final exam. included a singing and sight-reading unit, it was unlikely that

I'd be overlooked as a suitable candidate. So I accepted my fate, came to terms with the fact that I was the only one of the honoured class of eight who didn't play an instrument to a reasonable standard and, in due course, joined the choir as its youngest - if undistinguished - member.

I still wish though, despite achieving a respectable Credit in the School Cert. Music exam., that I could have learned to draw and paint something that is artistically pleasing - or at least recognisable.

Geography was now little more than strings of boring facts about foreign countries, which the teacher read from her notes in a dreary voice, and which we then went on to illustrate by labelling and colouring-in the Xeroxed maps she provided. Afterwards we were directed to the relevant pages in our text books and had to maker notes from them as our homework. The girls in my class refused to believe my description of the relaxed sessions at Blyth: how – in the drowsy darkness - the brightly-coloured slide shows of Venetian palaces, herds of Lapland reindeer, or the sunrise as seen from the rim of the Grand Canyon, were invariably accompanied by the surreptitious rustling of chocolate wrappers. I admit I learned more from the W.G.H.S. geography lessons but, because none of them managed to catch my interest, I rapidly forgot all the parrot-learned facts once I'd got my School Cert. Credit in the subject. But I did make sure, in later life, that I actually saw those palaces, Lap reindeer, and the Canyon sunrise for real.

History lessons, at first, offered few challenges. I'd apparently missed the sections of the course dealing with pre-history, cavemen, Vikings, and peasants' lives under the early English Kings. Once again, for my first two terms there, we concentrated on the years from the Norman Conquest to the end of the Tudor period, and then leaped over the next two hundred years or so to Queen Victoria's reign. My ideas about the intervening epochs, their achievements, issues, and far-reaching effects, consequently remained hazy for many years to come, especially as the focus of our later studies was on European history from the late 18th century to the end of the 19th. However, because the teacher was a lively, red-headed young woman who underpinned the inspiring descriptions of events with clear explanations from which we could make usable notes, I enjoyed every one of her lessons. Through her, I even became a fan of Napoleon and the logical reforms he introduced into the French systems of government and Justice.

We were all a little afraid of Miss Foote, our Maths teacher. She was somewhat fierce-looking, with an unflatteringly short haircut and a wardrobe of skirts and jumper in muted shades of grey. She stood no nonsense and was uncompromisingly determined that – through sheer hard work – we should all achieve mathematical understanding and examination success. And, gradually, we came to believe it too – and to appreciate her. Miss Tocher was, in most ways, just the opposite. Our class had a singing lesson every week with her and it was almost always a minor disaster. I never understood why the majority of these normally well-mannered girls just played around, defying all her panicky efforts to establish some kind of order. I don't even know if all her other classes were similarly riotous. The songs she chose for us were a happy mix of familiar, traditional folk songs and some new attractive items, and she was a very competent accompanist. It ought to have been a really enjoyable period but, for some reason, most of the girls refused to co-operate. They chatted loudly, clattered chairs, and either ignored her instructions or answered her admonitions with insolent scorn. Several of us pitied this plain, ineffectual mistress – though that title was hardly appropriate in her case! – and were embarrassed for her, but our protests were ignored or laughed at by the rest of the class. I've since wondered (though it was never actually said) if they thought her name indicated that she was of German or Austrian origin, and felt they should make her suffer for it.

Mademoiselle Blanc was also extremely plain. She was elderly, swarthy-skinned, and invariably dressed in a drab skirt, a long, shapeless cardigan, and thick woollen stockings, but we respected and were fond of her. She was born and brought up in Paris but we knew, from the anecdotes she occasionally told us, that her family lived mainly in Normandy and, one morning, we were surprised to see her looking oddly distraught. She tried several times to greet us as usual, then her face crumpled and she lowered her head into her hands and sat at her desk, visibly shaking, for two or three minutes. We sat in silence. Was she ill? Annoyed? Praying? Then she got up abruptly and blundered out of the room. Sympathetic anxiety kept us waiting in our seats, talking softly, and puzzled as to what to do next, but within a very short time another teacher arrived to take over.

'Mam'selle has had bad news, I'm afraid,' she told us quietly. 'As you may know, it was announced on the news this morning that France has fallen. I'm sure you'll understand what this means for her and for all of us. She'll be back with us tomorrow.'

She was and, although she seemed to have lost some of her usual verve, she was too experienced a teacher to bring any more personal distress into her classroom.

Two classes in each year not only did Latin as well as French (the third class did Spanish) but we also took Physics and Chemistry while the others took Biology. At that time I didn't realise there was a hierarchy implied, just as I failed to see there was any difference between the scholarship pupils and those who were charged full fees and had been accepted via a comparatively easy Entrance exam. This must mainly have been because the Staff deliberately made no difference in their attitude towards us, but I think it was also due to the fact that my parents didn't really grasp it either. They had virtually no experience, direct or otherwise, of higher education and the opportunities it could offer working and lower middle class people. They saw Harry Etherington's teacher training college course as a wise move rather than a minor achievement. Nevertheless, without putting any pressure on me whatsoever, they were keen for me to do as well as possible so that, when I left at sixteen, I would be able to go on to take some kind of follow-up course which would enable me to get a "good" job, preferably one with promotion prospects and – if I didn't marry – a pension at the end.

I simply accepted all the school's routines and organisational arrangements with very little thought and – except for Latin – enjoyed working at all the subjects. My father was particularly pleased when it became obvious that I was very much interested in the Physics and Chemistry sessions; if I needed support in those areas he was competent to help. One of the reasons I enjoyed them so much, though, was that the atmosphere during those periods was relatively informal. We conducted and wrote up all our experiments in pairs and could choose our own partners, so Marjorie and I were able to work together in those lessons for the next two years.

The weekly session in the gym was quite pleasant, though I was not much good at climbing the ropes, doing handstands or leaping confidently over the horse. I did take pleasure, though, in finding that – when we lined up in height order at the beginning and end of each lesson – in the space of two years I was moved from the middle of the column to just three girls from the end. I liked being tall! I also liked the weekly dancing lessons we had through out the winter and whenever the weather was really bad during the rest of the year. We did a little English country dancing but, most of the time we learned American Square dancing and that was pure delight for me.

My favourite subject, as always, was English and my class was lucky enough to have an excellent teacher. Miss Docherty was tall, very slim, and invariably beautifully dressed. Her auburn hair was fashionably styled, her rather sharp-featured face was carefully made-up, and her nails were discreetly polished. Some of the girls found her air of sophistication and her teaching-style slightly alarming. It was obvious that she had little time for those who weren't prepared to work at her subject with due concentration and at least a touch of imagination. Her remarks could verge on the sarcastic if someone displayed a stupid lack of intelligent thought, but all our written work was marked and responded to with meticulous care and real interest. I looked forward eagerly each week to reading the analytical comments and stimulating remarks which she wrote to justify the grade she'd given my latest effort. No one could be bored in her class, and the literature sessions were especially enjoyable. We were encouraged to enliven the Shakespeare plays and set books with dramatic readings and to explore the characters' emotions and reactions in relation to the behaviour of people around us.

Though I generally preferred one of the central desks I tried, whenever possible, to sit on the front row for her sessions, partly because I liked to see the details of whatever she was wearing. One afternoon, despite suffering from a very heavy cold and sniffing surreptitiously because my handkerchief was already way beyond further use, I sat enjoying listening to her reading a Keats poem. For some reason she had chosen to walk backwards and forwards across the room while she read and, just as she paused immediately in front of me, I couldn't avoid sneezing violently. The result was a repulsive mess! I gazed in helpless horror at the state of my hands and the lid of my desk, realising all too clearly the disgust Miss Docherty must be feeling as she looked down at my slime-covered face. But I was wrong – and I shall always remember with gratitude how she reacted so swiftly and sensitively to lessen my acute embarrassment that I don't think anyone in the class knew what had happened. Very quickly – hardly missing a beat as she read – she took her own handkerchief from her jacket pocket and slid it unobtrusively towards me. When she came to the end of the poem (and I had managed to make myself a little more presentable) she leaned down, gave me a tiny grin and murmured conspiratorially, 'If you want to go for a drink of water for that cough . . .' And, gratefully, I headed for the cloakroom washbasins. When, two days later I returned her carefully laundered hanky in an envelope containing a pretty thank-you card, she simply nodded and went back to her marking without further comment. As my American friend would say – she was a very classy lady.

NEW FRIENDS

At the beginning of my first spring term at the school it was announced that we would be staging "A Midsummer Night's Dream" at the end of May, and anyone who would like to be considered for a part should sign the list on the English noticeboard as soon as possible. Naturally, I raced to volunteer and, although the cast was mainly drawn from the older classes, I was lucky enough to get the part of Snout the Tinker. We rehearsed after school, of course, and I was told to bring a knife, a hunk of bread and an onion to all rehearsals; I was given an old leather bag to keep them in. I could then give a more convincing impression of being a "rude mechanical" by spending the gaps between my speeches munching greedily. I really don't care for onions very much (and, inevitably, eating them resulted in all the others noticeably backing away whenever I hovered near them) but I was more than willing to suffer for my art. And, as soon as I realised that I was the one who had to play Wall, it seemed even more worthwhile.

My Wall costume was impressive. I was provided with two sheets of thin plywood with bricks and mortar painted on them and they had strips of leather attached so that they could hang from my shoulders like the sandwich boards used to advertise a local café or to announce "The End of the World is Nigh". Stretching out my arm with two fingers splayed and dramatically declaring that this was the chink through which Pyramus and Thisbe could talk gave me such pleasure that, for the actual performances, I let my hand shake visibly and my voice rise to a trembling squeak as if Snout was overcome with stage-fright. This was never commented upon by any of my fellow actors, nor by the teacher who had directed our scenes, so I don't know if this rudimentary attempt at Method acting was appreciated or whether people thought I really was nervous. But from then on I decided that, whatever the play, I would resist the temptation to show off. I would always perform on the night in the way I'd acted in rehearsal. It might be easier on others' nerves.

As it happened, no more plays were put on by the school while I was there – perhaps because wartime pressures made this difficult – but the next year we had an inter-house poetry-speaking competition and I was chosen as the Year Three representative for mine. We won the cup, so I felt I'd compensated for any past transgression.

Within a few weeks of my arrival in Tettenhall I had been lucky enough to make a great friend. Brenda North was in my year but in a different class. However, as we both had to push our bicycles up the Rock on our way home - and nearly always around the same time - we began to wait for each other so that we could make the struggle together. A good gossipy natter made the effort less of a burden and the distance seem shorter. Very soon, instead of going straight home in the afternoon, we dawdled longer and longer, reluctant to part: there was so much to say, and we soon took to spending most of our free time together.

Bren, as she was known, lived about half a mile beyond our house, well into the highly desirable residences' area our estate agent had shown us. Her father was the managing director of a successful manufacturing business and they lived in a large house set in landscaped gardens. Occasionally, if Bren and I called in on a Saturday on our way back from a walk or a wander round town, I would be asked to stay for tea - though not, perhaps, with any great enthusiasm on the part of her somewhat dismissive mother who, once I was seated at the table, hardly spoke another word to me. I couldn't help being impressed (and, I admit, just a little overwhelmed) by the formal, oak-panelled dining-room and the luxurious comforts of their sitting-room. The kitchen was almost as big as our two main rooms put together, and Bren's pretty bedroom was divided from her older sister's by a shared bathroom complete with both a bath and a shower: a fairly unusual feature in those days. Bren, of course, took all this for granted so, apart from saying once or twice how pretty this or that was, I was clearly not expected to comment. So I didn't. I'm a quick learner.

Bren and I were very comfortable together. As a pair of young girls we had a good deal in common and shared a similar sense of fun. We took great pleasure in one another's company but - if anything - I was the leader in whatever we did. Bren had a generous, sunny personality and was, in most things, simply content to follow. She was, though, considerably more socially experienced than I was. Though no comparisons or direct references were made to this – and I don't really know if Bren was even conscious of it – I soon realised that, even at the age of thirteen, she was used to eating in restaurants from sophisticated menus, she'd been on holidays abroad, stayed in hotels, had riding lessons, and her simple, page-boy bob was always expensively styled at a leading salon. None of these things was likely to come my way - and I just accepted this, without envy, as a fact of life – but I was very much aware that I had a lot to learn before I could feel as casually confident in many social situations as she clearly did. Still, as I've already claimed, I'm a quick learner and I don't think many of my social gaffes were too obvious to the circle of friends and family she gradually introduced me into, however painfully embarrassing *I* found them. Or, maybe, they went unnoticed because I was merely Bren's school friend: of no importance whatsoever.

A week or two after "A Midsummer Night's Dream" was over, Bren asked if I'd like to take part in a play some of her sister's friends were trying to produce to make money for the Red Cross. It was their attempt, she said, to feel they were contributing something to the war effort and, without knowing much about it, I enthusiastically said yes. All I was told was that Bren's sister, Peggy (who was seventeen and very popular with a number of sixth formers from the Grammar School) was very friendly with one who was hoping eventually to follow a career in the theatre. He was a mature eighteen-year-old with a strong ambition to prove his talent by producing a Shakespearean play, and he'd persuaded a group of friends to join him. So Peggy had offered the North's house and garden for rehearsals and promised to ask around and find some girls who might like to take part. It was, I suspect, mostly and excuse for these youngsters to be able to get together – and why not?

When I joined them they had already had two meetings and appeared to know one another well, so I felt very shy, especially as they were all older than me. I'd come straight from school choir practice so I was still wearing my school uniform while the rest had somehow managed to change and were sitting about the room in casually smart clothes. Bren had no intention of taking a part – she said there was no way she could learn reams of flowery language - but she'd promised she would hang around to support me. Unfortunately she was in bed with a heavy cold that first afternoon and I was horrified to be given a copy of "As You Like It" - a play I'd never read and knew absolutely nothing about – and I was told I was to take the part of Audrey. I could have done with Bren's support. There were about ten of us sitting at the North's dining-table to read our scripts but I felt that the place was crowded with dozens of strangers – a daunting mix of laughing young men and confident, attractive girls.

All too soon we came up to my first scene and I suddenly realised that, not only was I completely ignorant as to the play's plot, but I had absolutely no idea of Audrey's character or background. Still, my experience of the heroines in "A Midsummer Night's Dream" – Helena, Hermia, et al – led me to expect I would be comfortable in the part. So I was not happy to find that, far from being a heroine, I was a lumpen bumpkin who Touchstone – for some unfathomable reason – was determined to marry. He was played by a fierce-looking, ginger-headed boy who eyed me doubtfully whenever I spoke and seemed to take great delight in saying lines which pointed out my undesirability.

'An ill-favoured thing but mine own,' he declaimed with relish, matched only by the pleasure he seemed to take in ordering me to bear myself more seemly!

Sheer nerves drove all sense out of my head and, for the first time in my life – and, thank goodness, almost the last – I was overcome by an attack of uncontrollable giggles. This reaction was politely ignored by everyone. They sat patiently waiting while I struggled again and again to recover myself but, every time it was my turn to speak, the silly giggling bubbled up once more. I was thoroughly ashamed of myself and only too relieved that we didn't get as far as my second scene that night.

We managed two more rehearsals – both without reaching my scenes, as it happened – but we had to give up. The comparative inaction of the early months of the war (now referred to as the Phoney War) had been followed by disastrous events in Europe. A series of German victories allowed Hitler's forces to overrun Belgium and the Netherlands, to sweep through France, and to drive the British Army towards the channel. The troops' desperate, fairly successful, evacuation to England from the beaches of Dunkirk was swiftly followed by the Battle of Britain for air supremacy. We now stood alone in our fight against the Nazis. "As You Like It" and a possible few pounds for the Red Cross seemed irrelevant now.

In any case our producer, who'd applied to join the RAF some months before, was almost immediately sent for pilot training and no one had the heart to suggest a replacement. I think I was more relieved than disappointed that the play had been abandoned but I was pleased to be asked some months later – I think, as Bren's friend – to join the group to go carol singing during Christmas week to collect money for the Red Cross. We only went to houses the young people had connections with – relatives, family friends, and neighbours – so we were invited into the hall or sitting-room of some of them and once treated to a small glass of sherry and a biscuit. This was my first taste of alcohol and I found it stung the back of my throat unpleasantly, but I revelled in the experience – and further opportunities to glimpse how the other half lived.

After Christmas there were no more links with the group and, though Bren and I still spent much of our time together, my main focus was home, school work and family concerns. At Easter I was distressed to be told that Bren would be leaving the High School in the summer. She was going to Abbotts Bromley, the famous boarding school Peggy had attended. At first Bren disliked the idea but she was soon caught up in the excitement of buying the new uniform and the prospect of exotic extras such as fencing lessons. I missed her very much when the autumn term came. We both expected to keep up our friendship yet it faded quite quickly; our letters stopped and, during the holidays, her mother made sure Bren's days were filled. But I remember our time together with affection and gratitude. I'd learned a lot.

VISITORS AND OTHER PROBLEMS

When France fell in 1940 the German forces were massed just a few miles away from our coast, and there was a very real fear that, within the next few weeks, Hitler would follow up this victory by invading Britain. This remained a strong possibility for a very long time and it was clear that some kind of emergency defence organisation was necessary; the surviving soldiers from the Dunkirk retreat would be needed elsewhere and for other purposes. An urgent appeal was broadcast for men, who were not already part of Air Raid Precautions teams, or Auxiliary Fire or Ambulance Services, to volunteer for the LDV (Local Defence Volunteers) which was rapidly being set up. There was an immediate response from thousands of men of all ages, willing to give up a great deal of their spare time to train and take on the heavy duties involved in preparing to defend this country. My father was one of them and, because of his comparative youth and practical skills, he was soon made a sergeant.

The story of this "army" - renamed the Home Guard - is still a very familiar one, so need not be retold here. But it is worth emphasising that for men like my father - who were in a reserved occupation because their work as civilians was vital to the war effort or the country's infrastructure, or who were too old or not considered physically fit enough for any of the Armed Services - it was a godsend. They could make an extremely important contribution to the protection of their local area and to the people's feeling of security.

My mother had joined the WVS (Women's Voluntary Service) some months before and willingly took on the responsibility of providing a hot dinner every Saturday for the ten firemen and four members of the ARP Control team on duty at the nearby Fire Station. She and Mrs Phillips, the charming wife of a master from the Tettenhall College, took it in turns to plan and shop for the ingredients. They then worked together preparing and cooking the meat, vegetables, and pudding, serving the meal, and tackling the mountain of washing up afterwards. Soon after I was fourteen I took over from my mother the task of scrubbing our kitchen floor, and cleaning and polishing the porch tiles most Saturday mornings. Sometimes, though, she had a migraine or bilious attack and I would go in her place to help prepare the dinner for the firemen. I found the sheer quantity of the materials to deal with and the speed at which we had to work really alarming, but I expect Mrs Phillips was even more alarmed when she saw that I was to be her partner that day. Because I was inexperienced I was slow and clumsy, and my willingness scarcely made up for these drawbacks, but she battled on cheerfully and treated me like a valued fellow-adult.

During the next twelve months we thoroughly enjoyed having a fair number of visitors to stay. My mother's cousin, Mirrie's son Albert, was now in the RAF and for several months was stationed close by. I looked forward to his visits. He had a talent for making his everyday experiences as an Aircraftsman sound hilarious - it was like listening to a popular radio comedian who didn't need to rely on jokes or slick one-liners to entertain his audience - and when his wife, Madge, came over for a long weekend it doubled our pleasure. From her point of view it was good to come because, not only could she be with Albert, but it gave her a much needed rest from the sporadic heavy bombing raids on Hull which had recently started.

She was, of course, especially welcome, because she was able to bring my mother up to date with news of Auntie Mirrie, and the rest of the Taylor relations. Auntie Mirrie kept writing to say that, though she'd love to see us and our new home, she felt she couldn't leave Uncle Tom to cope on his own with the haulage business and its inevitable wartime problems. And he certainly wouldn't take any time off to bring her. However, we were very glad to see Auntie Annie and Uncle Will arrive from Keyingham for a week to give Uncle a little rest. He had retired three years before, but the firm of solicitors he'd worked for had become so short-staffed because of employees leaving to join the Forces, that he'd been persuaded to return to work again as their chief clerk. At nearly seventy he was finding the responsibility, and the strain of travelling into Hull every day very tiring.

Not quite so welcome, though, was a sudden visit from Granny and Grandpa Langdale. A somewhat confusing phone call one evening from Grandpa (Granny couldn't use a telephone because of her increased deafness) informed my mother that they would be with us the next afternoon for a fortnight's "break". They'd apparently been given an unexpected holiday at very short notice.

When they arrived and had taken their cases up to their bedroom, my mother looked at me with a worried frown. 'I don't like it,' she said quietly.

'Why not?'

'Granny has lost all her bounce and bustle. Even her earrings seem to droop rather than dangle. She doesn't look in a holiday mood, and *he* looks as if he's lost a shilling and found a ha'penny.'

'Maybe they're just tired. After all they set off very early this morning. They've had four changes, and some long waits between trains, and they've carted a whole mass of luggage.'

My mother shook her head. 'I don't like that, either. Perhaps they'll tell Daddy what it's all about, when he gets home . . .' And she shrugged her shoulders gloomily.

She was right to be suspicious. Most of the time they hung around the house and garden rather than exploring the area or going on the kind of little trips they usually enjoyed. Nothing was said about their work or the Hospital and, as the fortnight neared its end, there was no mention of plans to leave.

'We've simply got to ask what's happening! And they've got to tell us,' said my mother.

There was a desperate edge to her voice which my father and I recognised. She was tired of sharing her home and her kitchen, and of being kept in the dark with no clue as to when the situation would change.

'If there's been some sort of kerfuffle at the hospital we need to know, and to help them make plans to move on,' she declared.

I wasn't there, of course, when the questions were asked and I never got round to asking how they were approached - the whole problem area was too sensitive - but my mother told me the next day that they'd lost their jobs and had left at a moment's notice. We were never told why and, untypically, neither even hinted that the other was to blame. There was no attempt to explain the surrounding circumstances. Frustratingly, the whole episode still remains an intriguing mystery.

It was two uncomfortable months before jobs had been found for Grandpa and Granny but, as usual, in the long-term they were fortunate. A wealthy, middle-aged business man had, just before war began, built a luxury house in a small village on the outskirts of Wolverhampton and he desperately needed a gardener/handyman and a housekeeper. Unsurprisingly, these were hard to find in 1941. He was a bachelor and, although he was away from home for much of the week, it was a relief to him to know he was coming back to a sparkling-clean house and a well-tended garden. He also liked to entertain sometimes at the weekends, so Granny's excellent cooking was very much appreciated. They were given a very comfortable living-room, a bathroom of their own, and a large, well-furnished bedroom overlooking open countryside. In effect, they had the sole use of a beautiful house for most of the time. Because their boss (or "Sir" as they always referred to him with semi-serious emphasis) was often travelling around, living in hotels, Granny had a considerable amount of freedom to plan her own timetable and choose the weekly menus. She could order whatever groceries she fancied, and use his ration book more or less as a supplement to theirs, so the three of them fed rather better, I think, than the rest of us.

I enjoyed visiting them occasionally; I even slept there once or twice when Sir was away. I was very impressed with his large bedroom. His bed was on a raised platform in an alcove and its dark red, velvet curtains could be drawn to separate it from the rest of the room, making it seem warmer and more private. And I loved the way the dining-room's stark white walls provided a striking background for the brilliantly coloured bird of paradise which Sir had had painted on the wall behind his chair at the end of the dark oak table. Its head was near the ceiling, its gorgeous tail feathers almost swept the floor, and it was skilfully positioned off-centre so that it would appear to be watching over him as he dined. But, best of all, I enjoyed being with the engaging springer spaniel puppy he'd bought as soon as he realised that Granny and Grandpa were always around to look after and exercise him. I was nearly as fond of him as I was of our Paddy.

We were glad, of course, that they were now so comfortably settled and even more glad to have the house to ourselves again. It was good to be able to have friends to visit, and family to stay with us. Whenever Uncle Bill - who'd been made Captain of his own merchant ship just before war began - docked in Cardiff, Auntie Nora would come to us for a few days on her way to be with him for a few days before he left to sail north to join up with a newly assembled convoy and set off on the Atlantic run once again. And it was even better when Uncle Bill came up to meet Auntie Nora at our house, and both would spend part of his leave with us.

Ever since our time together in Cornwall, Uncle Bill had kept in touch with me. I would get a long letter from him once or twice a year, full of funny anecdotes and detailed descriptions of places he'd visited and interesting people he'd met. He sent postcards and, nearly always, a birthday card too, and once or twice a telegram came to celebrate a special occasion such as when I passed my scholarship. Very occasionally he would send a present and they were always unusual - even weird. Once it was a pair of pale blue mules trimmed with marabou feathers. They had kitten heels and looked just like the ones American film stars wore with their glamorous negligees. Another time it was an armadillo shell. The tail was curved to stick into its mouth, forming a handle, and the resultant sewing basket was lined with orange satin and completed with a matching drawstring cover. It was creepy, but the girls in my class at school were quite envious - especially when I told them that he'd brought his wife a similar armadillo, flattened, with two slits in its shell to form a letter-rack which could be hung on the wall by its curved tail.

'It seems horribly cruel to me,' declared my mother. But Uncle pointed out that the South American people who'd made them were desperately poor, with very few natural resources or means of making any money to feed their families.

It was on one of these visits that Uncle insisted that I should call him and Auntie by their first names.

'You're almost fifteen and you look so grown-up now that, when you call us Aunt and Uncle, it gives people the impression that I'm a tediously garrulous ancient mariner, on my last sea-legs, married to some boring old lady. Yet we all know that, instead, I'm a dashing young sea-captain who's only just managing to hang on to this flirty young charmer of a wife! So, have a heart, Jean . . . please'.

I was delighted. I was even more delighted when, to seal the new arrangement, he suggested that I might like to go with him to a Music Hall in Wolverhampton the next evening to see one of his favourite comedians - just like my trips with Auntie Mirrie and Uncle Tom. Nora generously gave her blessing and, when I tentatively asked if he could wear his uniform, she was as surprised as I was that he cheerfully agreed.

'You're very privileged,' she said. 'You know he hates wearing it when he's on leave, and I never seem to be able to persuade him to wear it for me. And I'd so love to show him off.'

Looking back now, I realise just how generous Nora was being and I love her for enabling me to have - guilt-free - a wonderful evening to remember. For that's exactly what it was, from beginning to end. I was so proud to be seen with him and revelled in having him all to myself for a couple of hours. They left for Hull two days later and, for a little while, our daily routines seemed somewhat humdrum. But not for long.

Very soon after we'd arrived in Tettenhall the local council had offered all households an Anderson air raid shelter. These consisted of corrugated iron sheets - curved for the roof and flat ones for the end and the entrance - which could be bolted together and fitted into a deepish hole in the back garden. My father (already familiar with the task because of the shelter he'd built in our Norwich garden) had immediately begun digging into our lawn and, in no time, had the shelter in place and started lining the earth floor with wooden planks. He fitted it with four bunks, put two shelves across the sealed end, and managed to run a covered cable from a plug in the kitchen to provide us with electric light. Within five weeks it was finished. My mother had made some kind of thin mattress for each bunk and found a miner's lamp to use if the electricity failed, and my father had covered the curved roof with the turf he'd cut from the lawn. We'd all got used to making sure we put thick clothes into a carrier bag at the foot of our beds each night, to grab and take with us to the shelter if the siren sounded.

We offered our fourth bunk to June James, our hairdresser friend from two doors away, and it was gratefully accepted. Because her elderly father was so lame, he and his wife had been given an official alternative - a large, reinforced metal cage, which they could put a double mattress into. The idea was that they could crawl into it as soon as the siren sounded and lie in safety under its solid roof till the danger was over, but it seemed to us that this process would be even more difficult for Mr James racing to an ordinary Anderson shelter. However, when it was delivered, they got rid of their dining-table and draped the cage in a crimson chenille table cloth until the war was over. But I think sitting round it to eat their meals must have been pretty uncomfortable: there was no place to tuck their knees.

All these preparations were wise, though. One November, brightly moonlit night, before the mod. cons. in our shelter were complete, the siren sounded and within two or three minutes we heard the ominous throb of German bombers heading towards us, and a sudden, frightening explosion of noise as the ack-ack batteries surrounding the Wolverhampton area started up. It was early evening but I don't remember grabbing my coat, or running down the garden to the shelter - just crouching there in the darkness while my mother stood in the entrance, trembling as she breathlessly waited for my father to arrive with June. He'd insisted, apparently, on waiting to help her to safety. It was a grim night for us all. The noise was appalling. The bombers flew overhead for many hours with the ack-ack batteries thundering ceaselessly as they sent up a defensive barrage of heavy gunfire. Every so often we could hear metallic thuds and even my father admitted that he thought it likely that some bombs had been dropped nearby. Once or twice, when the noise eased slightly, he suggested that he should dash out to see if June's parents were safe (I think he really wanted to see what was happening and how much damage there was) but we all begged him not to leave us and, in any case, the full, terrifying racket always started up again before he could insist.

When, at last, the noise faded and the All Clear signal sounded, we stumbled out into the cold, grey morning hardly daring to look around us. But all seemed surprisingly normal, though my father picked up one or two chunks of shrapnel from the little path as we walked towards the back door.

'From our local guns, of course,' he remarked, with comforting confidence. 'But where on earth were those bombers heading?'

We were too dazed to hazard a guess and - let's face it - too tired to care. But later that day we all knew - it was Coventry. From seven o'clock that night until six in the morning, over five hundred German planes had not only bombed many of the important industrial targets which surrounded the city, but its centre had been devastatingly attacked too. We had simply been on the main route of their deadly journey there and back.

From then on we had many frighteningly disturbed nights. Coventry continued to be targeted from time to time until August of 1942; these raids were mostly relatively light but in April that year there were two more serious ones of seven or eight hours length. And we suffered, too, whenever planes flew over to bomb Birmingham and other Midland industrial centres but, though the noise and flying shrapnel continued to be nerve-racking, only one actual bomb was dropped anywhere near where we lived - and that was after the main hubbub from our local Bofurs had died down and the all clear was sounding. It was probably a lone plane getting rid of its last bomb to lighten the load. My father, and many others, believed that the German pilots used the reflection from Wolverhampton's large,open reservoir on moonlit nights to check their position, and it did seem that they made a definite change of direction when they were overhead.

I can't remember the school's ruling (we only had two or three raids during school time, forcing us to march hurriedly to the cold, damp shelters on the playing field) but I think we were allowed to arrive at school one or two hours later than usual if a raid had lasted after two o'clock in the morning. Quite quickly our Anderson was made reasonably comfortable, a routine for grabbing Paddy and a box of vital necessities was established, and we became used to responding swiftly to the siren's wail even if we were wakened from a deep sleep.

Familiarity lessened our fears a little and, because there were often patches of time (between the planes flying to their destination and their returning) when the guns were silent, we tried to forget our discomforts by playing guessing games and story-telling. The light was too dim to read for more than an hour at a time and, in any case - if I hadn't managed to complete my homework before the Siren sent us hurrying to the shelter - I had to crouch awkwardly in my bunk to finish it. Thank goodness, when summer's longer days and lighter nights began, there were fewer and fewer air raids in our area until they more or less ceased altogether. We could take up fairly normal lives again.

THE SCHOOL CERTIFICATE YEARS

When I think now of the dangers and the suffering so many people were enduring throughout the war - the bitter fighting, the dreadful casualties and the many serious hardships which permanently altered the lives of hundreds of thousands of people, from 1940 onwards - my daily experiences seem very limited and trivial. But I can only describe what it was like for me: a girl entering her teens, being brought up with middle-class aspirations, in a pretty conventional family, on a very limited income. Our hardships were comparatively very minor but they were a significant part of the fabric of our lives and, as such, must have affected my development and future attitudes - at least to some extent. I therefore have little hesitation in recording them.

Though my father and I were largely unaware of the day-to-day problems of feeding the family once food rationing had been brought in, it must have been a constant worry to my mother. It took a great deal of careful planning and ingenuity to provide satisfying meals for a man whose job and Home Guard duties involved a fair amount of physical activity, and to cater for an adolescent's growing appetite. The three of us ate all our meals at home. We had just the bare rations, no special allowances, no canteen provision, no little extras from friendly shop-keepers who'd served us for many years, and we certainly couldn't afford even an occasional cafe or restaurant meal. A large part of our small back garden was taken up by the Anderson shelter, so there was little room for the rows of vegetables my father had been used to growing when we lived in Hull. Nevertheless my mother managed somehow to keep us healthily well-fed and though - from time to time - we felt a sharp longing for some really fresh fish (instead of limp fillets, weary from their long journey to the Midlands), an orange, a jam sponge pudding, or a hefty bacon and egg sandwich, we always seemed to enjoy good, filling meals.

Clothes rationing presented some problems, of course. Unlike the well-to-do mothers of some of my Tettenhall friends, we weren't able - in the first few months of the war - to buy lengths of material for later use, or stock up our wardrobes. And, of course, our wardrobes weren't too lavishly stocked to begin with. So for the next few years a lot of thought was needed before any of our clothing coupons were surrendered. Granny Langdale did what she could for us, my mother knitted warm jumpers and cardigans (though, as new wool cost coupons, she often unravelled old ones - discarding the thin bits!) and we became enthusiastic make-do-and-menders. But shoes were quite a drain on our meagre allowance and the fact that I was rapidly growing out of many of my clothes didn't help. Like many other adolescents, I had no cupboards of garments which could be altered, turned, shortened, or cannibalised as many adults had, and no older sisters or cousins who could help out with hand-me-downs. It was fortunate that I'd been kitted out with my new school uniform before coupons were introduced and that it had been bought for me to "grow into". It was a good thing, too, that I stayed thin - my growing was upwards - but, as the months passed, I did get just a little tired of wearing that uniform for much of the time, especially our regulation, sky-blue dresses made of thick, stiff cotton reminiscent of sail-cloth. They had unflattering, removable, Peter Pan collars made of white linen with matching cuffs edging our puffed sleeves. With reasonable care, the dresses could be made to last for three or four days before they needed washing but the collars quickly attracted grime from the air polluted by the Wolverhampton industries and this meant they had to be taken off to be washed and starched at least every other day, and clean ones tacked on. Understandably, though my mother was prepared to do the laundering, she insisted that I did the necessary sewing.

There was a shortage of coal and so, usually, we could only keep one fire going at any one time. The stove in the stone-flagged kitchen was needed to heat the water so we ate most of our meals in there and only lit the living-room fire in the evening. Looking back now, I realise how fortunate I was that my father had to set off for work well before eight o'clock. He always got the kitchen fire going before seven, and the room was reasonably comfortable when I had my breakfast. We had some extremely cold winters and, because the house never really got warmed through, our bedrooms were places of serious discomfort for weeks - particularly mine, which was above the unheated dining room. We all took hot water bottles to bed and, if the night was very bitter, we'd put them in half an hour earlier, bring our night things downstairs, undress by the fire, then rush up to get under the warmed blankets and eiderdown without any chilling delay. Often in the morning there would be ice patterns on the inside of the bedroom windows, so eventually I took to putting all my underclothes for the next day between my top sheet and the blankets and eiderdown. At least, then, they were the same temperature as me when I had to put them on.

All too soon, though, our smooth-running family life was disrupted by an unexpected visitor: Mrs Henderson. She arrived, clip-board in hand and - brandishing copies of recent, enforceable regulations - introduced herself as the newly-appointed, local Billeting Officer.

'You have two rooms to spare: a double bedroom and a dining-room, plus a decent-sized, shareable kitchen,' she stated, uncompromisingly. She exuded business-like confidence. 'I'm therefore entitled to billet two people here - either service personnel or civilians who have been drafted to work in one of the local factories and have nowhere to live. You will be paid a small rent and you won't be expected to cater for, or look after them in any way.'

And that was that. We had no choice.

'At least we can't be asked to take in evacuees - children, I mean,' said my father comfortingly when he was told that night. 'This is not designated as a safe area, you know, and just think how much responsibility and work children would mean. We'll just have to accept this as part of our contribution to the war effort.'

Our first tenants arrived a week later: a young Dutch corporal, his wife and their small baby. Many of these young soldiers, who had escaped from Holland to join the Allied Forces at the time of Dunkirk, had been stationed in Wales for twelve months or so, and several had started families and married local girls - often in that order. We were somewhat taken aback by the baby, beautiful though she was, especially as Gwennie seemed to be only about seventeen and was, understandably, a very inexperienced mother, unused to housework. But who were we to grumble? Baby Megan was thriving and we had very few disturbed nights. They were transferred to another camp three months later and, apart from one or two unsightly rings on our piano lid left by the milk bottles Gwennie apparently liked to keep there, they might never have been part of our lives.

The day after they left, Mrs Henderson was again on our doorstep, brimming with excitement.

'I've got the ideal couple for you, dear!' She beamed with misplaced enthusiasm.

My mother was less enthusiastic and profoundly distrusted the use of the term "dear" by someone she hardly knew.

'Major Roberts has just taken over command of the military camp, and his wife will be arriving in three weeks time. This is just the place for them. Charming people! Regular Army, of course.' She dropped her voice conspiratorially. 'Real professionals, you know. Nothing jumped up about *them*.'

My mother wasn't entirely sure what Mrs Henderson meant - nor was my father - but from the day they arrived it was clear that Mrs H. was right: they were charming people. We actually saw very little of them. The Major worked long hours and almost always ate in the Mess, and Mrs Roberts spent most of her days working with and for the wives of the men under his command as a kind of domestic adviser, mother confessor, and social organiser. She, too, rarely ate at home and in the evening was constantly entertaining or being entertained in and around the camp. But when we did meet up they were invariably friendly, considerate and very appreciative of being able to share our house. They'd been stationed in India for several years before the war began and Mrs Roberts had some lovely clothes which she kept in meticulous order, washing them carefully by hand. Whenever I saw her leaving the house with her light make-up immaculate and her beautiful silk dress or cream linen suit newly pressed, I felt I knew the true meaning of the term "bandbox fresh". When they were moved on a few months later, she left me with a jar of Cyclax vanishing cream and a sound grasp of the high standards expected of a lady.

Major Roberts - staying on for two more weeks to smooth the take-over procedure for his successor - told us that he and his wife had wanted to show their gratitude for making them so comfortable but, unexpectedly, she'd had to go ahead to find them somewhere to live. So, on behalf of both of them, he invited a young sub-lieutenant and me (with a friend of my choice) to join him for dinner at a good restaurant in Wolverhampton. Madge was staying with us at the time and I was sleeping in the James's spare bedroom, so I asked June to come but she refused saying she was too shy. Madge was thrilled to accept instead. It was a really generous gesture of the major's, and we had a great time, but I realise now that he probably had quite a shock when he saw Madge's brash make-up and somewhat startlingly coloured outfit - we must have looked an oddly-matched group.

'I've got just the person for you now,' said Mrs Henderson, a fortnight later. 'An RAF officer attached to the Boulton and Paul aircraft factory. Flight Lieutenant Brown. He'll take most of his meals in their canteen, so you'll hardly know he's with you.'

This was true. He was a very reserved man who slipped in and out of the house with no fuss and very little noise, and for many weeks any communication we had was limited to exchanging an occasional smile in passing, and comments on the weather. We learned nothing whatsoever of his background. One evening, however, he stopped me in the hall to ask when I would be taking my School Certificate and, some days later, asked how I felt I was doing. I gave him a summary of the six I was reasonably confident about, plus a brief explanation of why I had almost decided to opt out of taking the Latin exam.

'But I still feel a bit doubtful about the French oral and I'm even more unsure of some sections of the Maths papers,' I confessed.

'I might be able to help you a little in both those areas,' he said tentatively, and when I said I'd be grateful for any help he could give me, he suggested I went to his room for an hour or so the following evening.

My father was pleased. He knew he couldn't help me with the French and was reluctant to tackle the maths weaknesses. I'd tended to get very touchy - even slightly tearful - when he'd tried in the past, maintaining that his methods of working through and setting down were muddlingly different from how we were taught. I think, though, that the real problem was much the same as that experienced by learner drivers: being taught by close family rarely works. Both parties involved can become seriously emotional.

So, over the next two months, I went to the flight lieutenant's room for an hour or so every week. We did almost no French - after the first session he declared I had little to worry about, advising me just to spend a few minutes every day increasing my vocabulary - but he quietly took me through any maths processes I was unsure of, patiently explaining procedures and the reasoning behind them. And he brought me several old School Certificate papers to work through with him. When he was suddenly transferred down south at the end of those two months we lost all contact with him. However, when his (shared) batman came later to pack up the rest of his luggage, my mother asked if he knew what the officer had been in civilian life.

'He was a house-master at a famous public school,' said the batman, proudly. 'I don't know which one, but I do know he taught maths.'

Given help of that calibre, I'd have been ashamed of myself if I'd got less than a Credit in both French and Maths.

AMATEUR DRAMATICS AND BEYOND

Once the two-year School Certificate course had started we were expected to devote much of our out-of-school time to studying for the coming exams but, of course, this was neither realistic nor desirable. From the ages of fourteen to sixteen we had a lot of growing up to do. After all, at that time, a large proportion of children left school at fourteen to begin their working lives. I knew I was fortunate in being able to stay on, at a really good school, working towards getting valuable qualifications. In addition, of course, I had a supportive home-life with lots of opportunities to meet interesting people of all ages. But what was most exciting for me was the unexpected invitation I had to rejoin the drama group which some members of the original cast of 'As You Like It' had now revived.

I'm not entirely sure how this invitation came about. After all, anyone in the group who remembered me would surely think of me as the silly giggler? Bren was still at Abbot's Bromley and had completely disappeared from my scene and so had her sister; Peggy, had married a young naval officer on her eighteenth birthday and now lived in Portsmouth. Many of the original members had moved on, and I had done no acting since the school play. However, John Roper – Lucy Dixon's nephew – had been a member of the cast with a very minor part. He was now a lower sixth-former and he sometimes caught up with me at the bottom of the Rock. He would then cycle home with me - still fairly tongue-tied and awkwardly short of conversation - and one day he abruptly announced that he nowadays took a very active part in the re-formed drama group, largely made up of school friends based in Tettenhall. I was surprised to learn from him that they had already put on a successful version of Ian Hay's "The Middle Watch" in the recreation room in the basement of a wealthy member's home and were now hoping to cast a light comedy called "Grouse in June", to be performed in a local hall. They wanted to know if I would be interested. I couldn't wait to begin.

They met for rehearsals in one another's houses and I naturally assumed that, if I promised that my homework wouldn't be neglected, my mother and father would have no objection. I was right - but only if I agreed to be home by ten o'clock at the latest. That was easy to promise. It seemed reasonable - I was not yet fifteen, it was early June and, because double summertime had been introduced, the evenings were light until quite late. The first evening I turned up I was asked to try out for one of the leading characters - a shy girl of nineteen or so, who is tentatively pursued by an equally shy man (one of the heroes) - and I read it eagerly, with not the slightest suggestion of a giggle. I was told immediately by John Denton, the young producer, that the part was mine. Looking back, I'm puzzled that he took such a risk casting an unknown quantity like me, but I'm inclined to think that it may have been - at least partly - because I looked young, and the other five girls in the group were around eighteen. They were probably more drawn to the other parts: sophisticated women, in glamorous clothes, with some amusing lines and the chance to display their skill with different accents. As John Roper would be playing my suitor, I couldn't have been happier.

Rehearsals went well and eventually I received my first stage kiss - though not until the Dress Rehearsal and, even then, John was far too shy to do more than brush his incipient moustache vaguely near my top lip. That was very disappointing - a non-event, in fact. *Nothing* like as exciting as the three or four I'd shared some months before with Roy Pickworth (my old friend from the Grantham days) when I went to stay for a long weekend with him and his mother, Jess, in the Nottinghamshire village where they now lived. Roy had grown into a tall, amazingly good-looking fifteen-year-old and I'll always be glad that my first kisses were romantic enough to give me a very satisfactory standard to compare any future experiences with.

However, "Grouse in June" was a great success and I quickly felt I'd been accepted as a full-blown member of the group even though I was two years younger than the rest of them - a significant gap when you are an adolescent. However, the gap did become more obvious when we started reading plays in order to decide on one for our next production. By then it was winter, with its strictly enforced black-out regulations, and my parents not only refused to extend the ten o'clock curfew to ten thirty, but they now insisted that someone must see me home. I was in despair and very tempted to imitate Cousin Shirley and, with more genuine justification, yell a defiant 'Cassigaydus!'

'The rest *never* leave till half past ten at the earliest,' I moaned. 'How can I ask anyone to come away at ten, just to walk me home?'

They were adamant. 'You are only fifteen. It's wartime and you don't know who's about in the black-out . . . The roads round here can be quite lonely because most of the houses are detached and well-spaced out . . . There may well be a sudden air-raid . . .' And so on.

Naturally, I could understand their point of view, but I wasn't going to admit that or accept it without a struggle. Inevitably, of course, I had to give in and, with considerable embarrassment, take my problem to the group. It seemed hopeless. John Roper had had to refuse to take part in any play during the next few months because of the pressures of Higher School Certificate and his Oxbridge ambitions, so he wouldn't be at rehearsals, and there was no rush of volunteers from the rest. Still, after a minute or two's agonising silence, Keith Wood (bless him!) said he would do it - but only if I agreed to being carried on the crossbar of his bicycle. It would be quicker than walking and therefore we could leave the group a bit later. And that's what we did, though I diplomatically forgot to mention at home the type of transport I'd agreed to. I always hated reminding him when it was ten to ten, and it was an extremely uncomfortable ride for both of us, but we managed to make it before the deadline - except for once when I was nearly ten minutes late. There were no recriminations. I was simply but firmly told that, should it happen again, there would be no more Yew Tree Dramatic Society for me.

While we searched for a suitable play, we put on a very successful dance to raise more money for the Red Cross and I was surprised and flattered to be asked to sing two songs as part of the entertainment we provided. (Had they remembered my contribution to the carol-singing evenings the previous Christmas?) I chose "A Brown Bird Singing" - a wistful little piece, which probably suited my light, soprano voice quite well - and "One Fine Day", which certainly didn't. Keith's mother accompanied me on the piano and though, when I went to practise at their house, she gently queried whether I felt I had enough experience to interpret the latter as emotionally as it deserved, she tactfully agreed it was worth a try. On the night, the audience were equally tactful with their applause.

Before we could choose the next play we had a completely unexpected request from the Wolverhampton Repertory Theatre: could we possibly supply two or three women to take part in their forthcoming production of "Cradle Song"? Such a request was extremely unusual but it appeared that John Denton was friendly with one or two of the regular actors there and, because the play needed one or two more females to act as extras, John's group was the obvious one to ask. For various reasons, Judy and I were the only ones who could hope to manage to take part. The others were very envious. Luckily for me Judy was a sensible eighteen year-old who could be regarded as a responsible companion, but my parents talked - on and off - for several hours about whether or not I should accept the offer.

'I don't know whether we're right to agree,' said my mother eventually, 'but it would be such an exciting experience for you that I don't see how we can rob you of it. You're never likely to get another chance. But you've *got* to promise that you'll always travel there and back with Judy, and that there'll be some place where you can be sure to do your homework between scenes.'

We rehearsed the whole of one Saturday morning and were measured for our costumes. All the scenes are set in a nunnery and we looked forward very much to learning how to dress as nuns. We had little more to say than 'Oh, what a lovely baby!' and 'How sweet!' when the abandoned baby was brought in from the nunnery steps, but we had to practise reacting appropriately to whatever else was happening. There was also a fair amount of gliding backwards and forwards, and sitting meekly around with demurely hidden hands in order to provide an authentic-looking background for the main characters' performances. I was amazed at the huge size and brilliant lighting of the stage, and the complexities of the backstage space and equipment, but I was slightly disillusioned to find that there were only two small dressing-rooms - one for the leading man and one for the leading lady. All the rest of the women had to crowd into one room little bigger than a bedroom and the men had to use a similar one. We were lucky that week though. There is only one man in "Cradle Song" so he used one 'star' room, Mother Superior had the other; the rest of us were able to spread ourselves around the two larger rooms.

Our costumes - which arrived just in time for the dress rehearsal in exciting-looking wicker hampers - were disappointingly rather shabby and not particularly fresh-smelling, but they looked very convincing once on stage, and Judy and I loved sailing smoothly about in ours, practising looking as if we travelled around on wheels. We'd have liked to wear stage make-up but that would have been inappropriate for nuns. The leading lady and man were kind to us, if a little distant - they both went on, a year or two later, to appear regularly in West End theatres - but the one who helped us most was Gwen Berriman. She owned and ran a baby-clothes shop in Wolverhampton during the day, but was so keen on acting that she was often asked to take small parts in this Repertory theatre's plays - and never refused. Her character part in "Cradle Song" was fairly substantial, but she always found time to chat or share a joke with us between scenes, or make one or two gentle suggestions to improve our performances. A few years later, she became known and very much loved all over England as Doris Archer, the farmer's wife in the five-nights-a-week radio serial which continues to attract large audiences in 2011! She was sadly missed when she died – still acting - in 1980. I'm very glad to have known her.

The performances were as thrilling as we'd hoped. We savoured every detail from the call boy's shout of 'Overture and beginners, please!' to the applause at the final curtain. But, around the middle of the week, there was a minor crisis. At the beginning of the second act, Judy and I went as usual to sit at the foot of the crib leaving Gwen in the dressing-room finishing a welcome mug of tea. She then had to come in a few minutes later to take her seat nearby and join in the discussion about the baby's future - only this time she didn't! I suddenly saw that Gwen's chair was empty and that Mother Superior was beginning to cast agitated looks towards me. Then I realised that I was hearing whole sentences which weren't normally in the script and I knew I had to do something - but it had to be in character. I got up and, keeping my hands tucked into my habit's sleeves, I bowed my head respectfully towards Mother and slid quietly into the wings. Bunching my long skirt up to my knees, I galloped down the corridor and burst into the dressing-room, gasping 'You're on!' to a startled Gwen.

She was distinctly plump and no spring-chicken, but she sped towards the stage like an Olympic medallist, paused to take a deep breath at the curtained entrance, then sailed serenely on stage as if she'd been lingering over private meditations in a nearby cloister. She turned to nod at me as I went back to my chair.

'Thank you, Sister Gabriel,' she said calmly, then respectfully asked Mother Superior if she might now give her opinion, and we were back on the script. She was a real trouper.

Of course my mother and father came to see the play on the Saturday night and one or two of our drama group came at some time during the week, but little fuss was made by any of them. We were only "bit players" after all, and I didn't tell anyone at school about it in case they thought I was boasting. The following Monday morning, immediately after Assembly, I had a message to say I was to see the Head, Miss de Zouche, at break time. I knew it couldn't be anything serious, so when she called me in I presented myself with a shyly confident smile.

'I'm shocked and horrified at your recent behaviour!' she

began. 'I want a full explanation of how you came to appear on that stage last week and why you thought it was acceptable for a member of this High School to take time away from her studies - without my permission - and, furthermore, to flaunt herself every night in public!'

It was my turn to be shocked and horrified. It had never occurred to me that I needed permission, and I couldn't grasp why acting a tiny part in a highly moral play, in a thoroughly respectable theatre, should be condemned so vehemently. I stumbled through a brief account of how I came to be asked to take part, trying my best to include references to our drama group's praiseworthy reputation and fund-raising activities, and the fact that - as a nun wearing a traditional habit - I was barely recognisable, but I still had to endure a full three minutes' tirade on the subject of my sins, my casual attitude to academic achievement, and thoughtless lack of consideration for others.

'I am very tempted to take away your Junior Prefect's badge,' she said solemnly, and dismissed me with a sharp nod and the final words, 'I'll let you know what I decide when I've had time to consider all the implications.'

She must still be considering it, for I heard no more. It was never referred to again, but later that day - when I'd had time to recover from the attack and to register my surprise that she'd even been to the theatre - I began to wonder how she'd recognised me. Then I remembered the programme my mother had brought home. Unexpectedly, my name was in the cast list: Second Nun. And Langdale is definitely not a common name in the Midlands.

Judy and I returned happily to the familiar background of our group's meetings feeling we'd done a reasonable job, but wondering if we'd ever again get used to a very small stage and an audience of only forty or fifty. We did, quite quickly. But the atmosphere within the group was beginning to change - and I wasn't. After our next play there was a certain amount of fairly haphazard pairing off among the seventeen and eighteen year-olds, a tendency to turn lights out for the last half hour of play-reading meetings leaving one or two of us sitting idly around while various couples became - rather obviously - somewhat entangled with each other. It was all very harmless, but it was embarrassing for non-participants and, though I had absolutely no wish to join in, I found I rarely looked forward to the meetings with my usual enthusiasm.

For several weeks I worried about what I should do. If I left, I would be relinquishing any chance of play-acting in the foreseeable future, I would be cutting myself off from regular contact with ten or more friendly, intelligent youngsters, and I would miss - very much - their stimulating conversation, the "in" jokes we shared, and the pleasures of being with people whose extended education and comparatively mature attitudes were continually stretching my understanding of the world. There would be no more invitations to pleasantly luxurious houses, or to join in the occasional visit to the theatre. On the other hand, I'd be free to concentrate more on schoolwork and school friends, I'd not have to worry about finding the money to pay for the occasional cinema or theatre ticket, and I'd no longer spend part of at least one evening per week feeling awkwardly de trop. It was a very difficult decision for a fifteen-year-old to make, especially as there was no one I could discuss it with.

OPTING OUT

I decided to resign. I knew I'd have to give an explanation for taking such an unexpected action and, for some reason, I felt unable to use School Certificate preparation as an excuse. Probably pride would not allow me to pretend I found studying a struggle. I decided to hint at the truth, but I took an easy way of doing it: I simply wrote a brief note to Judy and asked her to tell the group I was leaving, and to say that I felt I was on the fringe of everything and had decided I would be more comfortable spending time on other interests. I then told my parents I was pulling out because I was rather bored with acting just at the moment, and they accepted what I said without comment. I realised I was deliberately closing a chapter in my life and it left me a little breathless and startled at my own rashness. It had certainly been an exciting chapter for me and I must admit I was afraid I might not open another one as satisfying for a long time to come but, by making this gesture of self-reliance, I also felt I'd taken a significant step towards becoming my own person: one no longer entirely dependent upon others' opinions, advice or approval.

The journey from childhood to adulthood is never easy, though some travel it relatively smoothly and seem to reach a balanced maturity with very few problems on the way. Having wise and understanding parents can help, especially if they are able - unobtrusively - to provide their children with a set of sound values to guide them throughout their lives. It may well be quite difficult for youngsters growing up in this twenty-first century to understand how strongly parents used to influence the attitudes of girls, from families such as mine, towards sexual morality, and their general views and expectations of the life ahead of them. In some cases, in those pre-contraceptive pill days, it was achieved through inculcating stark fear of the dire consequences of straying from the paths of virtue, but in others it was more by good example and sensible discussions of other people's actions and choices.

My parents, in addition to the good examples they presented in their personal lives, used some fairly subtle techniques - though I'm not sure how much of this was a conscious ploy. Because we had always been able to talk frankly about most things - and we were all genuinely interested in the people around us - they were able, en famille, to express their views and reservations concerning others' ways of living, their successes or problems. And, though they were healthily broadminded, sympathetic towards individuals' foibles, and very tolerant of a multitude of eccentricities, it was privately made very clear what they believed was acceptable behaviour and what was not. A justifiable type of mild conditioning?

Because neither my parents nor I were church goers, religion played little direct part in forming my ethical principles but their own upbringing was strongly Christian and their basic beliefs were inevitably passed on to me from early childhood. As with most young girls, there were many other, minor influences which significantly affected how I saw the world and my future in it. Films played very little part - I went so rarely, and then only to popular dramas, musicals and comedies - but books played a major role in my leisure time.

The type and quality of those I read so eagerly varied enormously. The school's set books, plays and poetry - Austen, Hardy, Bronte, Shakespeare, Chaucer, Keats, Wordsworth, Sassoon - provided a solid, lasting foundation to build on, but my own choice (often guided by school friends' recommendations) ranged haphazardly from "Cold Comfort Farm", via Rudyard Kipling, Mary Webb, Evelyn Waugh, D.H. Lawrence, Gene Stratton-Porter, Dorothy L. Sayers and Robert Graves, to "The Story of San Michele". For some unfathomable reason my father urged me to try tackling "The Seven Pillars of Wisdom" but, not surprisingly, I couldn't get beyond the first twenty pages. At this stage in my life I suppose I was unconsciously using books to find out more about different life-styles, the exciting possibilities they offered, and how to cope with some of the emotions I might experience. The Seven Pillars - apart from being difficult to read - couldn't really provide information of much relevance to a fifteen-year-old girl.

So I took the easy way out; I regressed from time to time, and enjoyed an hour or so with the currently popular women's magazines our hairdresser friend brought us. Through them I was more or less permanently conditioned into accepting that true love was worth waiting for (I still think it is), that virtue will reap its own reward in the end (not *quite* so sure about that), and that the way to attract a man is to be pretty, full of charming foibles, and to display a certain amount of feminine helplessness (no comment!). It was also implied that the way to *keep* a man is to devote oneself to ensuring his domestic comfort and to providing him with superb, home-cooked meals (mmm - w-e-l-l . . .). Several pages in each of them were aimed at helping their readers achieve the necessary prettiness through careful make-up and clever clothes. There were articles on how to acquire charm and/or a talent for winsomeness, and a host of household hints and tasty recipes. It was assumed that we could all manage to fake the helplessness, when needed, without further training. Temporarily, these magazines also led me to believe that marriage should be the ultimate aim of every woman, and that - once married - one could expect to live happily ever after. It was also clear from their short stories that desirable girls had names like Lynette or Coral, or nicknames like Sunny, and that the most attractive men were called Martin or Simon, smoked pipes and worked in advertising. I felt sorry for the Muriels, anyone with a nickname like Pooky, the Ivors and the Sidneys, and men who were bank clerks or commercial travellers. They obviously didn't stand much chance of real happiness.

The Problem Page at the end of every magazine, however, was fairly helpful; in fact, like most people, I always turned to that first. It was good to know that other people found life difficult at times and, even though their problems were nearly always way out of my league, I felt that any Agony Aunt's wise advice might come in useful for me one day. I was intrigued by queries about how far one should let a boyfriend go - though the vague answers didn't shed much light on what exactly he might attempt, and the emphasis on "respect" tended to be unsatisfactory for anyone looking for practical measures to take. Even more frustrating were the answers to correspondents with nom de plumes like Worried, or S.T.H. of Bognor, whose dilemmas were apparently too intimate to be printed. Answers such as "This is quite normal, but may cause problems if care is not taken . . ." or "Do try to talk this over with your husband. Frank discussion should bring you nearer to a sensible compromise . . ." didn't give much of a clue as to the content of the question. I learned rather more *and* got a fair amount of enjoyment from some of my father's slightly bawdy jokes.

That summer there was an appeal to our school from local farmers for girls of fourteen or more to volunteer to go pea or potato picking. There was a serious shortage of labour to harvest these crops, so we would be allowed to take a week off school and were promised payment at the usual rates for the number of bags we individually filled. Fired with patriotic enthusiasm and a longing for extra pocket money, many of us decided to head for the pea fields - it seemed that might be a cleaner job than picking potatoes. Early the first morning a group of us from my class set off on bicycles for a farm three miles away. The sun was already hot and we had a great time, laughing and chattering, as if we were on holiday and going on a picnic, but we were somewhat daunted to find that, after parking our bikes in a barn, we still had about half a mile to walk to the field before we could begin to work. We were given coarse sacking bags and told to start picking at the far side of a huge field, working towards a gate in the hedge where we could take our full sacks to an elderly, sour-faced woman to be checked and recorded. We were warned that the pea haulms would be regularly checked too, to make sure they'd been completely stripped. We would find our pay docked if they weren't.

The sun was beating down relentlessly all day and it was surprisingly tiring, pulling the pods firmly from the plants, dragging the heavy sacks along as we worked our way down the rows, then lugging them to the woman sitting at the trestle-table by the gate. The hours crept slowly by and the bags were disappointingly slow to fill. When it was time to leave, it seemed we'd been there for a week - and earned very little cash to show for all our exertions. None of us was used to hard, physical work so the journey home was a real trial and we had no energy left for cheerful chat or teasing comments as we cycled. I was ravenously hungry and painfully thirsty by the time I got home but I was almost too shattered to eat, and I was longing for a long, cool bath to soothe my aching back, blistered hands and sore feet. I was not too happy, therefore, when my mother greeted me with the news that Keith Wood had rung to say he was coming to talk to me around seven thirty that evening. I was even more distressed to hear that Paddy, who'd been looking out of condition and strangely lethargic over the last few days, was clearly now in some discomfort.

By the time Keith arrived, I was freshly bathed, fed and - to some extent - rested, but my face and arms were scarlet with sunburn, and I was nursing a now unpleasantly smelly Paddy, trying to give him some comfort. I was in no mood to talk anything through if, as I suspected, Keith was coming on behalf of the drama group to ask for further explanations.

'Jean,' he began diffidently as soon as my mother had shown him into the living-room then tactfully left to join my father in the kitchen. Paddy gave a little whimper and Keith came over to stroke him gently. He looked carefully at the poor dog's eyes and commented on his rough, dry nose and I remembered that Keith had told one or two of us that he was in the process of applying for a place at a Veterinary College. For the next few minutes I was no longer the focus of his attention, except as a source of information about Paddy's recent history and, in a way, this made it easier for us to talk later about my leaving the group.

'How can you say you are in any way on the fringe?' he demanded. 'You're always asked to play one of the main characters, you are asked to sing at the dances, and you know perfectly well that - after you read that difficult, emotional scene in Priestley's "Dangerous Corner" the other evening, confessing you were the murderess - John told you he wanted you to take the part when we put it on in October. And that's the lead. You can't leave! We shan't be able to put it on if you do.'

I was tempted . . . It was a wonderful part . . . But I knew there was no way I could explain my real reasons for feeling embarrassingly isolated - and they had absolutely nothing to do with the fact that no one attempted to draw me into the late evenings' pairing off sessions. I was a romantic, and my upbringing, plus the type of books and magazines I read, made it difficult for me to accept the idea of close physical contact with anyone of the opposite sex unless one at least *imagined* oneself to be in love with them. However old-fashioned, prim, or prudish this might make me seem, I just couldn't be comfortable with casual kissing and caressing in public - or even in private. I also knew that pride in my newly-acquired sense of independence would not let me change my mind and slide weakly back into my old position. For ten minutes or so I stuck grimly to my decision, then Keith left, shaking his head in bewilderment at my apparently senseless stubbornness.

Next morning, when I might have been overcome with regret at having refused to reconsider my actions, I had other things to distress me. I was forced to stay in bed with a prickly heat rash and a severe headache, presumably caused by the previous day's sun, and my father had to travel without me when he carried Paddy to the vet's surgery in town. Quiet tears were shed by my mother and me when my father returned alone, with a worn lead and collar in his pocket. I never knew what he did with them, but many years later I cried again when I found a Wolverhampton bus ticket in the leather folder where his work records and Reference letters were kept. It was in an old envelope and, in his handwriting, it was marked "Paddy's ticket", followed by a date.

THE LAST YEAR AT SCHOOL

Although the threat from German aircraft flying over us on bombing raids to other Midland cities had become slightly less frequent during the latter part of 1941, the problems ordinary people throughout the country were facing were increasingly serious. News bulletins on the radio, anxiously followed by all of us, were grim. Every month, thousands of men and women in the armed services, and hundreds - including children - in Britain's bombed cities, were losing their lives or were being cripplingly injured, yet we seemed no nearer victory. German U-boats were fiercely attacking and sinking many Naval vessels and taking a severe toll of our merchant ships which were bringing desperately needed food and goods from the U.S.A. or transporting vital supplies to our fighting Forces. Surprisingly, though, the general morale remained high. Boosted, partly no doubt, by Churchill's speeches, patriotic songs, and some well-designed propaganda, nearly everyone hung on to an inner conviction that we British were in the right, fighting for the freedom of the people of Europe and beyond. We also found comfort and inspiration in the tradition that we always fought best with our backs to the wall. So we stoically put up with whatever was flung at us and got on with the job of winning the war.

In December 1941 the Japanese attack on Pearl Harbour brought the Americans into the war. For a short while this seemed to make little practical difference to us in Britain - we had already had a considerable amount of help from that country through the Lease Lend arrangement instituted by

President Roosevelt - and it was only to be expected that the U.S.A. would have to concentrate on building up their own Forces, training and weaponry, for some time to come. But, now that we officially had such strong, wealthy allies, the future did look somewhat brighter. In time, with their potentially powerful backing, many things should improve; meanwhile, though, ordinary daily life was often far from easy. Only a determination to see the funny side of things, and to make the best of whatever happened with cheerful willingness, carried most civilians through that winter's difficulties and deprivations.

School and revision for the coming exams took up a good deal of my energy. In those days, to obtain a School Certificate, one had to pass written papers in English, Maths, a foreign language (plus an oral test), and at least two other subjects. The exams all took place during three weeks or so in early summer and no course work was taken into consideration. If one failed any subjects, they could not be re-sat separately. The whole six had to be taken again, so the pressure to pass at the first attempt was very intense. The Certificate of Matriculation (a mandatory requirement for entrance to any university course) was only awarded to those who passed the basic School Cert. with at least five Credits and one Distinction. Under the difficult wartime conditions, most of us felt we'd be happy to achieve the basic Pass grades, with two or three Credits if we were lucky. During the spring term I decided to drop Latin, as I was far from confident that I'd made up for the "lost" year; but this still left me with the very acceptable total of eight subjects.

Just before Easter Auntie Mirrie rang to say she was determined to come to stay with us for a few days. This was very awkward as, by then, we'd had a departmental manager from the Boulton and Paul aircraft factory billeted upon us and he'd persuaded my mother to let him bring his wife and toddler to join him until they could find a suitable house to rent. My single bed and small bedroom were only just big enough for me.

'It's so long since we met,' said my mother, very near to tears, 'and Mirrie really does need a break from waiting every night for the odd plane or two to drop their remaining bombs on Hull on their way back from somewhere else, or for more nuisance raids to start up again . . . or even another blitz.'

For months I'd been pestering my parents to let me go up to Keyingham to see Grandma Taylor, Nora and my two cousins, and I wanted to see Auntie Annie and Uncle Will too. We knew that no bombs had been dropped on any of the East Riding villages and it seemed that there was currently a lull in the attacks on Hull. In any case, the raids were almost always at night, not during the day. It was therefore agreed, after lots of persuasion, that I could spend four nights at Grandma's on condition that I didn't visit any relations in the city (that would be dangerous) and didn't linger at the station - just in case. As it happened there was no temptation for me to linger. As the train trundled from the city's outskirts to its centre, I was too shocked and horrified by the sight of so much devastation, so many streets of ruined buildings, to even consider it.

Our trains must have passed each other but, of course, Auntie Mirrie and I didn't meet. I'm sure she enjoyed her time with my mother but, ironically, it was hardly a restful break. Heavy anti-aircraft fire drove them all into our Anderson shelter on two nights of her stay - unexpectedly, Coventry had been attacked again - and I too spent the two nights, lying on a folded eiderdown under the reinforced roof of the Maynor's broad hall with Nora and family, because there were two quite serious raids on Hull. So, though we could only just hear the guns firing and bombs falling eight or so miles away and were in no real danger, I realised that I would not be too reluctant to return home. But I've always been glad that Auntie Mirrie was able to visit then. She died a few months later, less than five weeks after her breast cancer was diagnosed. I was bitterly sorry that I had missed seeing her. Her loving generosity had made so many important differences to my life and I feel I had never thanked her properly.

*

It was always assumed, in families like mine and Marjorie's, that we would leave school once we passed our School Certificates. We would be sixteen then (in our case, just sixteen, for both our birthdays were in July) and it was time we started earning a living. For some years, whenever anyone asked what I wanted to be when I left school, I had always said, very definitely, 'I don't know yet - but not *anything* in an office and *never* a teacher!'

I'm sure, if I'd wanted to go on to some kind of college to learn shorthand, typing and book-keeping, my parents would have been more than willing to pay the fees and continue to support me throughout the course, but there was no pressure on me to make this or any other choice. There was no offer of career advice at the school during our last year and I was sensible enough to know that my long-standing wishes either to write books or to become an actress were not realistic. At one point I did hear that the Wolverhampton Grand Theatre was looking to appoint a new assistant stage-manager, and for a day or two I seriously considered applying. I was well aware that, for anyone of real talent, this was a recognised path into the profession, but I was honest enough to admit to myself that, though acting would always be a fascinating hobby, I just didn't have the burning desire for a stage career that all really successful actors possessed - and probably not enough talent either. The idea of spending every evening backstage for the next couple of years or so as an A.S.M., racing from one nerve-racking task to another in dim, uncomfortable surroundings when everyone else my age was able to enjoy some kind of social life, suddenly did not seem particularly appealing. There would be problems, too, with getting home late every night and it struck me that during the day, when I just might have some free time, all my friends would be working. So what else attracted me?

When I was about eight, I'd noticed a newly-completed building by the side of the main road between Hull and Hedon. It was white, modern, and seemed to me to exude an air of pleasant efficiency. I was told it was a laboratory and, somehow, I always looked forward to seeing it whenever I travelled to Keyingham. At that time I didn't know exactly what a laboratory was but it looked an intriguing place to spend one's working hours, and when I began taking Physics and Chemistry at High School I always thoroughly enjoyed time spent with test tubes, Bunsen burners and pipettes.

Having Marjorie as my partner for all the practical experiments and note-taking simply added to my pleasure. In our last year at school Marjorie and I had become even closer friends, so it was natural that we should begin to talk about what we might do when we left in July, and when we found out that there was a new Government-sponsored course at the Wednesbury Technical College which equipped its students to work in any laboratory concerned with metallurgical analysis, we both knew that this was exactly what we wanted to do.

There were obviously lots of advantages. The course sounded interesting and, because only applicants with a School Cert. would be considered, it seemed it was probably a fairly demanding one. It lasted just three months and this meant that we would very quickly be "qualified" and able to apply for a reasonably good job. We would be paid a pound a week throughout our training (about forty-five pounds in 2011 terms) plus our train fares to Wednesbury and we would really enjoy studying together. At last we'd be doing something for the War Effort! Apparently, because many of the young men employed in iron and steel laboratories had been called-up, there was a serious shortage of assistant technicians and this was now regarded as a gap which women could quickly be trained to fill. Working in a busy lab should, we felt, offer a measure of freedom and informality not to be found in the dull routines of office work, the stultifying activities which we believed occupied most of a secretary's day. And there would be the added satisfaction of feeling that we were breaking into what was generally regarded as a man's world. My father was delighted! At last I was moving towards his line of country, his enthusiasms. My mother, of course, just wanted to know about the chances of promotion, and if there would be a pension plan.

Once our decision was made I willingly queued up at the central Labour Exchange to collect the necessary application forms. I'd no previous experience of their procedures, so I was slightly surprised to hear some of the questions the sullen young woman in front of me had to answer – there was very little attempt, then, to maintain client privacy! When she was asked what experience of employment she had there was a lengthy silence. The queue behind me was long and inclined to mutter rebelliously, and the clerk was clearly short of time and temper.

'What work have you done in the past? . . . What *were* you?' he barked impatiently.

That she could answer. 'I was a lav-watcher,' she muttered.

I was glad he understood what she meant. It was several minutes before I did,

*

It's never easy waiting for exam. results, especially when the course of your future career depends upon them, but there were very few air raids on Hull at that time so I was able to go up to Keyingham again to stay with Auntie Annie and Uncle Will. It was a memorable ten days. For one thing, my visit coincided with the last four days of Bill's much needed leave (a whole three weeks ashore while his ship was being repaired and fitted with new equipment) and I was able to spend some time with the Storm family and Grandma Taylor at the bungalow, Maynor. Not *too* much time, of course - Auntie

Annie tended to be jealous and reminded me frequently that I'd already stayed with Nora and Grandma when I came up last time. Bill was relaxed and full of fun, Nora was happily savouring every moment of having him safely at home for a while, and Shirley and Michael were revelling in having their father with them again: like a real family, as Shirley said.

It was during this holiday that I began to appreciate my cousin Michael as a personality in his own right. He started to emerge as more than just a pleasant, background component of the Taylor/Storm ménage. He was now nearly seven; no longer merely a sunny little fellow, content to play quietly on his own, well away from the general hurly-burly of family life, but a highly intelligent boy with an almost adult sense of humour. It was obvious now that he'd found his own ways of coping with the unsettling impact of three very individual, forceful females upon him – a lone male – and he seemed to sense that, in some ways, I was on his side.

He was apparently aware that my stay with Auntie Annie could be extremely dull at times. Inevitably, as a teenager (though that term had not yet been coined) I very quickly got bored with Auntie's frequent demands to know which day Nora did her washing or whether girls' schools still teach darning, particularly by the third day of asking. He'd also gathered that I couldn't escape to Maynor too often without offending my affectionate aunt and uncle. So, one fine Saturday afternoon, he hatched a plot to extract me for an hour or two. Without saying anything to his mother he trotted down to West View intending to say that his sister Shirley needed some help with her homework, so could I come? This was quite brave of him, for he'd never been there before and was unlikely ever to have spoken to either of the Wrights, or even to Olive.

As it happened, when he arrived, Olive was at the far end of the vegetable garden so Auntie herself answered his knock and, perhaps because he'd interrupted her usual post-prandial nap, she was somewhat uncharacteristically snappy.

'What do *you* want?' I heard her say.

Michael blenched, and there was quite a lengthy pause before he could manage a reply. I strained to hear it, only to find my newly acquired dignity as a young adult slightly deflated.

'C-can Jean come out to play?' he blurted out. I think he found her answering nod rather alarming.

I went, of course, and enjoyed a relaxing hour or two even though I had to pay for it by putting up with a detailed examination of every page of Michael's stamp album. I really couldn't help wishing that Bill had restricted his ports of call to – say – Rotterdam and Cardiff, or at least had written to his son less frequently.

But getting to know Michael and appreciating his talents weren't the only pleasures of that holiday, for I was fortunate enough to meet John. He lived at the end of the lane in the old mill house where Granny and Grandpa had lived when they were first married, and he stopped to talk when he saw me cutting some flowers in Auntie's front garden. He was a couple of years or so older than me and had recently returned home after a terrifying trip of several weeks aboard a merchant ship sailing to various Russian ports inside the Arctic Circle. He had been accepted some months before for RAF aircrew training and had volunteered to serve as a temporary midshipman while waiting to be called up. He had a fund of stories about his extremely unpleasant experiences, but described them with such engagingly wry humour that my almost overwhelming admiration could be cloaked in laughter. I was particularly impressed by one. Apparently he was constantly seasick and was told by one old sailor that he would feel much better if he stayed up on deck, striding backwards and forwards, loudly reciting any poetry he could remember. From his vivid description, I could just picture the scene as he paced up and down in the freezing sleet, buffeted by icy winds, declaiming 'I wandered lonely as a cloud, that floats on high o'er vales and hills . . .' into the semi-darkness of the afternoon.

'Did it work? Did you feel any better?' I asked, breathlessly.

'No . . . But, judging from their raucous laughter, I think the crew did - especially when I got to the bit about seeing daffodils. So I started to spout 'O Wild West Wind, thou breath of Autumn's being . . .' instead but, as I turned to face into the ruddy wind for dramatic effect, I was violently sick again. That quite made their day.'

Almost every afternoon, for the rest of my holiday, we went for a walk and each day I looked forward so eagerly to our next meeting that I was unable to settle to anything for more than ten minutes at a time. I spent the mornings waiting for his knock on the door and counting first the hours and then the minutes as they dragged by with agonising slowness. One afternoon he took me into Hull to see a film (shyly holding hands in the warm darkness) but most days he fetched me to spend the evening at his home, where we could talk about the books we enjoyed, play Lexicon with his mother and young sister, or sing favourite songs round the piano. Very old-fashioned - indeed, virtually Victorian - but, nonetheless, very exciting for a naive fifteen-year-old like me.

The night before I left to go home we planned that, before he started his training at the Midlands R.A.F centre where he was expecting to be sent, he would come to stay with us for a few days at Tettenhall. Not surprisingly, my mother and father were far from enthusiastic about this, so it never happened and, after exchanging letters every few days for several weeks, the central focus of our lives changed rapidly. This - coupled with the fact that we were unlikely to be able to meet again for many months, even years – meant that our mutual interest inevitably faded. Nevertheless, the memories of those few days I spent with John are all happy ones and, when we briefly met by chance twenty years later, I could still see why I'd found him so attractive.

*

Both Marjorie and I passed the School Certificate, of course, and the postcards from our class teacher, giving us this good news, also contained her congratulations on our gaining comfortably more than sufficient Credits and Distinctions to Matriculate. This meant we would be accepted without question on the Metallurgy Course, and we were very grateful that the high-quality teaching at Wolverhampton Girls' High School had enabled us to do so well. It was many years before it dawned on either of us that the High School had, in quite important ways, failed us. As things have turned out, we are both very satisfied with the long term effects this "failure" has had upon our lives, but others who had a similar experience may feel rather differently. Our first question is: why was it never suggested we should stay on into the sixth form, not only to experience more advanced types of teaching and learning, but also to have the chance to take Higher School Certificate? We eventually realised that - as well as the three or four brilliant ones obviously heading for Oxbridge - a number of girls in our year who got no more than the basic School Cert. had automatically stayed on. We also learned that several others, whose results were exactly the same as ours, had also gone into the Sixth Form - and most of these went on to university or some form of higher education.

We've since concluded that the only differences between us were: we were scholarship girls, while the sixth formers with only the basic School Cert. had parents who not only paid full fees but could also comfortably afford to keep them at school till they were eighteen. Most of the rest staying on, who had matriculated as we did, came from families with academic backgrounds or who, at least, were well-aware of the importance of educational qualifications. Their parents knew the routes which led to higher education, and the methods they could use to make sure their daughters got the opportunity to take them. Our parents possessed none of these advantages.

The second question is: why did no member of staff warn us that a three-month course was unlikely to be more than a mediocre training exercise, and that opportunities for advancement in that type of lab would be severely limited? Neither of us had been a timid mouse who sat at the back of the class, unnoticed most of the time and, though we hadn't shone at any sport, we'd been Junior Prefects and had willingly taken part in the school's few extra-curricular activities. Our names were known, and (apart from my theatrical escapade) our copy-books were unblotted. I wish we'd thought to contact the school to ask these questions (perhaps helping to improve the situation for future pupils) but our lives were too busy for us even to realise there'd been a problem.

Although we'd been happy at the school, we were so looking forward to our future jobs that we weren't sad to leave. I did have one regret, though. We'd been told by sixth-formers that Miss de Zouche - or Dizzy as we now called her - always gave the leavers a talk on sex, and that we should on no account miss it. I can't remember why I couldn't be there - I only know that it was unavoidable - but, as with the first day at Newland High School, I've always felt I've missed out on yet another rite of passage. The frustrating thing was that, when I asked the rest of the girls what Dizzy had said, the only replies I got were infuriating giggles and the somewhat baffling statement, 'She told us we must never sit on boys' knees. Something might happen.' And even Marjorie said she couldn't remember more than that. It had all been too vague.

So, a few days after my sixteenth birthday, I left school looking forward eagerly to preparing for my working life and the stimulating prospect of being recognised as grown-up.

For my generation there was no chance of a gap year. The term "teenager" had not yet been coined and no one could expect a spell of carefree time between being a child and becoming an adult. On the contrary, being adult was what most of us had been looking forward to – what we *wanted*. I'm somewhat ashamed to confess, though, that I was only vaguely aware how fortunate I was that, whatever challenges lay ahead, I had the foundations of a secure and happy childhood to support me and build upon.

WEDNESBURY TECHNICAL COLLEGE

Clutching our precious weekly train passes, provided by the Labour Exchange where we'd originally applied to join the Metallurgy Course some months before, Marjorie and I breezed through the busy ticket barrier at Wolverhampton station trying to look as if we were regular commuters. Planning what we should wear now that we were free of the constraints of school uniforms had been quite a problem, but our parents had handed over a few of their clothing coupons and we'd acquired one or two hand-me-downs from more distant relatives and family friends. Thankfully the pale khaki lab coats (the rather unflattering "slops" we'd been advised to buy) cost very few coupons. We were, of course, understandably excited and just a little nervous in case the new experiences ahead should prove to be more demanding than expected, but at least we could share any problems and help each other with any practical difficulties.

We need not have worried. The taciturn, elderly tutor mainly responsible for our training was himself somewhat nervous, and obviously very shy of the ten young girls who made up the first intake on this new course. In some ways, *we* trained *him*, at least in what to expect from his students. We made him aware of the probable extent of schoolgirls' knowledge of elementary laboratory techniques, their surprising areas of ignorance, and – perhaps most important of all – their attitude towards him and their work. We respected him and were keen to do well but, though we recognised the vital need for scrupulous accuracy in the analyses we were learning and practising, we felt free to take full advantage of the informality of working in a lab. We could talk as much as we wished - which was nearly all the time - and even sing if we felt like it, which Marjorie and I did fairly frequently. No one seemed surprised at this, or complained, and our versions of the popular songs of the day were, in fact, often requested by many of the others who would sometimes then join in too. Overall it was a thoroughly enjoyable experience. We worked hard to refine our skills, to increase our speed in producing results, and to improve our ability to cope with several operations in parallel, but it was, to a large extent, ten weeks of comradeship and fun.

What we learned, however, was almost entirely practical. The Certificate awarded at the end of the course described each of us as a qualified Junior Metallurgical Analyst but, in fact, we learned to do little more than set up and maintain the appropriate apparatus, and concoct the various chemical solutions necessary for the eight or nine basic techniques we would be using to discover the percentage of silicone, carbon, or manganese, etc. in any given sample of metal. We had no sessions on the underlying theory, no real understanding of what we were doing, or its purpose, and no idea of the existence of other, more complex and difficult, procedures. There was no attempt to interest us intellectually and I can only assume that girls of our educational background and calibre were selected because it was assumed that – once in a job - we could be relied on to work consistently accurately and, if necessary, without direct supervision.

One incident, though, stands out clearly in my memory. Sometime near the end of the course we were all taken into the basement of the college, where various types of machinery were housed, and shown how to drill our own samples from small chunks of unidentified metal. Over the next week we were expected to go there with a partner and practise doing it for ourselves. One morning Marjorie and I decided to go down and take turns in producing a few usable samples from a likely looking piece of steel. Marjorie began to operate the elderly electric machine with cheerful confidence and I stood casually beside it, mesmerised by the sight of the pile of thin filings appearing – almost magically - on the steel's surface. Suddenly there was an anguished yell and I looked up to see Marjorie's head being dragged towards the rapidly revolving spindle at the top of the drill. Within about two seconds the switch on the side of the machine was turned off, but at the same moment – realising that her scalp was about to make disastrous contact with the whirling shaft – she fiercely yanked herself back, leaving a large lock of hair attached to the machine.

We could never decide what really happened. We knew *why* it happened: there was no fitted guard at head-height, and there should have been. Other serious omissions included the fact that we hadn't been given sufficient safety instructions or warnings of possible dangers and there was no rule - or even advice - about the need to wear a protective cap or net. And although Marjorie kept her naturally wavy hair fairly short, it should have been pointed out to her that the curls which fell attractively from the top of her head towards her brow were an obvious hazard.

And what we *didn't* know - then or now - was who had switched the machine off. Marjorie was convinced I had done it, though I have no recollection of any such action. She argued that there was no way she could have operated the switch herself and that leaning towards the whirling spindle in order to reach it was the last thing she would have wanted to do. Nowadays, of course, there would be justifiable charges of negligence and a case made for compensation to be paid, but at that time such action simply didn't occur to us. I don't know if our tutor realised the possible consequences for himself and the college but one of the other girls later said that, when she dashed up to the lab to tell him what had happened, he seemed panic-stricken. He hovered indecisively for a few seconds, then rushed down to see the damage for himself.

'Who is it? Who is it?' he shouted to the girl as he ran.

We've no idea why, when someone called to him that it was Marjorie, he wailed, 'Oh no! Not Marjorie!', but she really couldn't help being flattered. Naturally the pain and shock of losing a substantial amount of hair and the prospect of being left with an ugly bare patch for many weeks was very unpleasant, but Marjorie still insisted on our going to the theatre that night. We'd been saving up for this event for some time and were very lucky to get the tickets but, not surprisingly, she suffered a delayed reaction and we had to leave before the end so that she could get home and go to bed. But I've always admired the way she coped with the problems the accident brought, quietly refusing to make any fuss.

*

In the October my father decided to start applying for a better, more congenial job – one where he could take on more responsibility and be his own boss. It seemed a rather abrupt decision but I think he realised that I would soon be applying for a job myself and it would be best if I knew where we were going to live before tying myself to one which might be difficult for me to reach easily. He and my mother were hankering for the country so, once the decision was made, he sent off two or three applications for posts in rural areas. Two replies, suggesting dates for interviews, arrived within a few days.

The first was clearly unsuitable. The details originally sent to him had been misleading. It was a small, one-man pumping station almost on the Welsh border and though, after only four or five simple questions he was unhesitatingly offered the job, he couldn't even consider it. None of the three members of the local council sub-committee who interviewed him seemed to have any idea of what the job entailed and he'd been somewhat startled to be asked if he could "pack a gland" – which I understand is the equivalent of asking dressmaker if she could manage to use a treadle machine.

'Now, have you any questions you would like to ask us before you *finally* decide not to accept it?' said the farmer who was acting as chairman.

'Well . . . what arrangements would be made for me to have some time off each week – and for a week's annual holiday?' my father asked, more out of politeness than a need to know.

The three men facing him looked shocked. 'You surely wouldn't want to leave your little engines for someone else to look after, would you?' said the chairman.

My father thanked them for their time and left without answering.

The second interview - in a smallish, Shropshire town with the slightly unusual name of Shifnal - was very different. The questions were reassuringly technical as well as dealing quite searchingly with his background and personal suitability. He'd been able to find out a good deal about the area beforehand - and the probable future developments – so he was very glad indeed to be offered the job before he left for home. We were all pleased. It had so many advantages. The town is little more than thirty minutes from Wolverhampton by train, but is set in pleasant countryside a few miles from the Wrekin and we expected it would be possible for me to find and travel to a job in one of the steel works or foundries in the Black Country without too much trouble. My father would be in charge of a modern pumping station, situated nearly a mile from the outskirts of the town, and he would also be responsible for the water supply to quite a large rural area served by several small, "booster" pumping installations. He would have a working plumber as an assistant and the authority to take on one or two labourers as necessary. He was pleased, too, to find that George Thomas, the Town Clerk, had previously worked for the Council in Beverley and that his wife, Audrey, came from there.

'It'll be good to welcome another Yorkshire family to Shifnal,' George told him. 'And our Sanitary Inspector comes from Ossett you know!'

Best of all, it was part of his contract that he should occupy the comfortable, modern house which stood in a quarter of an acre of grassy garden surrounding the pumping station. The house was semi-detached, with white walls and a deep red roof, and our "half" was a good deal larger than the part where the assistant already lived. The resulting imbalance added to the charm of the architecture and, because the pumping station was deliberately set away from the house and its design was pleasantly unobtrusive, the overall appearance of the property was, he said, very attractive. My mother and I couldn't wait to see it.

But a few days later we had some terrible news. Bill's ship had been torpedoed in mid-Atlantic and sunk by a German U-boat. For almost two weeks Nora could get no further information but then she was told that the captain of one of the convoy's undamaged ships had reported that he knew that most of the crew had managed to get into two lifeboats and that their captain was in one of them. I don't know how Nora coped when she heard this – sadly, it was not possible for any of us to get to Keyingham to help her – but I can imagine how desperately she must have clung to the slender hope that he'd been picked up by another ship, unable to let the families know until they docked in an American port. The following weeks of waiting for news must have been almost unbearable, and she must have realised all too clearly the effect that the bitter November weather and the rough seas of the north

Atlantic would have on the wretched condition and misery of men surviving for days in an open boat.

There *was* no news. As with so many other people who lost relatives and friends during the war, Nora had to learn to live with the fact that she would never know how, or even when, Bill died. The children had to accept that they would grow up without the affectionate support of their father, and the rest of us who loved him had to come to terms with the fact that we, too, would never see him again. Even now it hurts to think that, because Shirley was barely ten and Michael only seven when Bill was lost, they hadn't had the chance to get to know him very well. He'd been at sea most of their lives and they rarely saw him for more than a few days every six or seven months. No matter how much we were able to tell them about his rare qualities, they could never fully appreciate the warmth and charm of his personality, the stimulating pleasure of his conversation, or how much fun he was to be with.

*

During the last month of our course at the Wednesbury Tech., two of the Department's tutors spent time finding us jobs. There were plenty of vacancies around of course, but they wanted to fit us all into the most appropriate niches, easy to travel to and best suited to our individual "talents". Marjorie was accepted by a firm which needed someone who could work alone in a small lab and take full responsibility for all the necessary analyses. I knew I would prefer, if possible, to be part of a busy team but this was just the type of work she would enjoy. In any case, I was more of a problem for them because our plans to move to Shifnal in December meant I would be living in Shropshire – hardly over-populated with iron and steel foundries! However, just a week before the course ended, I was told I'd been offered a job – no interview necessary - in a large works just four miles or so from my new home: the Lilleshall Company in Oakengates. The lab had a staff of five, I would be paid the going rate (£2 a week, which was about average for an inexperienced sixteen-year-old with only very elementary skills) and it sounded ideal. Oakengates had a pleasant pastoral sound to it and I accepted the offer cheerfully, with few qualms.

At home in Tettenhall, we were relieved to learn that the man and his family who had been billeted on us for the past few months were now leaving to live in a small, rented house nearer to his work. There would be no difficulties about giving them notice etc. so we now could concentrate on planning and packing up for our move to the Waterworks House. And planning would certainly be needed because, for unavoidable reasons, we *had* to move on Christmas Eve and I was to start work three or four days later. Because of College commitments and the obligatory attendance at the Wednesbury Town Hall for the ceremonial presentation of Certificates etc. to about a hundred students, I hadn't seen Shifnal or the lab before we moved, but my mother had visited the house and was very happy with it.

Ten days before we moved there was a peremptory knock at the door and, as soon as my mother opened it Mrs Henderson, the Billeting Officer, bustled into the hall, full of smiles and exaggerated good will.

'I've only *just* heard!' she trilled. 'Your rooms are free again, aren't they? And that solves a *big* problem for me. Everyone has always said how comfortable they've been here with you and now I have the ideal, PERMANENT tenants for you – at least for the rest of the war. If it's all right with you, my husband and I will move in next Thursday.'

We were *so* sorry to see how drastically her face dropped when my mother told her our news . . . well, almost sorry.

THE TAYLORS

MAY AGED ONE

AGED TWELVE

AGED EIGHTEEN

GRANDPA TAYLOR

AS VICE-PRESIDENT OF THE DEBATING SOCIETY

WITH GRANDMA NANCE AT ROBIN HOOD'S BAY

THE LANGDALES

GRANNY & GRANDPA
WITH FRIEND (1935)

AUNTIE ANNIE &
UNCLE WILL (1934)

FRANK: AGED EIGHT

ME

MINUS TWO MONTHS

WITH 'THE' PRAM

*OUTSIDE THE
ROBIN HOOD'S BAY
COTTAGE*

GRANTHAM

HARRY AND ERIC ON MY
FATHER'S BIKE

ME SHOWING OFF
AS USUAL

ROY AGED FIFTEEN

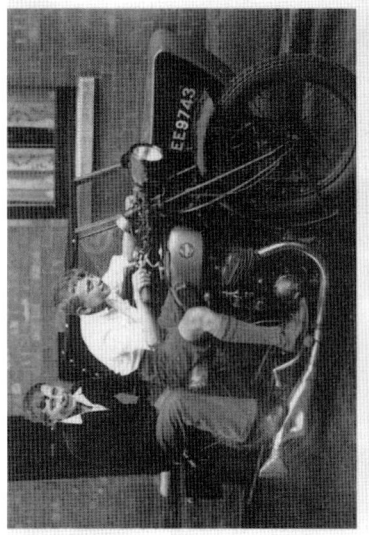

RELATIVES WHO WERE FRIENDS

MADGE AND ALBERT'S WEDDING

ANNE AND JOE'S WEDDING
-AT LAST !

UNCLE TOM

HARRY AND FLORRIE 1930

HOLIDAYS

*MUMMY AND DADDY
THE CORNWALL TRIP*

*UNCLE BILL AND ME
ON THE RIVER FAL*

*ME AND PADDY ON
HORNSEA SANDS*

CLOSE FAMILY

OUTSIDE MAYNOR
(top row)
FRANK, MICHAEL, NORA
GRANDPA & MAY.
ME *(with court shoes)*
and SHIRLEY

WITH
GRANDMA

WITH AUNTIE MIRRIE
(Soon after I'd had scarlet fever)

*MICHAEL PLOTTING
TO RESCUE ME*

*MARJORIE
A FRIEND FOR LIFE*

*ME: A JUNIOR
METALLURGICAL
ANALYST*